Discourse and Responsibility in Professional Settings

Studies in Communication in Organisations and Professions
Series Editors: Christopher N. Candlin† and Srikant Sarangi,
Aalborg University, Denmark

This series aims to build bridges between communication and discourse studies and a broad range of professional, organisational, and workplace sites by foregrounding authoritative analyses of real-life practice – in collaborative, informed and explanatory ways. The series provides an interdisciplinary and interprofessional forum for dialogue between academic researchers and professional/workplace communities and organisations. Examples of appropriate fields of inquiry include: social and community welfare, medicine and healthcare, counselling and therapy, education, law, media, management and business, policy and government and development studies. Coherence among books in the series is achieved through their common concern with cross-over concepts such as power, diversity, identity, agency, decision-making, expertise, risk, appraisal and evaluation.

Published:

Dialogue in Focus Groups
Exploring Socially Shared Knowledge
Ivana Markova, Per Linell, Michele Grossen, Anne Salazar Orvig

Writing the Economy
Activity, Genre and Technology in the World of Banking
Graham Smart

Forthcoming:

Understanding and Interaction in Clinical and Educational Settings
Barry Saferstein

Morality in Practice
Exploring Childhood, Parenting and Schooling in Everyday Life
Edited by Jakob Cromdal and Michael Tholander

Team Talk
Decision-making across the Boundaries in Health and Social Care
Edited by Srikant Sarangi and Per Linell

Interpreter Mediated Healthcare Consultations
Edited by Srikant Sarangi

Language and the Job Interview
Celia Roberts

Discourse and Responsibility in Professional Settings

Edited by
Jan-Ola Östman and Anna Solin

Sheffield, UK   Bristol, CT

Published by Equinox Publishing Ltd.
UK: Office 415, The Workstation, 15 Paternoster Row, Sheffield,
South Yorkshire S1 2BX
USA: ISD, 70 Enterprise Drive, Bristol, CT 06010
www.equinoxpub.com

First published 2016

British Library Cataloguing-in-Publication Data
A catalogue record for this book is available from the British Library.

ISBN-13 978 1 84553 914 6 (hardback)
         978 1 84553 915 3 (paperback)

Library of Congress Cataloging-in-Publication Data
Names: Östman, Jan-Ola, editor. | Solin, Anna, editor.
Title: Discourse and responsibility in professional settings / edited by
    Jan-Ola Östman and Anna Solin.
Description: Sheffield, UK; Bristol, CT: Equinox Publishing Ltd, [2016] |
    Includes bibliographical references and index.
Identifiers: LCCN 2015030996 | ISBN 9781845539146 (hb) |
    ISBN 9781845539153(pb)
Subjects: LCSH: Sociolinguistics. | Professional ethics. | Business
communication—Moral and ethical aspects—Case studies. | Communication
in organizations—Moral and ethical aspects—Case studies.
Classification: LCC P40.5.P76 D57 2016 | DDC 401/.41—dc23
LC record available at http://lccn.loc.gov/2015030996

Typeset by JS Typesetting Ltd, Porthcawl, Mid Glamorgan
Printed and bound by Lightning Source Inc. (La Vergne, TN),
Lightning Source Ltd. (Milton Keynes) and Lightning Source Pty
(Scoresby, Victoria).

Contents

Preface

The present volume has been in the making for well over a decade. One clearly discernible starting point was a panel on Ideology and responsibility organised in 1998 by Per Linell and Jan-Ola Östman at IPrA's Sixth International Pragmatics Conference in Reims, France. At this time, the editors of the present volume, Jan-Ola Östman and Anna Solin, were working in the project *Pragmatics, Ideology, and Contacts* (funded by the Academy of Finland), where in particular the expression of ideology and its relation to responsibility became increasingly central. The topic of ideology and responsibility has occupied us continuously after that, as can be witnessed in the collection *Issues of Minority Peoples*, edited by Frances Karttunen and Jan-Ola Östman in 2000; and in the volume on *International Communication Monitoring* put together by Jef Verschueren, Jan-Ola Östman and Michael Meeuwis in 2002.

The present volume has gone through many stages and changed shape and contents over the years. Getting a proper hold on responsibility has been a challenge, to say the least, and this volume is clearly only a first step towards getting a deeper understanding of the complexity of responsibility in discourse. With this volume we want to communicate what we see as the importance of issues of responsibility for research in language studies generally, and in professional settings in particular. We hope the volume will inspire readers to take part in a much-needed debate on the topic.

We are grateful to all who have inspired us with insights and comments over the years, particularly the contributors to the volume, and the series editors Srikant Sarangi and Chris Candlin. Finally, we want to thank the editors, contributors and Equinox for their patience and support in the final stages of preparing this volume.

Jan-Ola Östman & Anna Solin

Part I
Discourse and responsibility

The notion of responsibility in discourse studies

Anna Solin & Jan-Ola Östman

1 Introduction

This volume focuses on responsibility in professional settings and in particular on how responsibility is manifested, expressed, attributed, negotiated and contested in the discourses of professional settings. Taken together, the studies reveal the importance of analysing discourse from the point of view of discourse participants' agency, accountability and responsibility and thus add an important dimension to existing strands of research in discourse studies, in pragmatics, and in applied linguistics.

In discussions of organisational and workplace cultures, the notion of responsibility is typically framed as one concerned with professional ethics. Responsibility is analysed in terms of the different accountabilities that professional practitioners are purported to have in relation to their clients, audiences, funders and other stakeholders. So far, there has been little academic research combining such a perspective with a close analysis of language use. This is so despite the fact that discourse on or related to professional responsibility has proliferated in recent years both in public fora (e.g. in connection with corporate social responsibility reports) and in more local practices (e.g. as manifested in the publication of in-house codes of conduct). While there is much research on professional discourse and language use in the workplace,[1] studies rarely address the theme of responsibility explicitly and directly.[2]

The volume contains three theoretically attuned chapters in this first part of the book, and nine detailed case studies, which examine different types of contexts where the production of texts and/or interaction is definitional of professional practice: health care, social work and journalism. The types of data studied range from globally available mass-consumed discourse (such as news agency dispatches) to local face-to-face encounters (e.g. counselling sessions). The data come from a variety of linguistic and cultural settings: the UK, Norway, Sweden, the USA, Belgium, and Finland.

The chapters all stress the dynamic nature of responsibility. The discourse perspective adopted reinforces the view that responsibility relations need to be perceived as fluid, as negotiated and construed in interaction rather than as predetermined: responsibility has to do with how we position ourselves in context, in relation to our sense of ourselves, of agency, and in relation to our sense of others and of authority.

In the next section, we examine the notion of responsibility and how this notion is useful and timely in discourse studies. We discuss the various meanings of the term *responsibility* and present a number of key distinctions that we see as directly relevant in analyses of professional discourse. Section 3 gives an outline of the ways in which the contributions to the volume address issues and problems around responsibility and discourse.

2 The notion of responsibility

Responsibility is a central concept in many academic disciplines, including philosophy, political science, law and psychology. Unlike terms such as 'accountability' and 'ethics', it is also frequent in everyday usage. We constantly position ourselves in relation to our sense of responsibility to others and in relation to (different voices in) discourses about responsibility. Still, the concept of responsibility as such has not been prominent in discourse studies so far.

For some, responsibility may be an old-fashioned notion that suggests the existence of universal normative frameworks; the term may be seen to imply that there are unproblematic and widely shared criteria for what counts as 'responsible behaviour'. For others, the term has become an empty tool of corporate or political rhetoric. Moreover, as Harmon (1995: 13) points out, the literature on the subject tends to be negative in tone; *responsible* is often understood as a synonym for *blameworthy* rather than for *trustworthy*. Thus, the first step in establishing a viable scholarly approach with responsibility as the starting point is to show the scope and usefulness of the term from the point of view of discourse studies: the range of meanings of the term *responsibility* that might be relevant. Indeed, one can argue that Critical Discourse Analysis and related approaches are concerned with responsibility par excellence and have responsibility as an (often unexpressed) central theme. But irrespective of how Critical Discourse Analysis is practiced, explicit references to the concept responsibility are scarce in the literature. The concept thus clearly needs to be lifted up and be dealt with on its own terms.

Even scholars often use the term responsibility as a 'term of art', the semantics and scope of which are presupposed to be generally understood. The complexity of the term is at least partly due to the multiple and even opposing meanings it has. The adjective *responsible* can refer both to someone who is to blame (*He was responsible for the accident.*) and to someone who is trustworthy (*He is a responsible parent.*). The noun *responsibility* can also be used to refer to the duties attached to a particular position (*the responsibilities of a minister*). Indeed, Harmon (1995: 5) goes as far as to claim that since the idea of responsibility connotes 'multiple and conflicting meanings', the term is 'inherently paradoxical'. (See also Lakoff's chapter in this volume.)

In order for *responsibility* to work as an analytic term, it is necessary to make a distinction between primarily moral and primarily legal meanings (cf. Harmon 1995; Cane 2002). The meaning invoking moral judgments emphasises the way in which human behaviour is constrained by moral rules. Such rules 'mark out the things that are wrong for anyone' (Baier 1970: 104), in contrast to responsibilities attached to a social role or position. Examples of this first kind of usage are collocations like *responsible consumer* and *responsible citizen.*

The second meaning emphasises legal responsibility, for example a person's accountability to others because he or she has contracted particular duties or responsibilities. Here the person or collective is in charge of something, and may be prosecuted in case of neglect. This meaning is the more salient in the following example:

> Exxon still refuses to accept responsibility for allowing a captain
> it knew to be a lapsed alcoholic to take control of the ship in such
> dangerous and environmentally sensitive waters. (*Independent*
> 28.2.2008)[3]

While the distinction between moral and legal responsibility is by no means a clear-cut one (causing an oil spill certainly has both legal and moral implications), these two aspects of the concept of responsibility are often good to keep apart for analytic purposes.

The philosopher Hans Jonas (1984: 90–93) makes a distinction between *formal* and *substantial* responsibility. Formal responsibility refers to one's 'accountability for one's deeds', and has primarily legal significance: a person is held responsible for a deed, and may be made liable for it. In contrast, substantial responsibility involves a commitment to particular actions also in the future. This concerns 'not the *ex post facto* account for what has been done, but the forward determination of what is to be done' (Jonas 1984: 92). For example, parental responsibility is not usually (only) about being responsible for the actions of one's child (e.g. the child bullying another child at school), but also involves a broader sense of responsibility: taking care of one's children.[4]

In Jonas's terminology, substantial responsibility is a form of 'natural responsibility', in contrast to the 'contracted responsibility' at stake when one acts in one's professional capacity. In the latter case, the individual has a choice as to whether s/he wants to take on the responsibility, or s/he may choose to resign the responsibility, while the former is 'independent of prior assent or choice, irrevocable, and not given to alteration of its terms' (Jonas 1984: 94–95).

Another important distinction is that between individual/personal responsibility and collective responsibility. Jonas (1984) notes that in traditional conceptions of ethics, responsibility had to do mainly with relations between individuals: the individual was perceived as having responsibilities to his/her fellow humans. Responsible behaviour could be demanded from individuals who had the requisite agency and knowledge to act responsibly and who could be understood to act intentionally and out of free will.

However, ethical discussions have in recent decades broadened in scope: in the case of collective harms such as oil spills and corporate fraud it may be difficult if not impossible to point to single individuals who can be held accountable. We can thus also conceive of collectives such as organisations and corporations as responsible moral agents, i.e. as responsible in the sphere where evaluations of responsibility are made. In many cases, responsibility has been institutionalised, for example in the form of codes of conduct and ethics handbooks. The 'ethical universe' has enlarged in other ways, too. As Thompson (1995: 262) points out, much communication is no longer face-to-face but is mediated across great distances of time and space. This has important implications for how relations of responsibility are analysed: we may be analysing relations which are not between single individuals situated in the same temporal and spatial context, but for instance the relationship between a multinational media corporation and its global audience.

In addition to the general distinctions made above (moral vs legal and individual vs collective), we further see a need to distinguish between three different types of responsibility which operate on different levels of social organisation:

(i) *sociocultural responsibility* – responsibility related to societal and group ideologies and the values and practices of the culture and community in which one is operating;
(ii) *interpersonal responsibility* – in relation to one's co-participants in a communicative setting; and
(iii) *responsibility to self* – in relation to one's 'internalised', sub-conscious values and attitudes.

These three levels are often also taken as the bases in linguistic-pragmatic studies of discourse (cf. e.g. Östman 2005). The levels can be seen as framing three different types of restraints on what manifestation of discourse is appropriate or prototypical in a particular situation. Speakers are restrained by and interpret the world around them – and thus play out their sense of responsibility – in relation to (i) their cultural coherence, their tradition and history, the society that they live in, and its institutions; in relation to (ii) the interactive restraints, rules of turn-allocation and norms of politeness and tact that they have to take into account when they are interacting with other speakers; and in relation to (iii) the constraints on feelings and opinions, on the expression of affect and attitudes, and the prejudices that surround them as interactants and speakers. Discourse-(co)producers can – simultaneously or not, but typically implicitly – use linguistic markers to express their sense of responsibility on each of these levels. A variety of such markers are discussed in the case studies in this volume.

Finally, the semantics of the term *responsibility* needs to be discussed with respect to two related terms, *accountability* and *ethics*. Dictionaries often treat the adjective *accountable* as synonymous with *responsible*.[5] Unlike the term *responsibility*, however, the term *accountability* implies a process of describing and explaining ('accounting for') one's actions to someone with whom one is in a relation of power. Accountability is therefore often used to characterise activities that are explicitly performed ('with some effect') and invite direct negotiation. Moreover, one tends to be accountable for past actions, not for appropriate behaviour in the future.[6] The term refers to evaluations and measurements, control and monitoring. Often accountability is demanded of organisations and institutions which need to make their practices more transparent (e.g. for those who fund their activities; a good example is higher education, discussed e.g. in Strathern 2000).

Ethics is a subfield of academic philosophy, but the term itself is also increasingly salient in practical contexts where institutions and organisations negotiate their stand on responsibility issues in the form of different types of codes of practice (relating, e.g. to equality, human rights, environmental issues or research ethics). One might say that ethics has become an industry in itself, with the upsurge in institutional and corporate codifications of rights and wrongs. The number of ethics titles in bookstores is constantly increasing; recent titles include *Socially Responsible Investing* and *Nursing Ethics*. The array of what we might call ethics genres is also on the increase: besides codes of practice, these also include corporate mission statements and reports. Despite laudable ideals, statements of ethics have thus become tools for corporate rhetoric and political correctness. A further aspect of the difference between accountability and responsibility on the one hand and ethics on the other is that although all of these necessarily involve agentivity, the first two terms cannot be used without implying that 'someone' is accountable and responsible. The agency of being ethical can be more dispersed.

Although the focus of the present volume is on 'discourse and responsibility in professional settings', we have not imposed any one definition of responsibility on the respective authors of the chapters. Issues of accountability, ethics, agency and morality are inevitably touched upon in the analyses. We see this volume as a first stage in the exploration of how responsibility is at work in discourse that takes place in professional settings.

3 Analysing responsibility in discourse

The studies in this volume approach responsibility from a number of complementary perspectives. Since the focus is on professional settings and practices, most chapters address 'contracted' responsibilities related to discourse participants' professional roles, but also moral responsibility is being negotiated in the data sets analysed.

In all the chapters, the discourse perspective is evident in the way responsibility is conceptualised as both constructed and dynamic. Responsible selves, identities and relations are not perceived as predetermined and stable, but as construed and negotiated in discourse, in interactions and texts; responsibility can be taken on, denied, assigned to other participants and evaded.

A central concern in all chapters is the way responsibility relations are construed in a given professional setting. That is, the central aim is not to provide generalisations about what constitutes responsibility or responsibility talk. The chapters emphasise that responsibility is not a stable quality of individuals or organisations, but is negotiated in texts and interactions. Therefore, the analysis of responsibility requires attention to the details of language use as well as close contextualisation of the data. The analyses examine, in particular, the negotiation over roles, rights and obligations related to professional, institutional and personal responsibility.

The chapters analyse a specific setting, whether it be care-giving or counselling or broadcast political talk, and show how context constrains and frames the way responsibility is attributed to different participants. Given the particularity of each context analysed, the authors use different concepts and analytic tools to tackle the constructed nature of responsibility, and how responsibility is (often implicitly) enacted in discourse.

This first part of the volume is concerned with explicating the rationale for analysing discourse from the point of view of responsibility. In addition to the present introductory chapter, it contains a chapter by Robin Tolmach Lakoff and one by Srikant Sarangi, all three approaching the phenomenon of responsibility from slightly different points of view, and all three suggesting concrete tools for the analysis of responsibility in discourse.

In her chapter, **Robin Tolmach Lakoff** provides a many-faceted account of how and why it is important for linguists (and especially those working within pragmatics) to take the notion of responsibility seriously, and why it is necessary for scholars from any field to take a linguistic perspective on responsibility in order to understand the concept properly. Taking a linguistic perspective means looking at language on all levels, explicating presuppositions and tropes. For one thing, Lakoff points out, all languages have devices that make it possible for speakers 'to deny what they are doing even as they do it'; this applies equally to taking and evading responsibility (for one's meaning-making) as it does to any other linguistic activity. In her focus on how language is used to deny or mitigate speakers' responsibility for what they communicate, she discusses a wealth of cases where responsibility issues are salient and have linguistic implications, e.g. in contexts of law and politics. She raises several questions that are central to the possibility of demanding responsibility: Can responsibility be attributed to anyone else apart from a unitary subject/speaker? Can those who are not treated as autonomous and dignified fellow human beings (e.g. five-year-olds, psychiatric patients) be held responsible for their actions? For what parts of their communication should speakers be held responsible – the words, the tone, the gestures?

Whereas Lakoff in her chapter takes a partly philosophical and partly linguistic perspective and focuses on the implicit means of expressing responsibility, dealing with issues of agency and intentionality, **Srikant**

Sarangi in his chapter takes a role-relational perspective on responsibility. In his discussion of the rights, roles, and responsibilities of participants in discourse, Sarangi in particular stresses the importance of the changing and emerging roles that interactants have and take on in interaction. His empirical data come from health care encounters where responsibility issues are particularly salient: discussions between counsellors and parents about whether a child should be genetically tested. Sarangi distinguishes between moral and causal responsibility and examines how these two types of responsibility are negotiated in the interaction between parents, counsellors and medical specialists. In a role-relational perspective interactants are seen as evaluating their responsibilities in terms of the (sometimes conflicting) roles they have; thus, a parent may talk in the varying (and often overlapping) roles of mother, wife and reproductively active woman.

The importance of the roles that participants take on or are assigned in discourse, and how roles and relations become entangled with responsibility, is a theme that emerges as central in many of the other contributions in this volume.

The second and third parts of the volume present a set of detailed case studies of how responsibility is enacted in discourse. Part II is entitled ***Constructing responsibility in health care and social work*** and is made up of four chapters, each examining responsibility relations in different health care and social work settings. They emphasise the importance of seeing responsibility not as a stable quality of individuals or organisations, but as something (to be) negotiated in situated interaction.

The study by ***Gøril Thomassen, Srikant Sarangi*** and ***John-Arne Skolbekken*** focuses on health care. Thomassen, Sarangi and Skolbekken concentrate on the framing of parental responsibility in genetic counselling sessions. The assumption is that parents routinely assume responsibility for the health of their children and that this responsibility is particularly salient in a context where possible inheritance of a genetic disorder is being discussed. The authors analyse counselling sessions held at a Norwegian hospital, and focus, in particular, on how responsibility talk is framed by parents and how genetic counsellors respond to such talk. The study shows that while parents often express parental responsibility by emphasising potential risks to their children, counsellors may not necessarily align with such concerns but redirect the focus to the risks affecting the parents themselves. Counsellors also typically aim to retain a non-directive stance, expressing generic and tentative claims rather than attempting to explicitly influence the client's decision making.

The remaining chapters in this part of the volume focus on how responsibility is assigned and negotiated in social work settings. ***Outi Jolanki*** analyses the distribution of responsibility between different actors in the care of elderly people in Finland. Her data consist of interviews where family members of care recipients discuss the roles and responsibilities of professional care workers vis-à-vis the responsibilities of family members. This is a highly contested area, involving evaluations of both moral and legal responsibility: who has the responsibility to care for the elderly in welfare societies? In the interview talk, professional caregivers are attributed a variety of different roles, ranging from allies and co-workers to adversaries. The analysis focuses on how interviewees construct these positions and relations, what kind of conduct is linked to the different positions and what kinds of meanings are given to the notion of responsibility.

In her study on caseworker-client interaction **Maureen T. Matarese** focuses on the way a social worker constructs client responsibilities in interactions with four homeless clients in a New York City shelter. Here the focus is on how the social worker manages the tension between institutional demands (particularly regarding the length that clients are allowed to stay in shelter) and individual clients' varying needs. Through an analysis of the discursive choices of the social worker (e.g. deontic modals, personal pronouns and expressions of time and space), Matarese shows that the way the social worker construes responsibility relations in her talk is highly dependent on the institutional setting and the various policy constraints affecting her position. Of particular significance is the way in which the social worker displaces responsibility to the institution in order to make it possible for herself to align with the client.

In the fourth study in this part of the volume, **Chris Bulcaen** focuses on the self-reflexivity of practitioners in social work discourse, and in particular on the ways in which counsellors topicalise the institutional context in their interaction with clients and colleagues. The data come from action research at shelters for battered and homeless women. Bulcaen argues that reflexivity is intrinsic to social work discourse, but this does not mean that asymmetries between clients and counsellors are seen in the same way by practitioners and by an outsider analyst. The study illustrates the dilemmas that researchers may face when their analyses take on an exonerating role (e.g. by corroborating counsellors' existing views about institutional 'realities'), and when the research subjects' reflexivity acts not only as an ally but as an impediment to the researcher's ethical aims.

The chapters in Part III, ***Responsibility relations in the media***, examine how responsibility is assigned and represented in media settings, both in well-established genres like the broadcast TV debate and the print news story and in journalists' talk about professional responsibility. The underlying assumption is that responsible selves do not pre-exist media representations, but are discursively construed in them. The analyses show that in interactions and texts, particular individuals or groups may be assigned or denied the role of an accountable person or the role of an agent able to act on social problems. Or, as in the case of Stenvall's chapter, responsibility relations may be obscured through unclear attribution practices.

Anita Fetzer takes a close look at interactions in the genre of the political interview. She starts from the assumption that responsibility is the default state in dialogue. Working within a sociopragmatic and conversation analytic perspective, she examines cases where this default state does not obtain and where participants' responsibilities need to be explicitly negotiated. Her data derive from dyadic political interviews broadcast on the BBC. She focuses in particular on the ways in which the different responsibilities of interviewers and interviewees are negotiated not only between two participants but between them and their audiences: a first-frame audience (i.e. the live studio audience) and a second-frame audience, who are not physically present. Responsibility is thus not only anchored to the communicative action of interviewer and interviewee, but also to the specific, layered context in which their activity takes place.

Christian Svensson Limsjö investigates the different voices that can be heard in mediated debate programmes when he looks at the allocation of responsibility to different participants in a Swedish current affairs television debate. More precisely, he explores how social identity is attributed, explicitly and implicitly, through membership categorisation. He finds that the host and the producers of the programme exert considerable influence on the roles that speakers can take in the debate. The roles remain relatively fixed for the duration of the debates, and have direct implications for the distribution of responsibility: societal responsibility is mainly allocated to those in what Svensson Limsjö calls an Accountable role, while those in an Example or Expert role only have the responsibility to describe their experiences or provide specialist knowledge. Thus, while responsibility is seemingly discursively distributed in the ongoing interaction, it is heavily controlled by the programme format. On the basis of his analysis, Svensson Limsjö raises the pertinent question of whether democratic public dialogue is at all possible in a debate where social roles and responsibility relations are simplified in the manner prescribed by a format.

Maija Stenvall examines news agency texts from the point of view of the attribution of claims. She focuses on how responsibility for claims can be avoided by obscuring the sources of such claims. Much of the contents of news dispatches consist of reported speech and it is essential for the reader to gain a sense of who is responsible for particular claims, the journalist or some news actor. Stenvall provides several examples from news agency reports of how responsibility is negotiated between journalists and their sources. Attributions which risk blurring responsibility for claims range from the use of general terms such as *Iraq* (as in 'Iraq says…') to the use of unnamed sources.

Karin Tusting examines the construction of social responsibility in a British Catholic weekly newspaper. In particular, she analyses who is construed as having responsibility for social problems. In Tusting's study, responsibility is closely tied to the notion of agency: the analysis looks at who are given the role of agent (i.e. the capacity to act on social problems) and who are given voice (i.e. the capacity to speak out and express opinions on social problems). The study shows that responsibility in this particular newspaper tends to be assigned mainly to institutions and powerful individuals, but seldom to ordinary people. Tusting relates this to the tendency in high modernity for decision making to be increasingly passed over to 'expert systems': the ordinary person remains in the role of spectator, with little agency and little responsibility.

The final chapter in this volume is by ***Anna Solin***, who examines constructions of responsibility in the journalistic profession. The journalistic profession has been the focus and forum of extensive ethical debates, concerning for example such widely held ideals as objectivity and fairness. Solin's chapter examines how British environmental journalists describe their professional ideals with reference to reporting on environmental risks. Ideals such as accuracy and autonomy are construed as central to journalism, but also as being constantly at risk due to editorial pressure and competition within and between newsrooms. The practice of risk reporting is thus constructed as a conflictual one: responsibilities to sources, audiences and editors do not necessarily coincide.

Solin's analysis raises the question of whether it is possible to distinguish between contracted and natural responsibility. While journalists can certainly be seen as having contracted responsibilities (to their news outlet and to their readers) – e.g. to write accurate and engaging stories – it is not clear to what extent they should also be seen to have moral responsibilities (e.g. of being sincere and honest to their readers and informants), and to what extent such responsibilities are in fact 'part of the contract'.

4 The professional discourse of the researcher

The chapters in this volume have concrete implications for professional practice in that they allow practitioners and their clients and audiences to notice and reflect on the details of the interactions they engage in and the discourse they produce, and particularly on what effects different discursive choices might have both in the immediate context and more broadly.

Whether we are talking about professionals involved in health care, social work or journalism, the studies in this volume stress the importance of engaging in analyses which open up rather than evade such questions. However, not only the relation between professionals and clients/audiences is at stake here, but also that between researchers and their informants/ co-participants. As analysts we develop our own orientation towards the communities we study, make choices of how we relate to our informants and are constantly up against questions of how we contribute or 'give back'. The traditional emphasis on description rather than prescription might discourage the passing of judgments on language data. Moreover, it is often argued that moral issues need to be addressed in context and that an outsider analyst is not in a position to understand the situatedness and historicity of the data to a sufficient extent (cf. Thompson 1995:258; Sarangi 2007). This creates considerable challenges for those analysts who want to engage in more extended dialogue with the communities they study (see also Cameron et al. 1992).

The position of the analyst may usefully be approached through the concept of 'reflexivity', as Bulcaen does in his chapter. Sarangi and Candlin (2003: 278–280) argue that in any applied linguistic research in professional settings, the researcher's position is likely to be fraught with tensions – it is difficult to achieve a balance between reflexivity and relevance. They list a number of different participant roles that a researcher may take on (such as 'befriender', 'assessor' and 'consultant'), which may have important implications for both the success of the research and the way in which its results can be interpreted. Awareness is a key issue – awareness of both one's own role as researcher and the ways in which informants understand and orient to one's agenda.

Many of the chapters in this volume show that professional practitioners may have different and even conflicting responsibilities to different stakeholders in discursive events. They also describe ambivalences and conflicts, whether within a professional community or between professionals and clients/audiences.[7] They suggest that reflexivity on the part of the researchers includes attempts to anticipate ways in which research findings can be taken up in unpredictable ways, or even used to create further tensions; not every analysis will necessarily result in increased understanding.

The chapters in this volume take variable stances towards different researcher roles. Not all chapters suggest practical agendas for intervention in the professional settings studied. Many analyses focus on how responsibility is constructed in discourse, and include little explicit commentary for example on what might constitute responsible language use in any given institutional setting. However, most of the authors draw some critical conclusions on the basis of their analyses, and it is here that (implicit) sets of ideals or values of 'responsible discourse' emerge: sincerity and honesty towards one's interlocutors (e.g. Lakoff), transparency in the expression of who is speaking (Stenvall), support for democratic participation and dialogue (Jolanki, Svensson, Tusting) and reflexive awareness (Bulcaen).

The challenge of reflexivity is one that all scholars are up against in their everyday work. The way one writes a scholarly article is a matter of taking responsibility for presenting findings in a fashion that is as neutral as possible so as to interest the research community at large, and so as not to offend anyone. Scholars also have to consider in what ways they and their research can be beneficial to the community that is being analysed. We believe that the very act of writing about issues of responsibility is a challenge that we need to address more explicitly in our everyday work.

Notes

1   See, for example, Candlin and Crichton (2012); Christie and Martin (1997); Gunnarsson et al. (1997); Iedema (2007); Iedema and Wodak (1999); Linell and Sarangi (1998); Mullany (2011); Roberts and Sarangi (1999); and Sarangi (2005).

2   A notable exception is Atkinson (1999). Overall, there is a relatively limited amount of research in discourse studies focusing on responsibility. A key volume is Hill and Irvine (1993); other fairly recent studies include Brown and Rubin (2005); Johnson (2008); Kampf (2009); Rasmussen (2013); and Sneijder and te Molder (2005).

3   The Exxon oil spill is a notorious example of how complex responsibility attribution can get. The oil tanker Exxon Valdez spilled 11 million gallons of crude oil in Prince William Sound, Alaska, in March 1989. The argument over damages to fishermen and native Alaskans was only resolved some 20 years after the event.

4   A distinction between backward- and forward-looking types of responsibility is also suggested by Cane (2002: 5): *historic responsibility* is concerned

with 'allocating the costs of harm on an historic basis', while *prospective responsibility* is concerned with 'distributing risks of harm' with a future orientation.

5   The *OED* lists 'answerable, responsible' as part of the definition of *accountable*, while in the *Longman Dictionary of Contemporary English* (1995) *accountable* is defined as 'responsible for the effects of your actions'.

6   Cane (2002: 33) argues that accountability is therefore a more negative term than responsibility: 'Giving an account, whether or not it may lead to the imposition of some sanction in case the account is unsatisfactory, is a backward-looking and essentially negative process, whereas the idea of being a responsible person is forward-looking and positive.'

7   The intricacies of professional ambivalence and its relation to situational context are dealt with in relation to genetic testing in Arribas-Ayllon et al. (2009).

References

Arribas-Ayllon, M., Sarangi, S. and Clarke, A. (2009) Professional ambivalence: accounts of ethical practice in childhood genetic testing. *Journal of Genetic Counselling* 18: 173–184.

Atkinson, P. (1999) Medical discourse, evidentiality and the construction of professional responsibility. In Roberts and Sarangi (eds) *Talk, Work and Institutional Order: Discourse in Medical, Mediation and Management Settings* 75–108. Berlin: Mouton de Gruyter.

Baier, K. (1970) Responsibility and action. In M. Brand (ed.) *The Nature of Human Action* 100–116. Glenview, IL: Scott, Foresman & Co.

Brown, C. and Rubin, D. L. (2005) Causal markers in tobacco industry documents: the pragmatics of responsibility. *Journal of Pragmatics* 37: 799–811.

Cameron, D., Frazer, E., Harvey, P., Rampton, B. and Richardson, K. (1992) *Researching Language. Issues of Power and Method*. London: Routledge.

Candlin, N. C. and Crichton, J. (2012) *Discourse of Trust*. Basingstoke: Palgrave Macmillan.

Cane, P. (2002) *Responsibility in Law and Morality*. Oxford: Hart Publishing.

Christie, F. and Martin, J. (eds) (1997) *Genre and Institutions. Social Processes in the Workplace and School*. London: Cassell.

Gunnarsson, B.-L., Linell, P. and Nordberg, B. (eds) (1997) *The Construction of Professional Discourse*. London: Longman.

Harmon, M. M. (1995) *Responsibility as Paradox. A Critique of Rational Discourse on Government*. London: Sage.

Hill, J. H. and Irvine, J. T. (eds) (1993) *Responsibility and Evidence in Oral Discourse*. Cambridge: Cambridge University Press.

Iedema, R. (ed.) (2007) *The Discourse of Hospital Communication. Tracing Complexities in Contemporary Health Organizations.* Basingstoke: Palgrave Macmillan.

Iedema, R. and Wodak, R. (1999) Introduction: organisational discourses and practices. *Discourse & Society* 10(1): 5–19.

Johnson, A. (2008) 'From where we're sat…': negotiating narrative transformation through interaction in police interviews with suspects. *Text & Talk* 28: 327–349.

Jonas, H. (1984) *The Imperative of Responsibility. In Search of an Ethics for the Technological Age.* Chicago, IL: University of Chicago Press.

Kampf, Z. (2009) Public (non-)apologies: the discourse of minimizing responsibility. *Journal of Pragmatics* 41: 2257–2270.

Linell, P. and Sarangi, S. (eds) (1998) *Discourse Across Professional Boundaries. Text* 18.

Mullany, L. (2011) *Gendered Discourse in the Professional Workplace.* Basingstoke: Palgrave Macmillan.

Östman, J.-O. (2005) Persuasion as implicit anchoring: the case of collocations. In H. Halmari and T. Virtanen (eds) *Persuasion Across Genres. A Linguistic Approach* 183–212. Amsterdam: John Benjamins.

Rasmussen, J. (2013) Governing the workplace or the worker? Evolving dilemmas in chemical professionals' discourse on occupational health and safety. *Discourse & Communication* 7(1): 75–94.

Roberts, C. and Sarangi, S. (eds) (1999) *Talk, Work and Institutional Order: Discourse in Medical, Mediation and Management Settings.* Berlin: Mouton de Gruyter.

Sarangi, S. (2005) The conditions and consequences of professional discourse studies. *Journal of Applied Linguistics* 2: 371–394.

Sarangi, S. (2007) The anatomy of interpretation: coming to terms with the analyst's paradox in professional discourse studies. *Text & Talk* 27: 567–584.

Sarangi, S. and Candlin, C. (2003) Introduction: Trading between reflexivity and relevance: new challenges for applied linguistics. *Applied Linguistics* 24: 271–285.

Sneijder, P. and te Molder, H. F. M. (2005) Moral logic and logical morality: attributions of responsibility and blame in online discourse on veganism. *Discourse & Society* 16: 675–696.

Strathern, M. (ed.) (2000) *Audit Cultures.* London: Routledge.

Thompson, J. B. (1995) *The Media and Modernity.* Cambridge: Polity Press.

Anna Solin is a senior lecturer at the Department of Modern Languages, University of Helsinki, Finland. She gained her PhD in Linguistics at Lancaster University, UK, in 2001. She currently directs a research project on language regulation in academia, with a particular focus on the shifting norms of English use.

Jan-Ola Östman is Professor of Scandinavian Languages at the University of Helsinki, Finland, and President of the International Pragmatics Association. In addition to degrees from the Åbo Akademi University in Finland, he has an MA from Reading University, UK, and a PhD from the University of California at Berkeley, USA. He has previously worked as Professor of English, and Professor of General linguistics at the University of Helsinki, and as invited scholar and guest researcher in Antwerp, Brussels, Tromsø, and Freiburg. His research focuses on pragmatics, discourse and the media; constructional approach to language; minority languages, especially signed languages and immigrant languages; socio-dialectology and socio-onomastics; language contact; and language policy and the sociology of language. He is the co-editor of *Handbook of Pragmatics* (John Benjamins) and of the book series *Constructional Approaches to Language.*

Taking 'responsibility': From word to discourse

Robin Tolmach Lakoff

1 Introduction

If, as scholars principally concerned with language, we were to suggest to colleagues in other fields – or, even more so, to people outside of academia – that we had some special competency to discuss responsibility, we could well expect to receive some scepticism. What is 'linguistic' about responsibility? What does a field primarily concerned with the formal properties of language have to contribute to a discussion of what is a psychological, social, or political problem – anything but a problem of *language*?

In the conservative view of many 'core' linguists, an investigation of responsibility, or 'responsibility', cannot be the topic of a linguistically-oriented collection of studies. Traditional modes of linguistic analysis do not provide a natural or meaningful way to investigate connections between responsibility and linguistic form: it is not even possible, such scholars would say, for a linguist, *qua* linguist, to undertake such an investigation.

But drawing a connection between language and responsibility is both necessary (if we are to understand each of them fully) and possible (if we use the resources available to us). It is essential for students of language to take a broad perspective. The business of linguistics as a social science is to use language as a 'window into the mind' – into human cognitive and social processes. Responsibility plays a role in both of these, and therefore we might expect to find it represented in some way in our linguistic and communicative behaviours and structures. Therefore, a full understanding of language as a cognitive and social activity requires a search for linguistic forms that relate to responsibility, a search ultimately producing a full understanding of how humans express their sense of responsibility (or eschew it).

Other social scientists might contest those points. But human beings do what they do, psychologically, politically, and socially, very largely through the medium of linguistic expression. While arguably feelings of responsibility, or the desire to avoid it, originate in mental constructs or social organisations, we express those feelings to ourselves and others, and arrive at justifications and possible courses of action, via linguistic channels. If we cannot frame our ideas in language, we cannot appreciate or communicate those ideas. Thus, understanding how language enables speakers to approach, frame, and accept or reject notions like responsibility is basic to the analysis of the concept itself.

Nor can language be studied meaningfully as a collection of un-contextualised forms. The study of a syntactic process like passivisation without reference to the interpersonal functions it serves would not produce a complete and coherent analysis. Languages would not have passive or passive-like structures, which complicate basic sentence-forms and thereby slow down the transmission of meanings, unless the functional gain from the complexity outweighed the semantic efficiency lost by it. Likewise, languages would not include presuppositions and other backgrounded meanings in their lexical structures – making them harder to understand and more open to deception and unclarity – without some communicative advantage. One important gain in both cases consists in speakers' ability to absolve themselves of some responsibility for what they are saying. Language exists in order to meet human needs: one basic human need is to feel comfortable with ourselves and to represent ourselves to others as competent and virtuous. The evasive capacities of language are an inextricable part of its being a human artefact.

While the topic of this collection is 'responsibility', the positive perspective, more significant may be the ways in which language does the bidding of its human speakers in order to deny or mitigate speakers' responsibility for what they communicate. A search for the ways available to speakers of English for evading responsibility for the meaning of what they say uncovers a rich lode: at every level, from smallest forms to largest, most concrete to most abstract, English (like other languages) has devices enabling speakers to deny what they are doing even as they do it. This in itself suggests the importance of responsibility to human beings.

2 The complexities of 'responsibility', and responsibility

The definition of 'responsibility' has been important in many fields, some of which I discuss briefly in Section 3. The problems have become more pressing as more different kinds of people become treated as capable of full responsibility for their actions – a double-edged sword in many cases.

To approach these controversies as linguists, we may find it helpful to begin with an investigation of the origins and historical usage of the word 'responsibility' itself.

2.1 Responsibility: The history of a word

The source of the English word is the Latin verb *respondeo*, 'answer'. We still use *answerable* as a synonym for *responsible* in one of its senses. The Latin verb derives from an Indo-European root **spend-*, 'make an offering, engage oneself by a ritual act'. In 'engaging oneself' (as a member of a society within which a particular form of expression of that engagement is recognised), a person understands and accepts membership in the group, with all its implicit and explicit obligations and privileges. Such a person, engaging in such rituals, understands and accepts a duality in the relationship, encoded in the dual meaning of the word itself. At least as far back as the 17th century, according to the OED, *responsible* could be used in two nearly antithetical ways, one as 'accountable (for something bad)':

> (1643) To hold this Popish erronious opinion, that they are in no case responsible to their whole Kingdomes or Parliaments for their grossest exorbitances.

The other, 'capable of fulfilling an obligation or trust; reliable, trustworthy':

> (1691) Not knowing that the Bill or Bond is true or legal, or that the Man bound to me is honest or responsible.

At first the coexistence of these contradictory senses is mysterious. The problem has been discussed before (for other words), by Sigmund Freud. In his essay, 'The antithetical meaning of primal words' (1957 [1910]), Freud considers words with (as he puts it) 'antithetical' or antonymous senses, for instance, Latin *sacer*, 'holy' and 'accursed'; English *cleave*, 'split' and 'stick'. In some cases (like *sacer*) the apparently antithetical meanings coexist because while the asserted component of the meaning remains constant (i.e. 'related to the divine'), a presupposition shifts (here, from 'good' to 'bad').[1] *Responsible*, while hardly a 'primal' word in Freud's sense, similarly gets its two senses via the encoding of opposing presuppositions, 'good' and 'bad'.

2.2 The encoding and evasion of responsibility in language

2.2.1 Presupposition and other backgrounding devices

Presupposition is an important aspect of meaning at both the lexical and syntactic levels of analysis. As such it has often been discussed in several fields: logic, philosophy of language, lexicography, syntax, pragmatics, and sociolinguistics. There have been many attempts over the last century or so to define 'presupposition' precisely, starting with Frege (1952 [1892]) and continuing at least through the 1980s (for useful discussion see Levinson 1983). Much of the controversy has concerned the kinds of backgrounded propositions that are properly called *presupposition*: only entailments remaining constant under negation, or backgrounded assumptions of many other kinds. Languages and their speakers could not function without indirect forms of encoding meaning; if everything had to be expressed as assertions, communication would become redundant and perhaps impossible. But presupposition is also a means of evading responsibility illegitimately because part of responsibility is, as the word's etymology suggests, literal 'answerability'. But by encoding material in the form of a presupposition, a speaker renders it unquestionable, and therefore removes the possibility of an answer. A speaker who wishes to be underhanded can encode controversial matter in the form of presupposition, thereby disowning responsibility for it.

Within linguistics, presupposition was first discussed at length in the late 1960s under the rubric of generative semantics. Some of these early commentators discussed classical cases of 'true' presupposition: factive verbs (Kiparsky and Kiparsky 1971) like *realise* (vs *think*) and *regret*; verbs of judging (Fillmore 1971) such as *accuse*, *criticise*, and *blame*. Other cases are sometimes called 'presupposition' in the literature, sometimes 'pragmatic presupposition' or 'assumption': in these it is not possible to identify a proposition that remains constant under negation, but a part of the meaning of a word or grammatical structure is backgrounded: e.g. the distinction between *tú* and *Usted* in Spanish or the choice of honorifics in Japanese. A related case is conversational implicature (Grice 1975), in which the responsibility for the meaning of an utterance is shifted from speaker to addressee. As with other backgrounding devices, implicature may be used deceptively, but it is also an important tool for the creation of trust and intimacy: if I can trust you to make my meaning for me, I have to believe that we share background and interests, are the same kind of people. In all these cases, giving up full responsibility for meaning-making has two functions: not just self-protection but also positive politeness (Brown and Levinson 1986), the implication that participants are alike and capable of mutual trust.

Syntactic relationships may also express presupposed or backgrounded material. The syntactically marked passive construction in English may presuppose (in the broader sense) the speaker's authority (e.g. *I don't know how it got broken*) when s/he uses the agentless passive (*get* or *be*) construction.

Subordinate clauses also express presupposed or backgrounded content. In the sentence *Before Max won the Nobel Prize, he was a delight to have around*, the first (subordinated) part is assumed to be true. Coordinating conjunctions may also encode background matter, not necessarily as formal presuppositions. In *John is a Republican, but he is honest*, the conjunction *but* invites the hearer to share the speaker's inference that Republicans are normally not honest.

Speakers may avoid some responsibility for meaning via discourse markers (Schiffrin 1987) such as *well, but, I mean, you know,* which speakers use to direct addressees to draw desired inferences without explicitly telling them to do so; and conversational inferencing (Gumperz 1982), in which speakers, typically by paralinguistic or extralinguistic means, convey coded messages to interlocutors. Code-switching and style-shifting are other ways of expressing emotional and social connectedness ('secret handshakes'), without explicitly acknowledging shared group membership.

2.2.2 Rhetorical tropes

Fields other than linguistics have discussed analogous cases. For thousands of years rhetoricians have discussed 'tropes' or figures of speech, as adornments to oratory or poetics, but not as the intended communication itself. As with discourse markers and inferences (some of which have been discussed as 'tropes' as far back as Aristotle), figures of speech frequently minimise or alter the meaning or intention of some part of a communication, e.g. its information content or the force or strength of the illocutionary point (Searle 1979).

This is clearly the case with *meiosis*, or 'lessening' (*That was not such a great evening*, to describe a horrendous dinner party). But its apparent opposite, *hyperbole* (*This is the greatest country in the history of the universe*) paradoxically also diminishes the force of an utterance. In the first case the speaker does the job of minimisation; in the latter the addressee, through implicature, is encouraged to understand the speaker's utterance less forcefully. In the first case, the lessening of speaker responsibility is relatively explicit: the speaker disclaims the meaning the utterance would have if it were to receive its full force. In the second, the responsibility for diminution of force rests with the addressee. In such cases the speaker doubly avoids responsibility: first, by ceding interpretive control to the hearer; and second, by saying something meant to lessen the force of the utterance without explicitly acknowledging that fact.

All such devices carry some risk, even as they enable speakers to avoid other risks. As long as interlocutors share most of their linguistic and social background, they can reasonably expect understanding to be sharable via these devices. But if speaker and addressee differ significantly in their linguistic and interactional grammars, backgrounded devices are dangerous: one cannot count on one's interlocutor to catch the intended meaning.

There are many other forms we use to avoid direct confrontation – forms that can therefore be considered aspects of negative politeness (Brown and Levinson 1986), e.g. hedges and euphemisms. Both allow speakers to convey interactionally or emotionally problematic ideas to others without themselves or their interlocutors having to explicitly acknowledge the meaning of what is being said. Such devices have a positive politeness component as well, since being able to use and understand hedges and euphemisms means that all participants in the interaction feel a degree of trust in one another based on shared cultural connectedness. To understand *Harry seems to be a bit under the weather* as meaning 'Harry is drunk', a hearer must understand the euphemistic intention on the part of the speaker.

Some of the examples above have always been a part of traditional literary and linguistic analysis; most at least partly involve more recent additions to the linguistic armamentarium: pragmatics, sociolinguistics, discourse analysis. But all can be said to turn on specifically *linguistic* forms: words and syntactic constructions. In the remainder of this chapter, I will examine the expression of responsibility in larger and more abstract communicative contexts. These examples are 'linguistic' not only in that they make use of language, but also because they are situated within specific discourse types or genres, which are subject to rules and processes analogous to those of 'core' grammar (cf. Labov and Waletzky 1967 and Schiffrin 1994).

3 Responsibility in discourse: Some cases and some problems

3.1 The responsibility for narrative

Narratology, the analysis of story-telling, has become a major concern in many fields, within academia (sociolinguistics, literary theory, and anthropology), and outside of it (law, psychoanalysis, and psychotherapy). Each discipline asks its own questions and requires its own kinds of answers. In recent years, a connection has been created among these fields: the recognition that events and how they happen cannot always be known. The stories created by all participants are of equal validity. In the past investigators have been able to assume uncontroversially that the narrator with the most social and political power has the best, or even only, claim to truth. The political and social changes of the last half century are causing scholars and participants alike to discard that ancient assumption. And since the ability to tell a story deemed truthful enables its teller to bear the responsibility for that narrative, these social, psychological, legal, and political changes have extended access to discursive responsibility: if you have a reasonable chance of being believed, you need to be careful about what you say.

3.2 Responsibility in the law

Legal scholars and trial lawyers for some time have construed trials, especially criminal trials, as narrative competitions. More recently the relevance of narrative to law has been extended to the making and application of the laws themselves. In the past, the comforting assumption of the legal community was that the law was 'blind' – it did not differentiate in its meaning or application depending on the status or roles of participants. But some scholars currently make the opposite argument: by its very blindness, the law enacts and enforces bias. The reason for that conclusion is that members of different groups, having very different experiences of the world, construct reality very differently and hence tell radically different stories about 'what happened' and 'whodunit'. So a law that may work well for, and make perfect sense to, members of a powerful group may do harm to members of minority or disempowered groups. The stories encoded in legal statutes are not given or obviously true, but must be developed and contested again and again: a society has the responsibility to both make and vet the laws and the stories behind them (cf. Delgado 1989; Williams 1991; and on the other side, Farber and Sherry 1997). But if different groups enter that society with different experiences and expectations, that is, tell different stories about what happened and what it means, then what appears to be 'justice' to one group is seen as 'just-us' – i.e. the law is designed by white men ('us') to work well for white men – to another (African Americans) (Gates 1996). The sharp disagreement along racial lines about the O. J. Simpson verdict is one such case. The same superficial 'story' was available to all; but the veracity of the teller was questioned on one side, not the other. The black community, in the persona of a largely minority-female jury, demanded and got the right to take over the responsibility for the meaning of the story from the majority members of society, as expressed in its verdict – and the consequent shock of the aforesaid majority (cf. Lakoff 2000).

3.3 Legal responsibility confronts psychological responsibility

The problems of legal responsibility get worse when legal 'insanity' runs into psychiatric 'psychosis' and ordinary language 'craziness'. The three, often popularly conflated, are quite different in their implications. Concern is frequently voiced in the American media about felons who 'get away with murder' through verdicts of 'not guilty by reason of insanity' (although in fact this outcome is very rare). To many that seems like an abdication of responsibility for bad behaviour, the use of 'craziness' to absolve wrongdoing. Likewise, in recent years there has been much agonising in conservative circles over the 'abuse excuse', e.g. the argument by the Menendez brothers that their admitted murder of their parents was the inevitable outcome of years of child abuse. Post-traumatic stress disorder has been used as a mitigating argument by Vietnam veterans charged with violent crimes.

During the 1980s a great deal of psychological and legal attention was focused on the then-burgeoning fields of multiple personality disorder and satanic ritual abuse. In one case a woman who claimed to have multiple personalities accused a man of acquaintance rape on the basis that, after she had given consent, and events were proceeding to their conclusion, one of her 'multiples' emerged (the defendant was unaware of her condition) who had not given consent. This case, while arguably ludicrous, raises an interesting philosophical problem about the distribution of responsibility among multiple personae allegedly inhabiting a single body, particularly when each (as is typical) is unaware of the existence of some or all of the others. Can such a person (or persons) be held responsible for their actions – positive or negative? It would seem that, unless there is a unitary subject/speaker 'I', the performer of the Austinian speech act, there can be no unambiguous attribution of responsibility for anything. The law requires the identification of such a subject, but psychology argues that this identification is not possible in all cases.

One notorious case juxtaposed these two uneasily coexisting world-views. In 2001 Andrea Yates, a mother of five children under the age of five, drowned all of them in her bathtub. She then called her husband and the police. She had done it, she explained, to save them from Satan. The Texas jury had little difficulty finding her guilty and sane – the latter because, as the foreman explained to the media, she had called the police afterward, *so she must have known it was wrong.* (She is serving a life sentence without the possibility of parole.) The jurors have also explained that they believed the defence psychiatrist's diagnosis that Yates was psychotic, but that that had no bearing on their finding of legal sanity. The conflict arises because the American legal system permits only two kinds of 'explanation' or exculpation for criminal acts: how are we to determine whether someone (who has admittedly done something bad) is responsible for it? Finally, we have trouble even addressing the question that underlies these quandaries: are human beings free agents or constrained by their psyches, their genes, their prior experience – or, for that matter, the devil? Only if we are truly free can we ever have responsibility – either the good or the bad kind.

In our post-Freudian world, the psychologically sophisticated acknowledge that people do bad things that are beyond their conscious intention or control because of 'mental illness'. But that assumption runs headlong into other explanations, older and more powerful: that God, or the devil, is responsible for human actions; that people must take responsibility for their behaviour, or else society cannot mete out punishment appropriately so as to ensure proper behaviour. Many people hold both of these contradictory theories. Two venerable institutions, religion and the law, are at odds over them. The problem is compounded by the entrance into the fray of a third competitor, psychiatry, whose definition of 'mental illness' has little to do with either legal 'insanity' or religious 'sinfulness'. The lay public, when they function as jurors, increasingly demonstrates its contempt for both law and psychiatry by refusing to find defendants not guilty by reason of insanity no matter how 'crazy' they appear. Respected institutions are arrayed against one another; putative definitions permit an uneasy truce, but peace is achieved only by both jurors and professionals refusing to consider the crux of the difficulty: that a person can be partly responsible, or responsible from one perspective but not from another. Thus the inconsistencies and ambiguities that exist around the word and concept of 'responsibility' lexically, syntactically and semantically are reflected at the discourse level, in a not fully explicit dispute among three ways of looking at human beings, three professions, three philosophies.

3.4 Feminism: Are women responsible?

Consider the case of acquaintance rape. A woman goes out on a date which culminates in sexual intercourse. The woman says she said 'No' but the man didn't stop, and overpowered her, but she did not give consent. The man says that she went out on the date consensually, she came to his place consensually, used alcohol or drugs of her own free will, and engaged in pre-coital behaviour ('petting') consensually – all of which, to him, implied consent to something further. Was it rape? Feminists argue that 'no means no' – an expression of non-consent means that anything further constitutes rape. Conservatives argue that the woman 'led him on' (or at least, let him go on) and therefore bears some responsibility for what ensued. Feminists argue further that women are, to some extent, still subject to their historical roles: it is unladylike to refuse a man's attentions; there is a sexual double standard still in effect that penalises women more strongly than men for sexual activity, so a woman should (in order to equalise the playing field) be the one who calls the shots. The other side argues that that might have been reasonable in the past, but things have changed so much that the responsibility is now equal, like everything else.

This is one of those areas in which it is sometimes hard to tell who is a 'feminist', on the basis of beliefs. Is it feminist to attribute to women responsibility for their actions (good and bad) equivalent to men? Or is it feminist to insist that women still require extra protection, because true equality is still in the future. Conservative writers (e.g. Roiphe 1994) have been scathing in their denunciations of women who claim acquaintance rape as a result of intercourse under the influence of alcohol; on the other hand, the same writers are often ready to argue that, under identical circumstances 'boys will be boys' who cannot be held fully accountable for their behaviour, and it's the responsibility of women to know that and act accordingly. And the same conservatives who are willing to exonerate white college men in acquaintance rape cases seldom argue for diminished responsibility in 'real' rape cases, in which defendants are often members of classes or ethnic groups classed as 'non-us'. So the attribution of responsibility has strong political implications, in terms of who alleges it and of whom it is alleged. Sometimes it is convenient to see ourselves or others as responsible agents – sometimes not. Clearly responsibility is slippery, semantically and pragmatically.[2]

Another difficult case is that of spousal abuse or wife-beating,[3] also currently being re-evaluated in terms of the assignment of responsibility, for somewhat analogous reasons. Historically, wife-beating was seen as a husband's prerogative – just as a man might legally beat his horse or his child or his slave. Starting in the 1970s, with the rise of the modern women's movement, the situation was re-evaluated, with women seen as persons with individual rights equivalent to men's. With this understanding, spousal abuse became equivalent in the law to other forms of assault, and could be punished with prison terms: men were seen as instigators and aggressors, and the argument used in the past that 'she was asking for it' no longer was admissible in court. This change has been seen, and correctly so, as a triumph for women and feminism.

Now (in what is sometimes considered a post-feminist era) the question of the responsibility for spousal abuse has shifted – not quite back to where it was, but shifted nonetheless. For instance, Deborah Solomon (2002) argues that at least some women who have been beaten by their spouses want to divest themselves of the attribution of innocent 'victim', claiming that they played some kind of active role: drove him to violence and thus bore some responsibility for what happened. They want to see spousal abuse as a joint activity, and themselves as in some sense choosing to play the game. As with acquaintance rape, the argument is that it is better (for the one abused) to feel like an autonomous participant rather than as a passive victim. But, as with rape, which attribution is more accurate, and which, if either, is merely a palliative narrative designed to make someone feel better – but not a good match with the facts? And who gets to decide?

3.5 A tentative foray into Realpolitik

Political scientists – unlike lawyers and psychologists – often treat 'mere' language with disdain, as not a serious player in real-world politics. But the political scientist Michael M. Harmon (1995) considers the 'paradox' inherent in the meanings we give to the word 'responsibility', attributing to it three meanings: agency, accountability, and obligation, and noting that sometimes these meanings conflict. If, for instance, we mean by *responsibility* that people are the authors of their actions, autonomous beings, then what is the role of the second sense, in which to be 'responsible' is to be *accountable for* your actions to a *higher authority* (who interprets what your actions mean and determines their consequences for you and others)? If responsibility is located in an accountability to superiors, how can people also view responsible behaviour as a personal, internalised 'obligation'? All of these meanings are essential parts of our understanding of the word, but logically they are uneasy bedfellows. The fact that we use the terms as if there were no conflict leads to some of the most troubling ambiguities in current political discourse.

Moral philosophers too have spoken about what we mean by 'responsible' and 'responsibility'. For instance, Wallace (1994) sees the definition of 'responsibility' as involving several related but distinct concepts, all with both psychological and social implications: freedom, free will, choice, and rational thought. A person needs to have reached certain levels of education, maturity, and economic comfort to be reasonably expected to be 'responsible' – a point not always appreciated in current American public discourse. Those who are not treated as autonomous and dignified fellow human beings cannot be held fully responsible for their actions. So responsibility is a state of interdependence: if A treats B as worthy, B may be expected by A to display responsibility. (The connection between this position and the feminist/conservative positions outlined in Section 3.4 should be obvious.)

Political scientists and moral philosophers might also consider as a failure of responsibility the growing dependence of politicians on polling to provide them with opinions, justifications, and definitions, or rather, definition. Among its many evils, polling offers a means of putting the onus on others for the outcomes of one's action – 'the polls made me do it'. It is a way of not having to come to a genuine decision for one's own genuine reasons – an evasion of the responsibilities of leadership by resort to a false populism.

3.6 Paradox on the Right: Who's responsible, anyway?

While less commonly in the era of the Tea Party, one still sometimes encounters, in serious discourse, identifications of political conservatives as the intellectual heavy-lifters, versus liberals as warm and compassionate, but less smart. These assessments are based on the rhetorical practices of both sides. Conservatives are seen as avoiders of postmodern ambiguity, and the 'on-the-one-hand, on-the-other' arguments favoured by liberals. But many of conservatism's most attractively hard-edged rhetorical gambits depend on a premise that is based on unresolved paradox. I discussed above cases in which modern developments in psychology collide with ancient religious, moral, and political beliefs about choice and determinism to create a paradox over responsibility for one's actions. Two other modern developments, sociobiology (now more often called 'evolutionary biology') and genetic research, create problems for 'hard-nosed' conservative thought.

Many conservatives are enthusiastic supporters of evolutionary biology, particularly when it is applied to women and minority groups. The premise is that our genes dictate our options: that women must stay home and raise families, and are not aggressive enough to engage in combat, for instance, and that if we try to override our genetic makeup we are headed for disaster. Anatomy is destiny. Their essentialism dictates that we not experiment with innovation; indeed, essentialism pats us on the back for understanding how constrained we are. It's a kind of millennial Calvinism, very gratifying indeed to those whose genes predestine them to privilege (who do most of this sort of writing). Similarly, the argument is made (most notably but not uniquely in Herrnstein and Murray's *The Bell Curve* 1994) that the current social and economic disadvantages plaguing the African American community are genetically predetermined. Hence no social programmes, no affirmative action, can create equality. So it is right to do nothing: not just morally right, but intellectually – scientifically – right.

But a paradox emerges here. If genes control most of our capacities and behaviours, then we cannot be held responsible for the latter. The same people who believe that genes predict our human capabilities are also, most typically, the ones who argue for strict and severe penalties for criminal behaviour, for ending 'welfare as we know it', and against prosecuting acquaintance rape – because those involved ought to 'take responsibility for their actions/lives'. But holding both these positions is self-contradictory. If your genes made you do it, you cannot be said to have *chosen* your deplorable path; and if you cannot be said to have made a choice, based on free will and the capacity for rational determination, then by any of the definitions moral philosophers and others have offered for responsibility, you cannot be expected to have it, and you cannot be criticised or penalised for failing to use it. You might as well blame a blind man for failing to warn you before you get up to lecture that you have spinach in your teeth.

4 Communicative responsibility: The lie direct

Each of the examples in Section 3 examines, directly or otherwise, the rights, roles, and responsibilities of participants in discourse. Outright violations of Gricean conversational logic (e.g. lies as violations of the Maxim of Quality)[4] are dangerous for a social species that depends on mutual trust in order to survive. If we cannot count on one another's discourse as reliable and interpretable, we cannot continue to use language as a means of social cohesion. It is obvious that outright lying is apt to have this effect.

Plato addresses the problem, if ironically (at least for modern readers), when he banishes poets from his ideal Republic because poets 'lie'. The 'history' Homer provides is not literally true even to the degree that those of Herodotus or Thucydides are. Today we think we have become comfortable making distinctions between 'real' and 'fictional' worlds. Yet when we encounter amalgams and mixed genres – memoirs incorporating events that could not have happened; novels that include real-world historical characters engaging in fictitious events – we may feel discomfort. Even as sophisticated a personality as Oprah Winfrey (voicing her audience's discomfort as well as her own) demonstrated in front of the world, on television, her fury at a guest whose memoir was later shown to contain a few untruths sprinkled through a generally accurate account. Memoir, like history and autobiography, cannot lie. Makers of these genres must take responsibility for the absolute truth of the whole.

4.1 The lay of the lie

The problem is not purely literary. As a number of writers have shown (e.g. Coleman and Kay 1981; Sweetser 1990), determining whether an utterance is a 'lie' is a tricky matter. There are many kinds of utterances between the unvarnished truth and the lie direct, and assigning a particular example to one or another depends on the assigner's frames, contextualisations, beliefs, and more. What kind of distinction ought we to make between the outright lie and the many intermediate cases (for which English has names like prevarication, extenuation, fib, story, white lie, and many more)? It is normally assumed that lying is the worst of communicative sins. But at least, in lying directly, the liar undertakes to lie – knowingly and intentionally. Even if the deceptive nature of the speech act is hidden from the addressee, at least, in a true lie, the speaker knows what is going on. There is, in that weird way, honesty if not honour in lying – truth in lying.

Such intermediate and undecidable cases allow those with a need for evasion to remain unaware of, and thus not 'responsible' for, the misconstructions to which they have led their interlocutors. If exposed, they permit credible deniability: the speaker 'misspoke', was the victim of 'misinformation', or was 'misunderstood'. A true lie, once discovered, is hard to weasel out of; while prevarication and its relatives are capable of manipulation. So ought we to give more credit to the politician who asserts that Barack Obama and Osama bin Laden are bosom buddies, than to the one who claims that there *is* no sexual relationship between him and 'that woman, Ms Lewinsky' – meaning, or insinuating, that at the moment of the speech act, no such relationship is taking place?[5]

4.2 Responsible communication: Where is it found?

We humans are proud of being the only creatures with – in some sense of the definition – full-fledged 'language'. Because we so strongly privilege the verbal component of our communications, we disregard the paralinguistic and extralinguistic parts – or we think we do, or should. One consequence is that, as hearers, we are less than fully competent to grasp and interpret any lack of correspondence between the verbal and nonverbal aspects of communication. We may sense a mismatch; but we can't quite identify it, since our (verbal) language – so rich in ways of talking about verbal language – is remarkably poor in ways of discussing the nonverbal. And while we feel that it's proper and normal to comment on someone's verbal utterance – 'What do you *mean* by "there is no sexual relationship"?' – we often feel it is intrusive and impolite to question other aspects of the communication: we don't often say, 'What do you *mean* by that smirk?' We do not, in other words, hold speakers to a high level of responsibility for their para- and extra-linguistic performances. Therefore we are not likely to catch, and still less likely to take explicit notice of, mismatches between the verbal and nonverbal which (as students of nonverbal communication such as Ekman 1985 have noted) are very apt to signal deceptiveness.

Another question on the same general point is raised by the highly volatile discourse of much of the American political right wing, from the 'tea-partiers' to media pundits like Rush Limbaugh and Glenn Beck to many members of Congress. The discourse of this group has been highly, and unusually, inflammatory since the election of Barack Obama, but the incivility took a sharp turn upward in the spring of 2010. The rhetoric has gone from the merely, if bizarrely, offensive to direct encouragements of acts of violence, some of which have in fact occurred. Thus far those actions have not gone beyond hurling bricks through the office windows of congresspersons who voted for a bill or rifling their offices; but it is impossible to predict where they may end.

Now, I assume that most sympathetic hearers of this rhetoric understand – as its producers most probably mostly intend – that it is meant to be understood through the use of conversational implicature, as floutings of the Maxim of Quality, i.e. as hyperbole and metaphor. But there are always a few people in a crowd (and the right-wing media command a very large crowd) who have not signed onto the Cooperative Principle, and could take these directives literally. If events inspired by denunciations of the president as a traitor, un-American, 'worse than Hitler', and so forth evoke an unthinkable response, who should be held responsible?[6]

5 Conclusions

I have tried to do several things in this chapter. I have suggested that, to understand what we mean by *responsibility*, we have to consider the full range of linguistic analysis, from the smallest to the largest units. We need to look at discourse as we look at more concrete levels of grammar: all are rule-governed parts of our linguistic competence. The difficulties individual speakers have dealing with the idea of responsibility at the lexical, syntactic, or pragmatic level foreshadow, and are intimately connected to, the difficulties modern societies are experiencing at the level of public discourse. Paradox is inherent in our understanding of 'responsibility', and our language, at every level, reflects that paradox.

Notes

1   In the case of *cleave*, on the other hand, the antonymous meanings result from the accidental phonetic convergence of two separate Germanic roots, **kleub-*, 'cut', and **klai-*, 'stick'.

2   And even lexically, with the increasing preference of those who have suffered such crimes as rape or spousal abuse, as well as diseases like cancer, for referring to themselves as 'survivors', rather than 'victims', thus avoiding the presupposition of helplessness inherent in the latter.

3   I will use these terms equivalently, although it has been pointed out that men and non-spouses are sometimes the victims of 'wife'-beating or 'spousal' abuse.

4   As distinct from mere floutings of the Maxims, e.g. hyperbole in the case of Quality, which are expected to be understood and normally are, often as preferable to the direct equivalent – precisely because implicature signals to participants that they share enough of a world-view to enable indirectness to be understood.

5   I am inclined not to give much credit to either, but if we have to decide who is 'worse', we might think of a bumper sticker seen in some profusion in Berkeley during the Iraq War: When Clinton lied, nobody died.

6   First Amendment law currently holds that, absent 'incitement to imminent violence' (Brandenburg v. Ohio 1969) rhetoric alone, no matter how inflammatory, is constitutionally protected.

References

Brown, P. and Levinson, S. C. (1986) *Politeness.* Cambridge: Cambridge University Press.

Coleman, L. and Kay, P. (1981) Prototype semantics: the English verb *lie. Language* 57: 26–44.

Delgado, R. (1989) Storytelling for oppositionists and others: a plea for narrative. *University of Michigan Law Review* 87: 2411–2441.

Ekman, P. (1985) *Telling Lies: Clues to Deceit in the Marketplace, Politics, and Marriage.* New York: Norton.

Farber, D. and Sherry, S. (1997) *Beyond All Reason.* Oxford: Oxford University Press.

Fillmore, C. (1971) Verbs of judging. In C. Fillmore and D. T. Langendoen (eds) *Studies in Linguistic Semantics* 273–290. New York: Holt, Rinehart and Winston.

Frege, G. (1952 [1892]) On sense and reference. In P. T. Geach and M. Black (eds) *Translations from the Philosophical Writings of Gottlob Frege* 56–78. Oxford: Blackwell.

Freud, S. (1957 [1910]). The antithetical meanings of primal words. In J. Strachey and A. Freud (eds) *The Standard Edition of the Complete Psychological Works of Sigmund Freud XI* 153–161. London: Hogarth.

Gates, H. L. (1996) Thirteen ways of looking at a Black man. *The New Yorker,* 23 October.

Grice, H. P. (1975) Logic and conversation. In P. Cole and J. L. Morgan (eds) *Syntax and Semantics 3: Speech Acts.* New York: Academic Press.

Gumperz, J. J. (1982) *Discourse Strategies.* Cambridge: Cambridge University Press.

Harmon, M. M. (1995) *Responsibility as Paradox.* Thousand Oaks, CA: Sage.

Herrnstein, R. and Murray, C. (1994) *The Bell Curve.* New York: Free Press.

Kiparsky, P. and Kiparsky, C. (1971) Fact. In D. Steinberg and L. Jakobovits (eds) *Semantics: An Interdisclipinary Reader in Philosophy, Linguistics, and Psychology* 345–369. Cambridge: Cambridge University Press.

Labov, W. and Waletzky, J. (1967) Narrative analysis. In J. Helms (ed.) *Essays on the Verbal and Visual Arts* 12–44. Seattle: University of Washington Press.

Lakoff, R. (2000) Who framed 'O.J.'? *The Language War* 194–226. Berkeley: University of California Press.

Levinson, S. C. (1983) *Pragmatics.* Cambridge: Cambridge University Press.

Roiphe, K. (1994) *The Morning After.* New York: Little, Brown.

Schiffrin, D. (1987) *Discourse Markers.* Cambridge: Cambridge University Press.

Schiffrin, D. (1994) *Approaches to Discourse.* Oxford: Blackwell.

Searle, J. (1979). A taxonomy of illocutionary acts. In J. Searle, *Expression and Meaning. Studies in the Theory of Speech Acts* 1–29. Cambridge: Cambridge University Press.

Solomon, D. (2002) Fierce entanglements. *The New York Times Magazine*, 17 November, p. 52.

Sweetser, E. (1990) *From Etymology to Pragmatics: Metaphorical and Cultural Aspects of Semantic Studies.* Cambridge: Cambridge University Press.

Wallace, R. J. (1994) *Responsibility and the Moral Sentiments.* Cambridge, MA: Harvard University Press.

Williams, P. (1991) *The Alchemy of Race and Rights.* Cambridge, MA: Harvard University Press.

Robin Tolmach Lakoff is Professor Emerita of Linguistics at the University of California, Berkeley. Her research and teaching interests have included: Latin syntax; syntactic theory; semantics and pragmatics; language and gender; the relationships among language, gender, and power; psychotherapeutic discourse; language and law; and discourse analysis. Her publications include: *Language and Woman's Place, Talking Power*, and *The Language War*.

Owning responsible actions/selves: Role-relational trajectories in counselling for childhood genetic testing

Srikant Sarangi

1 Introduction: Conditions of responsible action

According to Niebuhr (1999 [1963]: 47), the term *responsibility* is 'a relatively late-born child … in the family of words in which duty, law, virtue, goodness, and morality are its much older siblings'. For Niebuhr, the original meaning associated with 'responsible' is 'correspondent': 'The mouth large but not responsible to so large a body'. A transformation of meaning has since occurred, as evident in expressions such as 'responsible citizen', 'responsible parent', 'responsible government', 'responsible society'. A sense of 'responsibility' is intricately woven into our everyday mundane as well as institutional and professional lives, both explicitly and implicitly. As Scheff (1968: 3) points out:

> The use of interrogation to reconstruct parts of an individual's past history is a common occurrence in human affairs. Reporters, jealous lovers, and policemen on the beat are often faced with the task of determining events in another person's life, and the extent to which *he was responsible for those events*. [emphasis added]

Intentionality behind agentive action is regarded as a cornerstone for imputing responsibility (and blame). Responsibility is a double-edged phenomenon – reporters and policemen are endowed with responsibility to determine whether their target of investigation is someone being responsible. Generally speaking, in a professional-client encounter context, professionals have the responsibility to monitor if clients are being responsible when seeking a service, e.g. parents requesting genetic tests for their children. In return, parents are expected to display their responsible selves and actions in order to procure the intervention, i.e. genetic testing, they want.

Of relevance here is Scott and Lyman's (1968: 46) perspective on accounts: 'a statement made by a social actor to explain unanticipated or untoward behaviour'. Along the lines of Austin (1991 [1956]), they suggest a distinction between excuses and justifications. 'Excuses are accounts in which one admits that the act in question is bad, wrong, or inappropriate but denies full responsibility.' Justifications 'are accounts in which one accepts responsibility for the act in question, but denies the pejorative quality associated with it' (Scott and Lyman 1968: 47).[1] In a sense, what constitutes an excuse or a justification may not be distinctly manifest at the discoursal level as the onus seems to lie on the characterisation of the action itself as untoward or otherwise. Moreover, as we will see, a request for childhood genetic testing may be framed by parents as a justification, which professionals might regard as an excuse on parents' part – as a means to an end.

According to Austin (1991 [1956]), excuses are the means by which we try to escape responsibility. An excuse amounts to acknowledging, retrospectively, that what happened was a bad thing, and that the person offering the excuse did it, but not boldfacedly or intentionally, and therefore s/he cannot be held responsible for the action in question. In a related paper, 'Three ways of spilling ink', Austin (1991 [1966]) offers a nuanced distinction between 'acting intentionally' and 'acting deliberately or on purpose'. He considers the example of feeding peanuts to penguins when there is a public notice announcing 'Do not feed the penguins'. In this case feeding the penguins may be regarded as intentional action, but not undertaken deliberately or on purpose to kill the penguins (especially if the person has not read the notice and/or is unaware that peanuts are fatal for penguins). Acting impulsively thus does not presuppose deliberation or motive.

Moreover, following Aristotle, individuals can be held responsible for only voluntary actions (as opposed to actions that occur under compulsion or due to ignorance). In their characterisation of responsibility, Hill and Irvine (1993) draw attention to the interface between knowledge and agency:

To interpret events, to establish facts, to convey opinion, and to constitute interpretations as knowledge – all these are activities involving socially situated participants, who are agents in the construction of knowledge as well as being agents when they act on what they have come to know, believe, suspect, or opine. (1993: 2)

Working within a framework of dialogicity and interactionism as far as meaning making is concerned, Hill and Irvine hold that *'responsibility* points toward the agency aspect of meaning while *evidence* points toward the knowledge aspect' (1993: 2; emphasis added). We may conclude that knowing – in both prospective and retrospective senses – is an integral part of responsible action, i.e. rational action based on available information on the one hand and projected calculation of future consequences on the other.

In the literature many taxonomies of responsibility have been proposed, usually with an adjective as a prefix such as: 'absolute responsibility' and 'relative responsibility' (Scheff 1968); 'agent responsibility' and 'task responsibility' (Baier 1991); 'moral responsibility' and 'causal responsibility' (Baier 1991; Fletcher 1967). The last distinction – moral and causal – is of particular relevance as it suggests a potential tension between action and self-other orientation on a temporal dimension. Moral responsibility includes autonomy (respect for persons, Kantian rightness and individual capacity to act in a self-determined way and avoid external influence) – as distinct from libertarianism (acting in any way one chooses) and from individualism (assertion of one's rights against the rights of others). According to Baier (1991), 'causal responsibility' conveys that a particular action has caused an outcome, but that something could have been done to avert it, as would be the case in opting for termination of pregnancy following a prenatal genetic test. By extension, causal responsibility can be expressed prospectively in justifying current action to prevent or cause future scenarios. Although the distinction between moral responsibility and causal responsibility is a nuanced one, it will inform my data analysis in later sections.

The chapter is structured as follows. In Section 2, I develop a role-relational perspective in terms of self-other dynamics by drawing attention to the potential tensions associated with acting responsibly within a given role-set. In Section 3, I contextualise this role-relational perspective with regard to the ethos of parental responsibility in child-centred healthcare. Section 4 introduces the counselling context of childhood genetic testing concerning polycystic kidney disease (PKD) where the analysis centres on parental 'role-relational work' with its manifest display of moral and causal responsibility in dealing with the benefits and risks of knowing a child's genetic status. In conclusion, Section 5 brings together the main analytic points and reassesses the merits of the role-relational perspective in discourse studies of responsible conduct.

2 Responsible self/action: Towards a role-relational perspective

In the Introduction I have drawn attention to the following as the conditions of responsibility: agency, intentionality, knowledge and rationality. A complement to this list is the self-other orientation, whereby the self is conceptualised in terms of the other that stresses the relational dimension. Following Mead (1934), 'self' is a socially situated reflexive process, which is made possible through the perception of alterity. Mead's argument is based on a complex characterisation of the 'I-me' distinction, which indexes a dialogic notion of the self. The 'I' conceives itself as another would conceive it by 'taking the attitude of the other'.

Niebuhr's (1999 [1963]) characterisation of responsibility along the following four criteria underscores the relevance of self-other relations: (1) response; (2) interpretation; (3) accountability; and (4) social solidarity. One's action is essentially an interpreted, accountable response, which is anticipatory and socially cohesive. For Niebuhr, 'response' – in retrospect and in prospect – lies at the heart of responsibility. The salience of 'response' is echoed by Fletcher (1967: 235):

> In every situation the probing question is not so much, *What shall I do?* as *What shall I do?* Responsibility is response, and only the decision maker in his personal being and autonomy can make a response. [emphasis in original]

The self-other dynamics brings us to the notion of role-set (Merton 1957; for its application to professional settings, see Sarangi 2010, 2011). Responsible action is inherently tied up with 'the notion of the agent as a strong evaluator' (Taylor 1991: 216). This is particularly evident in decision-making situations which routinely involve a role-relational dimension, i.e. one makes a decision in a certain role capacity and such decisions may have consequences for oneself as well as for others. As Emmett (1966: 15) points out: 'what people think they ought to do depends largely on how they see their roles, and (most importantly) the conflicts between their roles'. Decision-making thus indexes agency and rational choices based on knowledge systems and they are usually other-oriented, as we will see in the display of parental role-responsibility in genetic counselling sessions. Extended to the childhood genetic testing scenario, the decisional choices a parent goes through may foreground potential conflicts embedded in the available role-set: a mother, a grandmother, a wife, a reproductively active woman, etc.

In the genetic counselling setting, which is our research site, the decisions clients make may come across as I-actions, without much reflection on 'me' as 'others would see it', from another perspective. The counsellor's/ therapist's role then becomes one of filling this gap, in encouraging reflection on clients' part, both retrospectively and prospectively (Sarangi 2010). Although, for Mead (1934), the anticipatory responses are about 'the generalised other' rather than specific others, in the genetic counselling setting, both the generalised and the specific 'others' are at play as the 'common good' and individual family members become invoked.

3 The ethos of parental responsibility in child-centred healthcare

Parental actions and roles are often invoked in a range of institutional/ professional settings when the child's wellbeing is at stake: in education, law, social work, healthcare. Parents are the usual targets of blame, i.e. lacking responsibility, in the context of children's educational failure, antisocial behaviour, health status such as obesity, etc. In the healthcare setting concerning children, parents assume not only the responsibility of carer but also as decision-maker on behalf of the non-autonomous child. Strong and Davis (1978) suggest that parents have expert and detailed knowledge about their children, so the doctor's scientific and generalised expertise is bound to be contingent on parents' expertise. In highlighting the moral order of healthcare encounters (Goffman 1961), Strong and Davis identify two strategies that professionals deploy in their management of moral task: 'face work' and 'character work'. While the former deals with the surface level of performance, the latter is concerned with societal assessment of individuals in terms of criticism and exhortation in the 'ameliorative' sense. For instance, the parent's working-class background may be invoked as 'character work' to account for parental indifference to the child's wellbeing. I would like to suggest a third strategy – 'role-relational work' – which can be located in between 'face-work' and 'character-work'. 'Role-relational work' takes into account Goffman's (1981) participation framework and recognises how the available 'role-sets' (as conceived by Merton 1957) can underpin decision making in a given interactional setting.

Other studies have shown the complex configuration of cognitive, social and emotional dimensions in the participation structure of the paediatric clinic (Tannen and Wallat 1982) and the extent to which the medical and moral dimensions are in a constant flux in inter-professional talk surrounding a child's health (White 2002).[2] Silverman (1987) draws particular attention to the delicacy involved in balancing parental responsibility and the autonomy of adolescent children in the management of diabetes. The fine line between a 'nagging' parent and a 'responsible' parent has to be discoursally patrolled, especially with the use of mitigating devices. While Silverman (1987) attributes responsibility to both parents and professionals, he reserves the notion of autonomy for the adolescent patients. Interestingly, parental nagging becomes equated with responsibility, which suggests a sense of interference. By contrast, autonomy becomes characterised as freedom of the adolescent or non-interference by parents, although it remains the parent's responsibility to facilitate the adolescent's autonomy:

> To act 'responsibly' can lead to the charge of 'nagging'. Conversely, an emphasis on self-expression can be defined by others as uncaring 'permissiveness' and mean that parents can be sharply reminded that 'young adults' still need guidance and support. (Silverman 1987: 235)

In a sense, parental responsibility and parental rights become rolled into one. Communicatively, the medical consultation resembles a bargain encounter, with parents positioned in a no-win situation.

4 Parental responsibility and childhood genetic testing

Childhood genetic testing raises several issues of concern, especially from the perspective of genetic counsellors. Testing of healthy children is only recommended if there is clear benefit to the child (Clarke 1998; Clarke and Flinter 1996; Harper and Clarke 1990). The relevant concerns are as follows:

- What is in the child's best interest?
- Will the child benefit from the test medically?
- Is the parents' 'right to know' a sufficient ground for carrying out testing?
- Is the child's future autonomy being compromised in the process?

It is worth noting that in conventional medicine, tests and test results are aimed at uncertainty reduction and for confirmation of diagnosis – as a precursor to medical intervention. In the context of genetics, only a few diagnostic tests are currently available. The other types of tests – carrier testing and predictive testing – not only involve cumbersome and costly procedure but could fail to provide definitive results. Moreover, the adverse effects of a genetic test can include the following: the child may lose future autonomy to make informed decisions; the child may lose the right to confidentiality; the test result can have an impact on the child's upbringing; and the test can influence the child's future career options.

Several researchers (Arribas-Ayllon et al. 2008a, 2008b; Downing 2005; Forrest et al. 2003; Hallowell 1999; Hallowell et al. 2003, 2006) have examined themes such as genetic responsibility, blame and guilt on the basis of research interview data. However, there are very few attempts at examining aspects of responsibility and autonomy as they unfold in the genetic counselling setting (see Pilnick 2002a, 2002b; Sarangi 2000, 2010; Sarangi and Clarke 2002; Sarangi et al. 2011). In a single case study, Sarangi and Clarke (2002) examine the subtle negotiation of childhood carrier testing within an ethos of non-directive counselling by contrasting the child's future autonomy against the parent's rights and role-responsibilities.

The familial basis of genetic disorders puts the client in a range of competing role-set in the time frames of past and future events. It then becomes the task of the genetic counsellor to elicit what the attendant rights and responsibilities vis-à-vis self and other relations might entail in a given case. The notion of responsibility in its moral sense is relevant here, where right and wrong actions do become implicated as well as what ought to be done.[3] But more importantly, causal responsibility is also in play as far as potential consequences of actions are concerned. Both counsellors and clients move between the trajectories of responsible actions and responsible selves and it is this interface which is my analytic focus.

In what follows I focus on a particular genetic condition called polycystic kidney disease (PKD), normally associated with an enlarged kidney, which can present cysts at a later stage. The manifest symptoms are high blood pressure and urinary infection. The clinics I draw my data from are joint clinic sessions involving the parents (PF and PM), the children (CF and CM), the genetic counsellor (G1), the kidney specialist (K1) and the genetic specialist nurse (N2) (see Appendix for transcription conventions). In my analysis, I focus on how parents justify their need or right to know a child's genetic status and how in their accounts moral responsibility and causal responsibility are conflated vis-à-vis the healthcare professionals' commitment to safeguard the child's autonomy and best interests.

4.1 Balancing advantages and disadvantages of childhood testing

In the following case (PKD/E), as part of family history, PF's father was diagnosed with PKD when he was in his early fifties. One of the daughters (CF) has had a urinary infection which led to a scan of her kidney but no cysts were found. This negative test result does not guarantee that CF would not develop the condition later in life, given the typical late onset associated with PKD. The mother is inclined to test her two other children, partly prompted by the fact that one of the boys regularly wets the bed. Extract 1a opens with the kidney specialist (K1) outlining the potential advantages and disadvantages associated with the decision to test the children 'now'.

Data Extract 1a

```
01 K1: so one of the things we can discuss in (.)
       this clinic is (0.5) whether (.) you actually
       (.) wish for your children to have tests for
       this condition or whether (0.5) uh it would be
       better to wait until (.) they're older (0.5) um
       (.) because there are (.) some (0.5) potential
       advantages in (.) in knowing (.) whether or
       not they've got it and (.) there are also some
       drawbacks (.) so (.) it's quite good if you're
       aware of the (.) advantages and disadvantages
       of children having [tests]
02 PF: [you know um] (0.5) with uh my boy he wets the
       bed a lot (.) would that [have]
03 K1: [right]
04 PF: anything to (.) he's five now I know it's a
       common [(0.5)] it's common with boys but [(.)]
       he does wet it a lot [(.)] =
05 K1: [yeah] [yes] [yes]
06 PF: = would that have anything
07 K1: it's most unlikely to [be anything to do]
08 PF: [that's alright then]
09 K1: with it and I'd certainly wouldn't regard it as
       a sign that he's got weak kidneys or anything
       like that (0.5) it it's um (0.5) just very
       common as you say in five year old boys I think
       it's probably about one in ten (I'm not sure of
       the facts) but [(.)]
```

```
10 PF: [yeah]
11 K1: um was there any family history of bed wetting
       in (.) either of you (0.5) no 'cause that can
       run in families actually (0.5) um
12 PF: no (^^^) (.) mam hasn't said nothing (.)
       (^^^^^)
13 PM: no
14 PF: no you know it's just weird how he's ((laughs))
       (1.0) having (.) well (1.0) (very rare have a
       dry night) helps a bit
```

The kidney specialist (K1) opens the discussion by inquiring about the parents' level of awareness concerning the advantages and disadvantages of childhood testing. Rather than responding directly to K1's concerns, PF, in turn 2, nominates her reason for testing her son. We see here a form of lay diagnosis that bed wetting may be related to PKD. PF offers several epistemic assessments: 'it's common with boys' (typical case formulation); CM 'wets the bed a lot' (extreme case formulation); 'very rare have a dry night' (extreme case formulation). PF comes across as a responsible mother who has been constantly vigilant and seeks clarification about the possible link between bed wetting and PKD. This sense of responsibility – I ought to do something, in the least talk to a profesisonal – is implicitly contrasted with her mother's indifference – 'mam hasn't said nothing' (turn 12). In addition to a display of moral responsibility on PF's part, the causal responsibility is embedded in her clarification seeking in that if her assumption about the linkage between bed wetting and PKD has any basis, then CM is at risk of developing PKD. As a way of reassurance, K1 offers epidemiological figures ('about one in ten') and then goes on to seek family history of bed wetting which yields little certainty, followed by a discussion of advantages and disadvantages of childhood testing, which was temporarily interrupted (see turns 2ff).

Later in the session (Extract 1b), K1 orients to the moral/ethical issues surrounding childhood testing.

Data Extract 1b

```
01 K1: having them tested young (1.0) u:m (1.0) I
       don't know whether you've (.) thought at all
       about whether the children should have tests
02 PF: *mm*
03 PM: (haven't spoken ^^^)
```

```
04 K1: not really no no I mean it's not a pressing
        issue at all (0.5) um (.) then of course there
        is the question of whether the children should
        have the opportunity to decide for themselves
        (.) [and]
05 PM: [yeah]
06 K1: of course if you've already done it (0.5) then
        they don't have that (0.5) opportunity to
        decide for themselves (0.5) but it is worth
        thinking as they get to teenage (.) um that
        it's probably fair that they should at least
        have the knowledge that this problem is going
        on in the family because if they don't have
        knowledge (0.5) they don't have any (.) choices
        (0.5) and uh (1.0) again they themselves can
        ask either for more information (0.5) (okay)
        from yourselves or (.) or from ourselves
        whichever is easy (but quite often) the GP (.)
        and (.) they can (0.5) consider whether they
        want to be tested (.) um (1.0) in their own
        time a::nd um (0.5) they need to know about
        the advantages and disadvantages obviously (.)
        but in addition they need to be able to (0.5)
        um (.) take on board the fact that it is a
        genetic condition and therefore they might want
        to (0.5) take that into account when they're
        planning their own families
```

Prior to the opening turns, K1 has explicitly highlighted the disadvantages of testing, including potentially differential treatment as far as everyday parenting rituals are concerned, the possible closure of certain career opportunities as well as higher premiums for insurance cover. These material disadvantages assume diminished significance when compared to ethical concerns surrounding the child's autonomy, which is framed generically to add emphasis: 'the children should have the opportunity to decide for themselves' (turn 04). Parental responsibility to test the child, which was triggered by bed wetting, is thus confronted with professional responsibility to safeguard the future autonomy of the child. However, parents are seen as morally responsible for informing the child about PKD running in the family. There is, however, an overtone of causal responsibility: if the child does not know his/her 'at risk' status, s/he will be prevented from making responsible decisions about future career, reproduction, etc. (turn 06). The list of disadvantages outweighs the advantages with K1 deferring to the child the key decision-making role, which amounts to delaying the parental decision about testing. A regular check-up of blood pressure and infections, rather than a genetic test, is proffered as a justifiable solution (data not shown).

4.2 Benefits of knowing for present and future purposes

What is absent from the discussion of advantages above is the 'peace of mind' argument which is often advanced by parents as a compelling reason for childhood testing. This is often cast as a psychological imperative underlying parents' need to know, which does not sit comfortably with ethical and medical reasoning that the professionals embody. In our next case (PKD/B), the parents underscore the importance of knowing the genetic status of their child (CF), having already tested another child (CM) as being affected.

Data Extract 2a

```
01 PM: it's just (.) kno::wing is (.) well knowing (.)
       we just know (0.) peace of mind isn't it (.)
       you know it's [(.) yeah (0.1) (y- know (.)]
02 PF: [one way] or the other (.) but I mean (0.2)
       it's something (I usually) (.)
03 PM: It's not like every day like (.) it's (.) yeah
       y- you might (^^^^^^^^)
04 PF: no (.) it's just every now and again (.) you
       might think about it [^^^]
05 G1: [but it's] not (.) sort of (.) yeah (.) it's
       not (.)
06 PF: and (.) feel a bit sad about it (.) but (.)
       no:: (.) it's not something you dwell on
07 G1: it's not playing on your mind [(.)]
08 PM: [no::]
09 PF: [no::]
10 G1: no (.) and [(.) (>>I mean<<)]=
11 PM: [especially the way] he is [(.) 'cos he's such
       a live wire]
12 PF: [oo:::h: hh (.) o::h:: ] he's full of it
       (laughs)) that's why we didn't bring him today
       [(.) he'd just demolish the place in five
       minutes]=
```

12 G1: [no (.) (oh well) (.) tha- thanks (0.1) yeah]
13 PM: [(you know (0.1)]=
14 PF: = [but u:h:]
15 PM: = (he ^^^ or anything like that)
16 G1: yea::h (.) and so you don't have any regrets
      (.) [about]
17 PF: [no]
18 G1: having tested him [(.) tested (he-) an tested
      him (0.1) done with ((CF))=
19 PF: [no (.) no (.) no (.) well we wouldn't have (.)
      u:h: (.) no and I =
20 G1: = (.) if you had
21 PF: = mean (.) it's just a case of [rather (0.1)
      knowing (0.1) yeah they're=
22 PM: [(realising (.) he's gotta have the treatment
      when or whatever (.) straight =
23 PF: = started right from the off then aren't they
      (.) it's it's] (.) that's the thing =
24 PM: = away (.) yeah (.) that's the way I look at it
      (.) yeah (.) (^^^) (.) =
25 PF: = (.) if they're found to have it (.) (then)]
26 PM: = yeah]
27 G1: yeah (.) >>I mean that's<< if (.) if ((CF))
      tested (.) and (.) turned out the same as
      ((CM)) (.) obviously you'd be disappointed (.)
      again (.) wouldn't you [(.)]
28 PF: [yeah]
29 PM: [yeah]
30 G1: but (.) but again you'd feel (.) you'd take it
      in your stride (0.1) the same way (0.1) d- you
      think
31 PF: [ye::s (.) u:h]
32 PM: [we were a little bit upset] for a while
      weren't we (.) and we had a bit of a
33 PF: I think you were worse than me really [(.)
      weren't you]
34 PM: [yeah (.) bu-]
35 PF: because as I say (.) I've been (.) I mean
      ((CM2)) (.) my oldest son isn't ((PM))'s so I
      mean (.) and he's fifteen now I've lived with it
      a v- a very long time [(.)]
36 G1: [ye::s]
37 PF: and uh (.) I think ((PM)) was a bit more upset
      than I was even [(.)] =

```
38 G1: [yeah]
39 PF: = but u:h:m (.) no I think i- i- it's better to
       know [(.)]=
40 G1: [yeah]
41 PF: = for them as well [really (.) you know]
```

Wanting to know is typically foregrounded as a justification in favour of childhood testing (Clarke et al. 2011), but this may be seen as an excuse, a means-to-an-end stance, as far as the professionals are concerned. Note that wanting to know equates with 'benefits of knowing' rather than 'risks of knowing' (Sarangi et al. 2003). Here PF downplays the risks of knowing when she says 'it's not something you dwell on' (turn 06). There is a side sequence about CM's hyperactive behaviour which is given as a justification for not bringing him to the clinic, bordering on causal responsibility – if we brought him 'he'd just demolish the place in five minutes' (turn 12). G1 (the genetic counsellor) now enquires, retrospectively, if their decision to test CM has led to any regrets (turn 16). Appeal is here made to causal responsibility: how that prior decision may have had an impact on decision making in the present time. It is fairly apparent that the prior decision to test CM has contributed to the current decision to test CF. The prior decision, and presumably the current decision, is justified by the parents in terms of possible benefit as far as future treatment is concerned (turns 22–26), even though that might be a remote reality. The recurrence of latching and overlapping talk indicates a sense of unanimity and harmony in PF's and PM's thinking about the positive aspects of testing and also about how to cope if CF were to test positive. The differences between PF and PM are acknowledged, given that PF's wealth of experience is owed to her exposure to her older son's PKD status from a previous marriage, which once again underscores causal responsibility. Overall, it seems justifications for actions take the form of causal responsibility: finding out the child's genetic status can lead to accessing treatment – by extension, not testing and not finding out CF's genetic status will amount to depriving her from receiving treatment. Causal responsibility is formulated in the 'if-then' format: *if* parents decide to test *then* certain outcomes/consequences will eventuate.

In the following extract, which continues from Extract 2a, G1 explores how the parents would cope if CF's test results were to prove negative, which might be regarded as a preferred outcome from the parents' perspective.

Data Extract 2b

```
42 G1: wha- what if ((CF's name)) (.) turned out the
       other way (.) what if (.) sh- you know (.) she
       didn't have it (.) uh (.) do you think that
       would (.) do you think that would ever create
       any difficulties (.) between the two of them if
       you like (.) or
43 PF: no::::::
44 G1: no (.) you're not worried about that at all
45 PF: no:::::::
46 PM: (it's a case of ^^^ ^^^^ ^^^ ^^^ ^^^ ^^^ ^^^^)
       isn't it
47 PF: h:::m::: well (.) it's the same with me and my
       little brothers and sisters (.) two of us have
       and two of us haven't [[(0.1) but uhm]]
48 G1: [[yeah (.) and that's never been an issue]
       between you [(.) I suppose =
49 PF: [well no (.) I mean (.)] i::n reality it's a
       blessing really (.) 'cos if =
50 G1: (^^^ ^^^^ ^^^^)
51 PF: = anything happened (.) my sister said she'll
       give me one of hers ((laughs)) =
52 PM: I doubt I want one of hers though
53 PF: ((laughs)) no joking (.) uh (.) you know so I
       mean really I suppose it could be a blessing
       [(.) you know i- if you look at like tha::t (.)
       if =
54 G1: yes:: (.) I suppose I hadn't thought of it like
       that (.) yes (.) yeah]
```

G1's opening question implicitly introduces the issue of 'risks of knowing' (Sarangi et al. 2003) even in the event of a preferred (negative) test outcome. If CF tests negative, then there is the potential risk of differential treatment of the two children – one affected and the other unaffected – which can stretch the role-set of parenting (note the elongated, emphatic 'no' in turns 43, 45). PF downplays the issue of differential treatment of the two children and chooses not to issue a justification (turn 47). We can read causal responsibility into PF's account: obtaining a sibling's healthy kidney is consequent upon a positive test result. The role-relational work assumes significance as PF draws parallels to her own experience ('it's the same with me and my little brothers and sisters (.) two of us have and two of us haven't'), which can be extended to her own children's future experience. The overall reasoning is that whatever the outcome of testing, 'it's better to know … [for us and] for them as well' if CF were to test positive or 'in reality a blessing really' if the results were to be negative.

4.3 The role-relational work underpinning childhood testing

My final case (PKD/A) is more complex as far as childhood testing is concerned. PKD runs in the family (PF's mother, her mother's father, her mother's younger sister have all been affected). PF was scanned and tested positive after she had her child (CM), so she wants to see if she has passed the faulty gene to CM and, additionally, if her affected PKD status would have any consequences for future pregnancy. She thus approaches the genetic testing scenario in the role-set of the current mother of CM, a future mother of an unborn child and also as a woman in her own right. PF formulates her situation as follows:

Data Extract 3a

```
01 PF  'cause um in when I went to the clinic (.)
       with ((CM)) they were going to discharge him
       but when they knew I had polycystic kidneys
       they didn't want to discharge him just in case
       (.) he had it and they did say oh there's um
       a blood test that you can have (.) so this is
       what I want to find out you know do I need to
       have it done or is it (.) is it not worth it I
       I dunno
02 G1  right (.) okay
03 PF  obviously if it's going to cause him pain and
       it's not (.) 'cause like it's not the end of
       the world [(.)] polycystic kidneys and I think
       is it =
04 K1  [mm]
05 PF  = worth (.) do I really want to know (.) you
       know will it stop me having any more children
       if I want any more (.) you know [(.)] =
06 G1  [right]
07 PF  = 'cause if like ((CM)) hasn't got it there's
       nothing to say that (.) if I have another child
       (1.0) they won't have it 'cause (1.0) you know
       some might have it you know
```

PF is genuinely ambivalent, unlike the parents in PKD/B, about testing ('do I really want to know') and would like to weigh the available options. It is worth pointing out that she has been referred to this specialist clinic and thinks that a genetic test involves a simple 'blood test', while also being aware of the fact that PKD is 'not the end of the world'. We see here elements of both moral responsibility and causal responsibility. There is a sense of guilt and the question remains whether she would have made different reproductive choices if she had known her genetic status prior to her pregnancy with CM. She now wants to see if testing CM would influence her future decisions about reproduction (turn 05). Her formulation – 'will it stop me having any more children' – is indicative of causal responsibility as knowing CM's at-risk status is likely to have a bearing on her future reproductive choices. There is some blurring of reasoning here as the risk of her transmitting the faulty gene to a newborn baby still remains at 50 per cent given her own genetic status, irrespective of the outcome of CM's test results. Unlike the parent in Extract 2, PF talks about causal responsibility from her own perspective – future reproductive choices ('will it stop me from having any more children', framed in a question format) – rather than from the perspective of the child. In previous examples, we have seen parents talk about benefit of treatment accruing from early diagnosis. Causal responsibility can thus play out at different levels taking different perspectives – parental versus children's.

Later in the session, the mother displays causal responsibility with regard to how CM's at-risk status came to light. She narrates the circumstances concerning CM's attack of meningitis which led to timely parental actions to contain the condition: it is presented both as a case of opportunism ('luckily enough we caught it before it went any further') and as an extreme case scenario ('if I'd left it another day he probably wouldn't be as healthy as he is now').

The discussion now shifts to the procedure of having a genetic test. Of relevance is the fact that a proper genetic test which looks for alterations in the gene would require blood samples from a number of family members, which PF had not realised (see extract 3a where she mentions a simple blood test involving the at-risk individual, see also turn 13 below).

Data Extract 3b

```
01 G1: in a family like yours it'd be difficult (.)
       maybe not impossible but it'd be difficult to
       work out which of those (.) two genes it was
```

```
           (.) that (.) was responsible for the problem
           in the family (1.0) so we could track (.) if we
           knew which one it was then we'd be able to track
           it [(2.0)] but that's right (1.0) um (.) and =
02 PF:     [track it but it's finding out which one]
03 G1:     = if there were (.) if the family was a bit
           bigger (.) and there were more people in the
           family (.) uh (.) either definitely with it
           or definitely without it (.) then it would be
           easier to (.) to work out which of the two
           different genes (.) was responsible (2.0)
           um (2.0) so (.) if I suppose if you were (.)
           saying that (.) you (.) very much wanted to (.)
           wanted to have a test carried out on (.) ((CM))
           (.) y- were (.) very keen for us to go ahead
           and do that now (1.0) uh (.) what what would
           I'd be suggesting (.) would be (.) getting
           blood samples from as many people in the family
           as possible really
04 PF:     I think as long as he's having (.) being
           checked out (.) once a year I think that'd be
           [(.)] yeah
05 G1:     [be enough] right no well that's that's fine =
06 PF:     = as long as I don't think that I haven't done
           anything [(.)] [to] =
07 K1:     [yeah]
08 G1:     [no]
09 PF:     = prevent it 'cause I mean I know you can't
           stop it happening
10 G1:     no (.) [right] so you're you're not telling me
           (.) you're you've r- that =
11 PF:     [um]
12 G1:     = you're really keen that we go ahead [and (.)
           do all this]
13 PF:     [>>oh no << (.)'cause (.)] the way that um (.)
           in this the clinic oh he can have a blood test
           (.) an I thought oh that'll be simple enough
           'cause the way he said it (.) to me sounded as
           if he just had a blood test yes he's got it or
           he hasn't so I thought oh (.) but the way that
           sounds it sounds a bit [(1.5)] yeah
14 G1:     [it's complicated] and it (.) it would (.) it
           would not give a one hundred percent [definite]
           result (.) it would give (.) we we might be
           able to =
```

```
15 PF: [mm]
16 G1: = say it's a bit more likely or a bit less
          likely [(.)] there would there =
17 PF: [yeah]
18 G1: = would [be]
19 PF: [I] think as long as he's being checked like
          you said once a year (.) I think [that'd be]
          (.) [okay] 'cause like you said it's not as if
          it's um life threatening
20 G1: [mm okay (.) well no well I'm]
```

Prior to the opening of the extract, G1 has offered a very elaborate explanation about the functioning of genes and chromosomes. The complexity involved ('getting blood samples from as many people in the family as possible', turn 03) in mounting a genetic test in order to get a definitive result as far as CM is concerned is seen as a difficult, if not impossible, option. In light of this awareness which remedies her previous misperceptions about what a genetic test might imply and that a test result may not be conclusive, PF juxtaposes her sibling role and her parental role and settles for routine annual blood checks for CM (turn 04, turn 19). This may be seen as an adequate display of moral responsibility under the circumstances ('as long as I don't think that I haven't done anything', turn 06). The causal responsibility is implicit: if I get CM tested then I can be cautious about future pregnancy and be protective about the future child. The complications associated with the testing procedure are directly contrasted with a sense of moral obligation, which echoes the 'no win' situation in Silverman's (1987) sense. G1's comment that even an elaborate family-wide blood test may not generate 'a hundred percent definite result' aligns with PF's position, especially since PKD is 'not life-threatening'.

The interaction continues as follows, as the topic shifts to a possible future pregnancy and the associated risks:

Data Extract 3c

```
21 PF: just (.) um like if we I was to have any more
          children it's not as if (.) you're saying you
          shouldn't have any more children because of
          this polycystic kidneys [(.)]
22 G1: [no]
23 PF: that's what's worrying me you know (.) as
          well if I wanted another child (1.0) am I
```

                    endangering it by (1.0) you know if I had
                    another child would I be endangering the
                    child (.) if this (.) if (.) if they both had
                    polycystic kidneys [(.)]
    24 G1: [no]
    25 PF: like the way I'm feeling now I mean there's
                    nothing wrong with me at the minute [(1.0)] so
    26 G1: [yeah] >>I think<< obviously another child (.)
                    there would be this fifty fifty [chance]
    27 PF: [yes]
                    [07 turns omitted where G1 prioritises PF's own
                    health status concerning her future pregnancy]
    35 PF: = basically I think I just want someone to say
                    (.) no you shouldn't have ch- any more children
                    or yes you will be okay to have children
    36 G1: right [((laughs))]
    37 PF: ['cause ob- you know]
    38 K1: the ch- you n- I mean the the decision about
                    having children [(.)]
    39 PF: [mm]
    40 K1: that's for you and your husband (.) what we can
                    do is try and help you understand the risk [of]
                    (.) [of (hel-) to your health (.) and(^^^^)]
    41 PF: [yeah] [well I mean I don't want to have (.)
                    have any more children]if it's going to in-
                    (1.0) do you know what I mean if it's going to
                    (1.0) I *d- (^^^^)*
    42 K1: well you had a good [pregnancy]
    43 PF: [yeah]
    44 K1: (.) and therefore even though you've got
                    polycystic kidney [disease]
    45 PF: [mm]
    46 K1: (.) it doesn't seem as though (.) from what
                    you've told us this pregnancy (.) put any
                    damage on your [kidneys]

As we can see, PF frames her dilemma in an 'if-then' format (turn 23), as one bordering on both moral and causal responsibility in urging for a categorical answer to her anxieties about future pregnancy (turn 35). But K1 skillfully steers clear of a direct response by refocusing on PF's own health during the pregnancy (turn 28–30), given that she is susceptible to infections and high blood pressure. In turn 41, PF again resorts to an 'if-then' formulation, albeit cut-off, to foreground her sense of causal responsibility.

In response, G1 refers to PF's previous pregnancy experience despite her
PKD status in turn 42 ('you had a good pregnancy'). The decision is left to
PF and her husband, aided now by relevant risk information.

In the final extract below, PF's continuing concerns about moral and
causal responsibility, bordering on guilt, become pronounced.

Data Extract 3d

```
01 PF: you know would it be cruel if I had another
       child if they got it when they're older
02 K1: so so we were just talking about (.) your
       health in pregnancy (.) then the other thing is
       [(1.0) (giving you)]
03 PF: [they have you know if I have any]
04 K1: you have a risk of passing (.) the gene on (.)
       um ((CM)) might have it fifty fifty the next baby
       might have it fifty fifty chance the next baby
       might have it [(.)] fif- =
05 PF: [no ((laughs))]
06 K1: = (.) so um (.) uh so there s- two slightly
       separate [things]
07 PF: [yeah]
08 K1: for you to think about obviously both related
       to the [polycystic]
09 PF: [yeah]
10 K1: kidney disease but one is (.) uh you know w-
       is it putting a stress on you and of course
       now you've got one child (.) you don't want to
       risk your health so you couldn't look after the
       present child and and [the]
11 PF: [mm]
12 K1: next child (.) u- that doesn't sound like a a
       big problem *at the moment* um and the other is
       the risk of passing it on (.) to your babies
       (.) but since you haven't had much contact with
       people who've had any complications from the
       polycystic kidneys it's difficult for you to
       [envisage isn't it]
13 PF: [yeah (.) yeah]
14 K1: (.) um (.) but I I don't think anything that
       you've said would make me feel (.) it would be
       (.) [particularly]
15 PF: [mm]
```

```
16 K1: dangerous for you to have a baby (.) but you
        know you should if you were planning to go
        ahead with another pregnancy just check with
        your own doctor [(.)]
17 PF: [yeah]
18 K1: uh that there wasn't any information he had
        that that was contrary to that (.) that's all
        (2.5) it's not for [us to say that you =
19 N2: [does that answer your question]
20 K1: = should or you shouldn't]
21 PF: yeah I think I just wanted um (.) a bit more
        knowledge about what could happen because (.)
        like you said I could go through life and have
        (.) no problems at all in (.) but I d- (2.0) uh
        I didn't know whether (.) would it be selfish of
        me to have more children and pass it on to them
        then they'd have to (.) deal with what [(0.5)
        you] know I di- =
22 N2: [mm yeah]
23 PF: = you know that I'd have to pass on all what I
        know about all this [(.)] like mammy's had to
        tell me (.) what she knows about it
24 N2: [yeah]
25 K1: I mean do you understand what are (.) the worst
        [possible things]
26 PF: [yeah yeah]
27 K1: that can happen so (.) [you know (^^^^^) at the
        best end of the situation]
28 PF: [but when you look at it like that you think
        well (.) yeah that's it yes]
```

At the outset PF appeals to her parental moral responsibility and possible
guilt ('would it be cruel', 'would it be selfish') and whether she could
adopt a position of causal responsibility and stop passing the faulty gene
to her unborn child. This co-existence of moral and causal responsibilities
is apparent as PF now orients to the child's perspective unlike earlier.
There is also a shift in the role-set from being a mother to being a
woman of reproductive age (K1, turn 2). K1 feels compelled to recycle
previous information (turn 04, turn 12) – both specific to PF's case and
to the general population. Note also the reference made to PF's parental
moral responsibility (turn 10) in relation to looking after more than one
child, i.e. her responsibility as a carer. Such lifeworld circumstances need
to be borne in mind when considering a future pregnancy. PF, however,

acknowledges the value of genetic literacy and is willing to transmit to her children the knowledge she has had to obtain from her mother (turn 23). The role-relational work again takes centre stage as G1 continually plays down the risks involved. The implicitly positive endorsement for a future pregnancy is facilitated by discounting the chance of a young baby inheriting PKD (turns 29–37, data not shown). This no doubt contributes to an understanding and assessment of causal responsibility. The knowledge that a genetic test procedure involves more than simple blood extraction from herself and that an elaborate testing protocol involving other family members can still deliver an inconclusive result contribute towards PF's decision not to go ahead with the test, which is evidenced at the close of the encounter.

5 Conclusion

The notion of responsibility is manifest in accounts underpinned by agency, intentionality, epistemic stance as well as orientations to self-other relations. In the context of seeking childhood testing, parental accounts of genetic responsibility can take the form of moral and causal justifications. The findings suggest that parental accounts orient towards the following: balancing of advantages and disadvantages of childhood testing; benefits of knowing for present and future purposes; and the role-relational work underpinning the decision about testing.

Although professional stance against childhood genetic testing seems to align with the code of practice, the different client scenarios do not always fit a neat pattern. As we have seen, professional task responsibility is manifest clearly in the outlining of advantages and disadvantages of childhood genetic testing. Attention is also drawn to the fact that the test results may be inconclusive and, where more definitive, the 'benefits of knowing' the child's genetic status cannot override the 'risks of knowing'. This then forms a robust basis for genetic counsellors to remain committed to safeguarding the child's autonomy and their best interests.

The parental reasoning behind the request for childhood testing can at times undermine the child's future autonomy, including the latter's right not to know, as is clearly evident in the case of PKD/B. The right to make informed decisions is in effect being taken away from them as, given their young age, they cannot participate in the decision-making process. This issue is also of significance in the case of adolescents and adults. The 'moral' right of parents to know the child's genetic status for their own 'peace of mind' then becomes a one-sided, means-to-an-end excuse, which professionals wish to guard against, especially if there are no immediate medical benefits on offer in terms of treatment and cure and if the disadvantages outweigh the advantages. Parents, however, tend to legitimise their right to know, as not doing anything could possibly be seen as irresponsible indifference. Causal responsibility thus comes to the fore in parental accounts.

What does emerge from the preceding analysis is the difficulty in keeping moral responsibility and causal responsibility apart. As we have seen, causal responsibility, both retrospectively and prospectively, is articulated in the 'if-then' format – explicitly and implicitly – and is nested within moral responsibility. Although I only briefly refer to autonomy and leave out discussion of potential blame, these notions are intertwined when we focus on accounts of responsible actions/selves. The notion of role-set, and attendant role-relational work, is found useful, especially in the discussion of PKD/A: childhood testing needs to be contextualised not only in relation to the parental role as far as the unborn child is concerned but also in relation to other children while bringing into the equation one's own reproductive status as a woman. A role-relational dimension brings out the different perspectives – real and hypothetical – that are recruited into the accounting practices. It is the strategic and context-specific imputation of different self-other perspectives that facilitates certain types of decision-making trajectories.

Notes

1   See also Taylor (1972). The notion of blame is implicated in responsibility (Pomerantz 1978; Shaver 1985).
2   See Tates and Meeuwesen (2001) for an overview.
3   At the linguistic level, responsible action is routinely realised in terms of deontic (ought/should) and epistemic modalities (Hare 1964). The analysis presented in the next section broadly follows theme-oriented discourse analysis (Roberts and Sarangi 2005).

References

Arribas-Ayllon, M., Sarangi, S. and Clarke, A. (2008a) Managing self-responsibility through other-oriented blame: family accounts of genetic testing. *Social Science & Medicine* 6: 1521–1532.

Arribas-Ayllon, M., Sarangi, S. and Clarke, A. (2008b) Micropolitics of responsibility vis-à-vis autonomy: parental accounts of childhood genetic testing and (non)disclosure. *Sociology of Health and Illness* 30(2): 255–271.

Austin, J. (1991 [1956]) A plea for excuses. In P. French (ed.) *The Spectrum of Responsibility* 39–54. New York: St Martin's Press.

Austin, J. (1991 [1966]) Three ways of spilling ink. In P. French (ed.) *The Spectrum of Responsibility* 55–61. New York: St Martin's Press.

Baier, K. (1991) Types of responsibility. In P. French (ed.) *The Spectrum of Responsibility*, 117–128. New York: St Martin's Press.

Clarke, A. (ed.) (1998) *The Genetic Testing of Children*. Oxford: BIOS Scientific Publishers.

Clarke, A. and Flinter, F. (1996) The genetic testing of children: a clinical perspective. In T. Marteau and M. Richards (eds) *The Troubled Helix: Social and Psychological Implications of the New Human Genetics* 164–176. Cambridge: Cambridge University Press.

Clarke, A., Sarangi, S. and Verrier-Jones, K. (2011) Voicing the lifeworld: parental accounts of responsibility in genetic consultations for Polycystic Kidney Disease. *Social Science & Medicine* 72: 1743–1751.

Downing, C. (2005) Negotiating responsibility: case studies of reproductive decision-making and prenatal genetic testing in families facing Huntington Disease. *Journal of Genetic Counselling* 14(3): 219–234.

Emmett, D. (1966) *Rules, Roles and Relations*. London: Macmillan.

Fletcher, J. (1967). *Moral Responsibility: Situation Ethics at Work*. Philadelphia, PA: The Westminster Press.

Forrest, K., Simpson, S. A., Wilson, B. J., van Teijlingen, E. R., McKee, L., Haites, N. and Matthews, E. (2003) To tell or not to tell: barriers and facilitators in family communication about genetic risk. *Clinical Genetics* 64: 317–326.

Goffman, E. (1961) *Asylums: Essays on the Social Situation of Mental Patients and Other Inmates*. Garden City, NY: Doubelday.

Goffman, E. (1981) *Forms of Talk*. Oxford: Blackwell.

Hallowell, N. (1999) Doing the right thing: genetic risk and responsibility. *Sociology of Health and Illness* 21: 597–621.

Hallowell, N., Arden-Jones, A., Eeles, R., Foster, C., Lucassen, A., Moynihan, C. and Watson, M. (2006) Guilt, blame and responsibility: men's understanding of their role in the transmission of BRCA1/2 mutations within their family. *Sociology of Health and Illness* 28(7): 969–988.

Hallowell, N., Foster, C., Eeles, R., Ardern-Jones, A., Murday, V. and Watson, M. (2003) Balancing autonomy and responsibility: the ethics of generating and disclosing genetic information. *Journal of Medical Ethics* 29: 74–83.

Hare, R. M. (1964) *The Language of Morals*. Oxford: Oxford University Press.

Harper, P. S. and Clarke, A. (1990) Should we test children for adult genetic diseases? *The Lancet* 335: 1205–1206.

Hill, J. and Irvine, J. (eds) (1993) *Responsibility and Evidence in Oral Discourse*. Cambridge: Cambridge University Press.

Mead, G. H. (1934) *Mind, Self, and Society: From the Standpoint of a Social Behaviourist* (Edited with Introduction by C.W. Morris). Chicago, IL: University of Chicago Press.

Merton, R. (1957) *Social Theory and Social Structure*. Glencoe, IL: Free Press.

Niebuhr, H. R. (1999 [1963]) *The Responsible Self: An Essay in Christian Moral Philosophy* (Introduction by J. M. Gustafson). Louisville, KT: Westminster John Knox Press.

Pilnick, A. (2002a) What 'most people' do: exploring the ethical implications of genetic counselling. *New Genetics and Society* 21: 339–350.

Pilnick, A. (2002b) 'There are no rights and wrongs in these situations': identifying interactional difficulties in genetic counselling. *Sociology of Health & Illness* 24(1): 66–88.

Pomerantz, A. (1978) Attributions of responsibility: blamings. *Sociology* 12: 115–121.

Roberts, C. and Sarangi, S. (2005) Theme-oriented discourse analysis of medical encounters. *Medical Education* 39: 632–640.

Sarangi, S. (2000) Activity types, discourse types and interactional hybridity: the case of genetic counselling. In S. Sarangi and M. Coulthard (eds) *Discourse and Social Life* 1–27. London: Pearson.

Sarangi, S. (2010) Professional values in interaction: non-directiveness, client-centredness and other-orientation in genetic counselling. In S. Pattison, B. Hannigan, R. Pill and H. Thomas (eds) *Emerging Values in Healthcare: The Challenge for Professionals* 163–185. London: Jessica Kingsley.

Sarangi, S. (2011) Role hybridity in professional practice. In S. Sarangi, V. Polese and G. Caliendo (eds) *Genre(s) on the Move: Hybridisation and Discourse Change in Specialised Communication* 271–296. Napoli: Edizioni Scientifiche Italiane (ESI).

Sarangi, S and Clarke, A. (2002) Constructing an account by contrast in counselling for childhood genetic testing. *Social Science & Medicine* 54: 295–308.

Sarangi, S., Bennert, K., Howell, L. and Clarke A. (2003) 'Relatively speaking': relativisation of genetic risk in counselling for predictive testing. *Health, Risk and Society* 5(2): 155–169.

Sarangi, S., Brookes-Howell, L., Bennert, K. and Clarke, A. (2011) Psychological and sociomoral frames in genetic counselling for predictive testing. In C. N. Candlin and S. Sarangi (eds) *Handbook of Communication in Organisations and Professions* 235–257. Berlin: De Gruyter Mouton.

Scheff, T. (1968) Negotiating reality: notes on power in the assessment of responsibility. *Social Problems* 16(1): 3–17.

Scott, M. H. and Lyman, S. M. (1968) Accounts. *American Sociological Review* 33: 46–62.

Shaver, K. G. (1985) *The Attribution of Blame: Causality, Responsibility and Blameworthiness*. New York: Springer-Verlag.

Silverman, D. (1987) *Communication and Medical Practice: Social Relations in the Clinic*. London: Sage.

Strong, P. and Davis, A. (1978) Who's who in paediatric encounters: morality, expertise and the generation of identity and action in medical settings. In A. Davis (ed.) *Relationships Between Doctors and Patients* 48–75. Farnborough: Saxton House.

Tannen, D. and Wallat, C. (1982) A sociolinguistic analysis of multiple demands on the paediatrician in doctor/mother/child interaction. In R. J. di Pietro (ed.) *Linguistics and the Professions* 39–50. Norwood, NJ: Ablex.

Tates, K. and Meeuwesen, L. (2001) Doctor-patient-child communication: a (re) view of the literature. *Social Science & Medicine* 52: 839–851.

Taylor, C. (1991) Responsibility for self. In P. French (ed.) *The Spectrum of Responsibility* 214–224. New York: St Martin's Press.

Taylor, L. (1972) The significance and interpretation of replies to motivational questions: the case of sex offenders. *Sociology* 6: 23–39.

White, S. (2002) Accomplishing 'the case' in paediatrics and child health: medicine and morality in inter-professional talk. *Sociology of Health and Illness* 24(4): 409–435.

A version of this chapter appeared in *Journal of Applied Linguistics and Professional Practice* 9:3.

Srikant Sarangi is currently Professor in Humanities and Medicine and Director of the Danish Institute of Humanities and Medicine (DIHM) at Aalborg University, Denmark. He continues as Honorary Professor at Cardiff University. In 2012, he was awarded the title of 'Fellow' by the Academy of Social Sciences, UK. In 2015, he was elected as a 'Foreign Member' of The Finnish Society of Sciences and Letters (Societas Scientiarum Fennica). His research interests are in institutional/professional discourse studies (e.g. healthcare, social work, bureaucracy, education) and applied linguistics. He is author and editor of 12 books, guest-editor of five journal special issues and has published nearly 200 journal articles and book chapters. He is editor of *Text & Talk*; *Communication & Medicine* and *Journal of Applied Linguistics and Professional Practice*.

Appendix: Transcription conventions

G1	genetic counsellor
K1	kidney specialist
N	genetic nurse
PF/PM	parent female/parent male
CF/CM	child female/child male
(.) (..) (…)	micropause/pauses up to one second/pause exceeding one second
((gap))	an interval of longer length between speaker turns and an approximation of length in seconds
word	decreased volume
>> <<	accelerated pace
<u>underlining</u>	increase emphasis as in stress
question mark [?]	rising intonation
-	cut-off of prior word or sound
[text in square brackets]	overlapping speech
((text in double round brackets))	description or anonymised information
(text in round brackets)	transcriber's guess
(^^^^^^^)	untranscribable
=	a continuous utterance and is used when a speaker's lengthy utterance is broken up arbitrarily for purposes of presentation.

Part II
Constructing responsibility in health care and social work

Negotiating parental/familial responsibility in genetic counselling

Gøril Thomassen, Srikant Sarangi &
John-Arne Skolbekken

1 Introduction

Within the family sphere, parents routinely assume responsibility (and are attributed blame) with regard to their children's wellbeing, especially in terms of education and health. In the context of healthcare, such responsibilities are manifest at the level of decision making targeted at minimising present and future risk to children. Our focus in this chapter is two-fold: (i) how parents frame their responsibility during genetic counselling and (ii) how genetic counsellors respond to such framings. We aim to demonstrate how shifts in framing are tied up with participant structure and how together they provide a basis for examining responsibility talk.

Given the familial basis of genetic disorders, the discharge of parental responsibility vis-à-vis risk of inheritance of genetic conditions becomes an imperative. As d'Agincourt-Canning (2001: 231) observes: 'genetic information belongs to and may benefit not only a single individual, but also members of a biological kinship'. Taylor (2004: 137) makes a similar observation in stressing that decisions about genetic testing have 'implications for self and others'. In the context of genetic counselling, genetic risk is often talked about in terms of individual risk and familial risk, which in some instances (e.g. breast cancer) can be framed and understood with reference to population risk. Because discussion of familial risk is integral to genetic counselling, parents who are either affected or have a carrier status often want to reassure themselves of the risk status of their children through seeking a genetic test for themselves and/or for their children. This is what we refer to as parental responsibility. Brief examples from our data corpus of how this is framed are as follows:

'What kind of risk is there that my children get it?'
'I would check how dangerous it is for her'
'I want to do the test for my kids'

'Isn't it natural if she faints and is anaemic she should have such a
test?'
'Should I talk with my children about it at this present moment?'
'I don't want to cause any unnecessary worry by telling them about
my genetic status'

Parental responsibility of the kind we are concerned with in this chapter fits
into the broader issue of families' need to play a protective role (Kessler
1998). As far as familial genetic conditions are concerned, the responsibility
for testing oneself and/or one's child inevitably takes on a psychological as
well as sociomoral character (Sarangi et al. 2011).

In what follows we first outline the notion of genetic risk and responsibility in light of relevant literature. We then provide details about our
data, methodology and analytical framework, which is followed by data
analysis. Our conclusion draws attention to the tensions experienced by
both parents and genetic counsellors when accounting for responsible
actions.

2 Genetic risk and responsibility

Previous studies dealing with genetic risk, responsibility and decision
making fall into three broad categories: interview-based (Arribas-Ayllon
et al. 2008; Downing 2005; Forrest et al. 2003; Hallowell 1999; Hallowell
et al. 2003; Skirton 1998); ethnographically grounded (Bosk 1992;
Featherstone et al. 2006); and clinic communication oriented (Pilnick
2002; Sarangi 2010; Sarangi et al. 2011, 2003).

Focusing on breast/ovarian cancer, Hallowell (1999) argues that women
conceptualise genetic risk responsibility as a moral issue, foregrounding
womanhood, motherhood, and as carers of others (see also d'Agincourt-
Canning (2001) on the gendered dimension of disclosure of genetic risk).
The women in Hallowell's study positioned themselves as 'at risk' before
they attended the clinic, and their decisions and motivations reported after
counselling concerning risk management were formulated as responsibility
for the care of others. This position was evident even when the women did
not have a need to know their genetic risk for their own sake, and when
medical interventions could be potentially risky for themselves. Hallowell
claims that the women's perceptions of risk and responsibility vis-à-vis risk
management are based on a construction of identity as 'self-in-relation'. In
a further study of women who had undergone genetic testing, Hallowell

et al. (2003) show that these women's accounts of moral responsibility in generating genetic information raise ethical dilemmas in the context of disclosing this information to others. The moral responsibility to provide genetic information by undergoing a test is overshadowed by a sense of responsibility to protect and prevent any harm for their kin that disclosure could cause.

Forrest et al. (2003) draw attention to barriers and facilitators in risk communication in the family – who to tell or not to tell. They find that telling about genetic risk is considered an important part of displaying familial responsibility. Forrest et al. refer to generational responsibility, where younger generations are implicated when making decisions about disclosure of genetic information. This is echoed by Skirton (1998: 107): 'Whether parents intend to tell their offspring about the risk of genetic disease is related not only to their attitude to the condition, but also their belief in the inherent right of an individual to information which has important personal implications.'

That genetic risk communication in the family is dynamic and nuanced is further endorsed by other researchers (Arribas-Ayllon et al. 2008; Downing 2005; Featherstone et al. 2006). For example, Downing (2005) observes in her case studies of families facing Huntington's disease how responsibility is a jointly negotiated process when making decisions about genetic risk communication. In a study involving a range of genetic conditions, Arribas-Ayllon et al. (2008) argue that family communication about genetic risk and responsibility is dependent on existing alignments and misalignments in family relations (see also Featherstone et al. 2006). This is explained with reference to a balancing act between parental responsibility and the child's (future) autonomy.

While the above mentioned interview-based studies focus on how people account for their genetic responsibility, in an ethnographic study of a paediatric hospital setting, Bosk (1992) examines how genetic counsellors provide pointers towards what constitutes reasonable and responsible action on the face of available genetic information. He suggests that although the counsellors remain committed to nondirective, neutral, information-based counselling, there is evidence of counsellors making statements to their patients that clearly imply what a reasonable and responsible person would do with genetic information. Such communicative outcomes may be seen as an unavoidable consequence of conflicting role expectations – the neutral expert on the one hand and the good Samaritan on the other. In ethical terms this could be described as a conflict between the principles of autonomy and beneficence. Responsibility resides squarely with the patient when patient autonomy takes centre stage, whereas a more paternalistic stance is involved when the counsellors communicate in a subtle manner what they presume to be in the best interests of the patient. Note that Bosk's discussion does not take on board the potential tensions between parental responsibility and the child's autonomy as Arribas-Ayllon et al. (2008) attest.

With regard to communication in the clinic setting, Pilnick (2002) draws our attention to how counsellors allude to 'what other people do', similar to what Bosk (1992) reports, when conditions for advice giving arise. Her main focus is on how counsellors shift between directive and non-directive stances when responding to clients' need for expert advice. The formulation of 'what other people do' indexes a preferred state-of-affair, and its consensual character implies a directive stance.

More recently, Sarangi (2010) has proposed a distinction between 'general others' (as suggested in Pilnick's work) and 'family-others' vis-á-vis role-responsibility. With regard to the 'family-others', he draws on Mead's (1934) notion of dialogic self in outlining different types of family-other orientation, categorised as 'self-vs-other', 'self-as-other' and 'self-and-other' (for a detailed discussion, see Sarangi 2007). More specifically, this differentiation is made to capture the dynamics between clients' and counsellors' orientation towards absent and co-present others in the decision-making process. Of particular relevance is Sarangi's (this issue) role-relational perspective on responsibility, i.e. how clients routinely take the 'self-and-other' (or what Hallowell (1999) calls 'self-in-relation') orientation into account when making decisions about undergoing genetic testing or disclosing genetic test results (Sarangi et al. 2011).

3 Data and methodology

Our data consists of 20 genetic counselling sessions (audio recordings and transcripts) within a hospital department of medical genetics in Norway (following usual ethics protocol, including informed consent from both counsellors and families). The clients are either affected by cancer or at high risk of inheriting cancer because of family history. These are mainly first consultations, with the exception of two sessions. The family pedigree is usually constructed during the opening phase of the first consultation, which subsequently constitutes a communicative resource for exploring patterns of inheritance risk. We select six extended examples (see Appendices for transcription conventions and for original transcripts in

Norwegian) involving breast cancer and bowel cancer in terms of explicit marking of parental responsibility (e.g. 'what kind of risk is there that my children get it?'; 'I would check how dangerous it is for her'; 'should I talk with my children about it at this present moment?').

In our fine-grained discourse analysis we demonstrate how responsibility talk is framed by parents and how such responsibility talk is responded to by the genetic counsellors, spanning the genetic risk assessment, the testing process and the dissemination of test results.

4 Data analysis

Our first case concerns a man (PM) in his mid-forties who is referred to the genetics clinic after he has had a polyp removed to assess whether there is familial risk concerning bowel cancer. As the encounter evolves the client obviously is more concerned about his children in his protective role (Kessler 1998) than about his own health condition. He nominates 'the risk for my children' as his main concern for this visit after the counsellor has presented some sort of preliminary formulation indicating future interventions for the client (turn 01). As we will see, the client comes across as a responsible parent and foregrounds his parental role-responsibility by orienting explicitly to his children's wellbeing.

Example 1: 'what kind of risk is there that my children get it'

```
01 GC1: but either way now we have to follow you up with a
        new colonoscopy and see how things develop (.) but
        what we will do is to see if we can find anything
        in the laboratory that can in a way confirm or
        disprove that there is a (.) an increased risk
        (0.5) eh: .hh and possibly then also say something
        about how often we think that it would be OK for
        you to be examined
02 PM1: yes [well]
03 GC1: [but]
04 PM1: the most important for me now because they have
        after all found things and I am after all being
        followed up
05 GC1: yes
06 PM1: and it's maybe not that which is the most
        important for me <that I am followed up is
        important> [((laughter))]
```

```
07 GC1: [yes yes]
08 PM1: but what is most important for me in this
            connection here is after all more that what kind
            (.) of risk is there that MY CHILDREN get it
09 GC1: =yes
10 PM1: = and then it is after all then sort of how they
            will be followed up eh: that is the [reason that]
11 GC1: [yes yes]
12 PM1: am here now
13 GC1: yes yes .hh so we have there are several factors
            (.) eh: (.) I don't know what you know about genes
            in general
14 PM1: ºa little bitº
15 GC1: a little bit (.) eh: well we do have along this
            DNA strand of ours (.) which is packed like chunks
            in these chromosomes in the nucleus (.) so these
            genes here lie a gene is an area on the DNA strand
            where there are recipes for important [proteins]
16 PM1: [yes]
17 GC1: a:nd most of them <so we inherit well well a set
            from father and a set from mother> and most of
            them are important from when we are a fertilised
            egg for us to develop at all (.) and then we have
            other genes that are more important later in life
            for maintenance (.) and if you think of a sort of
            colon cancer protective gene then (.) most people
            will after all be born with normal genes
```

In turn 01, GC1 outlines the investigation and surveillance procedure to manage the individual risk concerning PM1. In turn 02, PM1 offers a minimal acknowledgement, followed by 'well' which overlaps with GC1's 'but' – both turn initiations suggesting there is something else to talk about. In turns 04 and 06, PM1 begins to offer a comparative perspective underlying the decision to undergo follow-up tests – which is framed in terms of prioritising the motivation, marked temporally with 'now'. In turn 08, there is a shift of attention from PM1's own 'increased risk' to 'what kind of risk is there that my children get it' and how they can be followed up (turn 10) if they were found to be at risk.

Here parental responsibility is explicitly framed in the form of a question as the parent offers his reason for being tested by foregrounding an other-orientation (08, 10, 12). As can be seen, parental responsibility overrides individual responsibility, especially in turns 08 and 10, when PM1 shifts attention from his at-risk status to his children's future risk of developing bowel cancer ('but what is most important for me in this connection here is after all more that what kind (.) of risk is there that MY CHILDREN get it'; 'then sort of how they will be followed up eh: that is the [reason that]'). GC1 responds to this framing of parental responsibility by providing more information about genetic risk (13–17). In doing so, GC1 does not manifestly endorse or dispute PM's other-orientation as the reason for testing. Instead he readily adopts an information provider role by embracing a non-directive stance.

It is worth noting that PM1 asks two questions – what the genetic risk status of his children might be and what kinds of follow-up procedures are in place. As we can see, GC1 responds to the second question only minimally (13), but the first question is reframed in terms of PM's knowledge about genes rather than as risk of inheritance as far as the children are concerned ('I don't know what you know about genes'). What follows in turn 15 therefore is a textbook style explanation of how genes mutate. Later in the session (not shown), GC1 returns to the specific issue of risk inheritance after he has offered more general information about genetic risk associated with bowel cancer.

In the following extract, which is also taken from the same session, the father directly asks the counsellor for advice – whether he should inform his children about his decision to undergo genetic testing (including the testing of his father's tissue).

Example 2: 'should I talk with my children about it at this present moment?'

```
01 PM1: but do you think I should talk with MY children
        about it at this stage?
02 GC1: (1.5) <.hh> .h °n-° (2) well <it> >.hh< (1) mm um
        it depends how > um ho-< how invol- well IS IT
        something they have been involved in (1) well I
        think about grandfather and illness and-
03 PM1: (0.5) yes <mm> not really like- they were after
        all quite small when
04 GC1: (0.5) >yes<
05 PM1: (1) he died <so[o>]
06 GC1: [>yes<] .hh well because kids notice very often
        if someone like a parent goes to be examined at a
        hospital and then it may [be a li]ttle
07 PM1: [°yes°]
08 GC1: anxiety concerning that
09 PM1: >YES< <it> is not basically (1) °um° problem now
        at this s- stage at [least]
```

10 GC1: [no] no.hh <um> (1) what you <should keep in mind>
    as far as children are concerned it is after all
    that (1.5) or that goes for EVERYBODY .hh that
    what one imagines tends to be worse than what is
    [the reality]
11 PM1: [yes yes] that is why I ask act[°ually°]
12 GC1: [yes]
13 PM1: (0.5) (°right°)
14 GC1: .hh <e>mm (1) °eh° so it is a bit like up to you
    <whether you> say <it> that <you um> that we are
    thinking of investigating (1) this to see if there
    may be any risk .hh um (1.5) <n> that I think will
    be up to you what you- .hh NO BUT what [you must
    be aware]
15 PM1: [((clears throat))]
16 GC1: of is (2) is <that> there may <be> communication
    across the oth[er kids]
17 PM1: [YES YES no] °I understand [that°]
18 GC1: [>yes<] .hh <like if> your sister's children for
    instance get informed AND they talk together THEN
    [that will]
19 PM1: [yes]
20 GC1: be unfortunate
21 PM1: .hh yes
22 GC1: so if one gets going with assessment then it is
    a good thing that <one> maybe within the family
    agrees on WHEN one <ta[lks]>
23 PM1: mm yes
24 GC1: and WHAT one [says] then
25 PM1: [yes]
26 GC1: yes
27 PM1: .hh but after all it will depend a lot on (x) how-
28 GC1: >°yes°<
29 PM1: well 25 years old the daughter WILL soon be 25
    after all
30 GC1: [>yes<]
31 PM1: [.hh] <so> it is obvious that <if> yes
32 GC1: = >yes< (3) .hh <so is>
33 PM1: = but what do we do – how long does it typically
    take before one <has e> finished this assessment?
34 GC1: (1) .hh well it will take around THREE months

PM1's question in turn 01 about disclosure signals a return to the
counsellor's topic agenda initiated in the previous extract – the testing

and treatment options concerning PM1 himself. PM1, however, deflects this topical focus by nominating a related topic – disclosure of his genetic status. His question can be regarded as a variant of the so-called 'famous infamous question' in genetic counselling – 'what would you do if it were you?' (see Sarangi 2000). The asking of the question itself embodies other-oriented responsible action. However, such questions are directly addressed at the genetic counsellor, requesting a response. In a sense, such a question prepares the ground for professional advice disguised as personal preference. While genetic counsellors routinely avoid offering direct advice (Sarangi 2000), on occasions, such questions are responded to by what others do (Pilnick 2002), which may be seen as endorsing a preferred state of affairs.

Here PM1's question draws attention to his parental responsibility with regard to (non)disclosure of genetic risk information. What is implied in the question is the ambivalence surrounding risks and benefits of knowing one's and others' genetic risk status (Sarangi et al. 2003). Turn 02 is a possible slot for GC1 to report what other people do in such circumstances, but he chooses to give an 'it depends' response – which underscores the situatedness of the case in hand. This means the discussion remains focused on an assessment of the specific family circumstances rather than following a routine imperative based on what other people do. Generalised explanations, however, are offered later – how children become anxious when someone in the family is hospitalised.

PM1's parental concerns about whether or not to tell children are initially met with hesitation on GC1's part before s/he enquires about the children's level of awareness of the genetic condition in the family, especially their experience of the illness and the grandfather's death. When PM1 points out that the children were too small to remember the circumstances of their grandfather's death, GC1 shifts from this specific family situation to making general claims about children (how they get anxious when someone goes into hospital (06–08); and later, in more explicit terms (10), 'what one imagines tends to be worse than what is [the reality]'). Here is a hint that a disclosure of risk information can be beneficial in preventing undesirable imaginaries. This leads PM1, in turn 11, to reiterate his motivation for seeking direct advice ('that is why I ask actually'). Rather than offering a definitive 'yes/no' response, in turn 14 GC1 returns the decision making to the parent ('it is a bit like up to you whether you say it').

There is further qualification, which is temporally grounded, concerning communication between the other children. In turns 18 and 20, GC1 projects a hypothetical adverse scenario ('if your sister's children for instance get informed and they talk together then that will be unfortunate'). Although framed hypothetically, it seems such a scenario could very likely happen. So there are risks in one's children getting to learn about their genetic risk status from an alternative, dispreferred, source than their parents. By extension, parents need to take precaution to prevent the occasioning of such an adverse scenario. In this regard, GC1's formulation of this projected adverse scenario is meant to function as a contra-indication, implying that parents perhaps should directly disclose information about genetic status to their children. Such a generic formulation of do's and don'ts is a variation on 'what other people do' (Pilnick 2002). In turns 22–24, we notice a shift from whether or not to tell the children to 'when one talks' and 'what one says' – still retaining the generic and tentative tone.

Our next case concerns a mother (PF1) in her forties, diagnosed with breast cancer a year ago, who is accompanied by her 24-year-old daughter (PF1 is currently divorced from the father of the daughter). As in the previous case, the mother is more concerned about the future risk for her daughter than for herself, as she acknowledges explicitly 'I've already got breast cancer'.

Example 3: 'I want to check how dangerous it is for her'

```
01 GC2: eh I have got a referral and actually this
            referral is for you (.) but I see that it is your
            daughter who has filled out ((laughter))
02 PF1: yes because [it is]
03 GC2: [yes]
04 PF1: is m- the referral was for her I thought
05 GC2: exactly
06 PF1: I have already got [breast cancer]
07 GC2: [yes]
08 PF1: what I want to check is how dangerous it is for
            her
09 GC2: right I see
10 PF1: and so on
11 GC2: eh: at least it says here that you at the age of
            46 (.) that is a young age
12 PF1: .hh yes
13 GC2: actually got breast cancer eh: .hh and then I do
            understand that both you and your daughter have
            some thoughts and so you filled out the family tree
            here right
```

```
14 PF1: .hh yes
15 GC2: and there we have drawn a chart (.) and shall we
          have a look at that we start with that ((sniffles))
16 PF1: mm
17 GC2: eh: and then in our world we are simple so that
          women are circles and men are squares ((laughter))
18 PF1: ((laughter))
19 GC2: and then we find you there 46 years old (.) as I
          said young of age <but you are ok now>
20 PF1: yes I am having radiotherapy now almost done with
          it so
21 GC2: have you been to any checkups and: (.)
22 PF1: not yet
23 GC2: not yet
24 PF1: no I guess we need to finish all the treatment first
25 GC2: yes right
26 PF1: before we test
27 GC2: but the doctor is optimistic?
28 PF1: well I am now optimistic at least >I don't ask the
          doctor< ((laughter))
29 GC2: sounds good
30 PF1: ((laughter))
31 GC2: sounds good
```

In turn 01, GC2 addresses the mother as the primary participant in the session, not the daughter, as he implies that there might be a misunderstanding about who has the ratified entitlement for referral to the genetics clinic. The very fact that the daughter is co-present ('the referral was for her I thought') is already indication of parental responsibility. This is further explicated in turns 06–08 where PF1 states that her daughter's risk of inheritance rather than her own risk of recurrence constitutes the main purpose of the clinic visit. This reasoning resembles that of the parent in Extract 1. However, GC2's response here differs considerably from what happens in Extract 1. Rather than delve into an explanation of patterns of genetic inheritance, here GC2 is oriented to PF1's own current status, which is framed in a light-hearted manner by alluding to PF1's age (46 years, and being 'young of age'). In turn 13, however, GC2 aligns with the parental concerns about the daughter's risk of inheritance. This then forms the basis for a discussion of the family pedigree, again maintaining a light-hearted ethos as evidenced by mutual laughter. In turn 19, GC2 successfully foregrounds PF1's risk status as the topic, which is followed by questions about her treatment regime. PF1 responds favourably and paints an optimistic picture of her future, independent of her doctor's expert opinion, which is significant given her concerns about her daughter who is co-present. In other words, PF1 displays her other-oriented parental responsibility even when the talk is centred on her current risk status and future prognosis.

In the next extract, towards the end of the same session, PF1 returns to her concerns about her daughter (CD). It transpires that her ex-mother-in-law also had breast cancer, which means that the 24-year-old daughter runs the risk of inheriting breast cancer from both parental sides. Previous to this extract they have talked through the family pedigree and GC2 has just suggested that they inform PF1's ex-husband about the risk and the opportunity for him to undergo a genetic test (since her divorce, PF1's ex-husband (CD's father) has got a new family with one son and three daughters).

Example 4: 'if that gene is from my side'

```
01 PF1: mm but if that gene is from my side then it
            shouldn't after all make any difference to her
            siblings who don't
02 GC2: [.hh no]
03 CD:  [but you] don't know where it comes from
04 PF1: <but we don't know that [then]>
05 CD:  [mm]
06 GC2: = no but that-
07 PF1: = is it possible to find out that then
08 GC2: yes it is possible to [find out]
09 PF1: [mm]
10 GC2: and that is why I thought of doing it on both of
            you
11 CD:  mm
12 PF1: mm
13 GC2: simply
14 PF1: yes because if I have it [then]
15 GC2: [e:h] while I am now sitting just looking at the
            family tree I notice that there are actually three
            daughters on the other side here and
16 PF1: mm
17 GC2: ((clicking sound)) (1)
18 PF1: there are you see
19 GC2: ((sniffles)) (1.5) and then it is maybe not such
            a bad idea after all (0.5) that we try to get in
            touch with ((father's name)) (1)
20 PF1: °mm°
```

```
21 GC2: and if he wants to then it is easier that we take
        a blood sample there then
22 CD:  mm
23 GC2: because [then]
24 CD:  [yes]
25 GC2: we actually check out four girls in one [test]
26 PF1: [mm]
27 GC2: don't we (.)
28 PF1: mm
29 GC2: to find out something about risk there
30 PF1: .hh yes mm
```

Here we see that while PF1 is framing parental responsibility, rather categorically, with regard to her daughter's risk of inheritance, GC2 is interested in implicating the ex-husband and his new family to arrive at an accurate calculation of CD's risk status. In turn 03, CD expresses doubt about her mother's understanding of genetic transmission, which sets the scene for GC2 to expand the circumference of risk assessment involving CD's father. As can be seen, PF1 immediately aligns with her daughter – first by echoing CD's interjection by repeating her words and then by framing a question about inheritance: 'is it possible to find out' (07). GC2 responds affirmatively when he says 'that is why I thought of doing it on both of you' (10). In what follows (turns 15ff), GC2 invokes the family tree to justify why 'it is maybe not a bad idea after all that we try to get in touch with ((father's name))' (19). The economy and efficacy of the testing protocol is justified in turn 25 ('we actually check out four girls in one test'), which helps to displace the burden of parental responsibility PF1 seems to be carrying. The need for contacting the absent father thus becomes necessary.

Our final case concerns a woman (PF2) in her late forties who comes from a family with high prevalence of bowel cancer. She has been referred to the genetics clinic by her family doctor to ascertain if the family have a genetic risk of developing Lynch syndrome. Her main concern is her 27-year-old daughter who has polyps and is generally anaemic. PF2 has previously mentioned the worry she has about her daughter's susceptibility and returns to the topic by asking a question which is prefaced by her subjective medical knowledge.

Example 5: 'the fact that it is deep inside the intestine'

```
01 PF2: >eh could I ask you about something<
02 GC1: yes
```

```
03 PF2: the fact that it is deep inside the intestine
        almost
04 GC1: almost by the colon
05 PF2: yes yes so in the transition there yes
06 GC1: yes yes
07 PF2: and it can stop bleeding and it after a long time
        then it can give
08 GC1: yes so you can say that (.) eh a polyp which stays
        there or and after a while maybe a tumour that
        develops to the end of the intestine you might
        have symptoms
09 PF2: mm
10 GC1: but did it [start on the right side]
11 PF2: [mm yes]
12 GC1: then many many years pass before you get symptoms
        because what comes from the small intestine is so
        thick that it will flow past (.) mucus and blood
        will usually form very quickly so that you do not
        see it eh not that much blood then there are some
        people who (.) discover colon cancer because they
        become anaemic and then if one becomes anaemic
        without any other explanation one m- then one
        MUST ALWAYS check the intestine IF there may be
        something bleeding
13 PF2: .hh isn't it- isn't it NATURAL then for for <eh>
        HER then who has had (xxxx)
14 GC1: °m[m°]
15 PF2: [or] HAS [for that]
16 GC1: [°mm°]
17 PF2: has not yet been taken
18 GC1: no
19 PF2: isn't it natu- natural for a doctor to THINK that
        then? if <she xx> faints [and]
20 GC1: [°mm°]
21 PF2: is anaemic and has very little iron in her blood
        [and-]
22 GC1: [m]°m°
23 PF2: and is that something that she should have a test
        like that?
24 GC1: yes [<well>]
25 PF2: [that she must check] it out <and eh> all in
        [all?]
26 GC1: [°yes]°well you can say that which is (2) ALSO a
        challenge as far as such (1) a <a> if one thinks
        of such a familiar occurrence .hh it is after all
```

```
                 that .hh (1) THIS is NOT something one THINKS of
                 AT that YOUNG AGE [UNLESS]
    27 PF2:  [°n.hho°]
    28 GC1:  there is no particular reason for that (3) but
                 well she was born in
    29 PF2:  eighty two
    30 GC1:  = eighty two yes and is it a long time since she
                 was- she was in colonoscopy?
    31 PF2:  yes of course and she has removed <[a]>
    32 GC1:  [>yes<]
    33 PF2:  yes but is it is let's see could it be four years
                 ago now?
    34 GC1:  °mm. (1) okay°
    35 PF2:  (2) more or less
    36 GC1:  yes and now she is anaem[ic and]
    37 PF2:  [.hh ho] is (xx) has been on sick-leave she do you
                 understand (x) months
    38 GC1:  (x[x)]
    39 PF2:  [<and]> (without them finding) (xxx)
```

In the opening turns, both PF2 and GC1 can be seen as negotiating the
biomedical facts surrounding intestinal polyps leading to symptoms of
bowel cancer, with GC2 offering extended explanations in turns 08 and 12.
Of particular relevance is the linkage between unexplained anaemia and the
possibility of colon cancer (12), which allows PF2 to articulate her nagging
concerns about her daughter's risk. This leads her to voice her disquiet
about her family doctor's failure to undertake a proper risk assessment
despite the obvious signs (e.g. she 'faints', 'is anaemic' and 'has very
little iron in her blood', 13–23), which is accompanied by GC1's minimal
acknowledgements. PF2's account points towards a moral stance realised
in the form of a question in turn 23 ('is that something that she should have
a test like that?), which is reinforced in turn 25. GC1's immediate response
in turn 24 ('yeah well') is further qualified in turn 26 as she draws attention
to other complicating factors in genetic risk assessment than the ones PF2
has pointed out. Rather subtly, GC1 challenges PF2's potential accusation
of the doctor acting irresponsibly ('this is not something one thinks of at
that young age unless'). In a strategic move, GC1 then shifts the topic
to seek further information about the daughter's age and relevant medical
interventions to date.

In sum, the mother shows concern about the daughter's at-risk status
by foregrounding a link between anaemia and bowel cancer. GC1 first
provides an explanation, ending with: 'if one becomes anaemic without

any other explanation one m- then one MUST ALWAYS check the intestine IF there may be something bleeding' (turn 12). This prompts PF2, in turns 13–23, to return to her opening question and specify its force using a list-structure for emphasis – that the daughter faints, is anaemic and has very little iron in her blood. The question that follows may be heard as an implicit accusation for overlooking obvious symptoms: 'isn't it natural for a doctor to THINK [...] that she should have a test like that?' (turn 19). Note the generic formulation here, 'a doctor', which can function both to question the competence of the individual doctor concerned, while underscoring the fact that any doctor would have picked up the symptoms, followed by an immediate offer of a test. In response, GC1 mitigates this intended blaming on the part of PF2 by appealing to the young age of the daughter, thus endorsing the other doctor's decision not to offer a test.

Our next extract is taken from the same clinical encounter. Leading up to this point, the genetic counsellor has indicated that, based on the family pedigree, the family does not meet the criteria for being labelled 'at risk'.

Example 6: 'I wonder if it can skip a generation'

```
01 GC1: so there is no strong evidence that you have to go
        [<home>]
02 PF2: [no no]
03 GC1: to [say]
04 PF2: [but] I wonder if it can skip a generation and
        then to (.) °like to° e:h if- .hhyes <do you know
        what I mean>
05 GC1: =yes hh
06 PF2: .hh yes
07 GC1: [e:h]
08 PF2: [in relation] to my daughter
09 GC1: =yes but not not e:h that young
10 PF2: no
11 GC1: well since you have s- soon will turn fifty and
        haven't found anything with you then then (.) then
        can (.) then it is highly unlikely it will start
        like that
12 PF2: mm
13 GC1: =yes
14 PF2: mm (1) but there doesn't necessarily have to be
        anything with her either that is not what I am
        saying
15 GC1: [.hh no no]
```

    16 PF2: absolutely I really hope not <u>that</u> but I do not
           like the [development]
    17 GC1: [.hh no] no and then you can say that there <u>is</u> a
           <u>difference</u> because they haven't <u>seen</u> anything with
           her because (.) your colon (.) or well you have
           probably not been able to <u>check</u> that <u>carefully</u>
           because I take it you have been troubled (0.5) .hh
           but your colon you have like pavement epithelium
           like we have on
    18 PF2: mm
    19 GC1: all surfaces we have cells like this <u>mucosal</u> (0.5)
           and they are <u>formed</u> down in these

Following GC1's summary assessment of familial risk in turn 01 ('home' referring to family), PF2, as a responsible parent, seems reluctant to accept a 'no risk' scenario. This prompts her, in turn 04, to initiate a discussion not about the immediate risk to her daughter, but about the impending risk for the future generation, given that 'it [gene] can skip a generation'. The framing of an adverse hypothetical scenario is evidence of parental responsibility, which also appeals to shared knowledge signalled by 'do you know what I mean?' (04). GC1 in the subsequent turns (09–11) dismisses PF2's worries on the basis that they have not found anything to warrant further worries even though she 'will soon turn fifty', followed by a firm assessment: 'it is <u>highly</u> unlikely it will start like that'. What we see next is a subtle challenge of this assessment, when PF2, in turns 14–16, issues her own assessment of the present and future scenarios, while highlighting a preferred outcome: 'I do not like the development.' These types of parental assessments echo Sarangi's (this issue) findings in his study of parents' accounts in the context of childhood genetic testing in the UK. Overall, the mother comes across as a responsible parent in seeking clarification about her daughter's and the future generation's risk status with regard to development of colon cancer. In turn 17, GC1 finally initiates a shift in focus from assessing the family risk as such to a general genetic explanation of how bowel cancer may evolve. This shift is framed by GC1 to underscore how the client has spent more time worrying about her daughter than appraising her own level of knowledge about genetic risk and bowel cancer.

5 Discussion and conclusion

Our discourse analytic insights about parental genetic responsibility corroborate earlier findings based on interview accounts of parents as reported by Hallowell (1999) and Arribas-Ayllon et al. (2008). This suggests that parental genetic responsibility, whether examined via interviews or in clinic settings, is manifest in similar ways – familial risk management is framed as responsibility for the care of others, here children and grandchildren. The findings of the present study with regard to the discursive resources mobilised by parents in their accounts and by the genetic counsellors in their responses complement previous research findings based on comparable data settings in the UK (Sarangi et al. 2003, 2011, this issue). This observation points to cross-national parallels in terms of communicative processes characteristic of genetic counselling for inherited disorders.

The present study shows that parental responsibility is paramount in the context of familial genetic conditions – both in relation to decisions about testing oneself or others and concerning decisions about disclosure of one's or others' genetic risk status. The 'self-and-other' dynamics (Sarangi 2007, this issue), including absent others, typically characterises the counselling encounter. However, at a micro-level, parental responsibility is framed and responded to differently. As we have seen, parental concerns range from being protective to acting proactively in the best interests of the children. For example, PM1's reason for testing foregrounds a protective stance towards his children as he puts family risk (and family responsibility) at the centre stage of his decision, while also orienting to his own individual risk as part of the decision-making process. We notice that PF1 does not take into account her own risk like PM1 does, but simply focuses on her daughters' risks of inheritance. She comes across as someone who is protective and other-oriented when accounting for her reason to seek genetic counselling. PM2, on the other hand, signals a proactive stance when framing the reluctance to accept a 'no risk' scenario for her daughter. In highlighting her daughter's risk status by providing detailed evidence, and through questioning the doctor's decision not to offer the daughter a genetic test, PM2 acts proactively in anticipation of a hypothetical future scenario.

Such display of parental role-responsibility is not specific to the genetic counselling setting; one may notice parallels in the context of paediatric consultations. But what distinguishes genetic counselling from other settings such as paediatric consultations are the response-types from genetic counsellors. Given the familial nature of genetic risk, the counsellors, as we have seen, may revert the discussion to the current and future risks of the parents themselves. Even here one would expect considerable variation in counselling practice, although such practices generally embody a nondirective stance about decisional outcomes, while the counsellors may come across as being somewhat directive about the decision-making process itself. The findings of this study attest the fact that the role-responsibility of the genetic counsellor is crucial in keeping the discussions process-driven rather than outcome-driven, while providing necessary information for a sound basis for decision making. When parents initiate other-oriented responsibility talk surrounding the risk status of their children or grandchildren, genetic counsellors tend to orient not only to individual risk scenarios but also to the other familial roles and responsibilities the parent as a client of genetic counselling may have. Allusions to what other people (might) do and potential adverse scenarios also become part of the counselling agenda to drive home the nuanced notion of parental (ir)responsibility.

References

Arribas-Ayllon, M., Sarangi, S. and Clarke, A. (2008) Managing self-responsibility through other-oriented blame: family accounts of genetic testing. *Social Science & Medicine* 6: 1521–1532.

Bosk, C. L. (1992) *All God's Mistakes. Genetic Counseling in a Pediatric Hospital.* London: The University of Chicago Press.

d'Agincourt-Canning, L. (2001) Experiences of genetic risk: disclosure and the gendering of responsibility. *BioEthics* 15: 231–247.

Downing, C. (2005) Negotiating responsibility: case studies of reproductive decision-making and prenatal genetic testing in families facing Huntington Disease. *Journal of Generic Counselling* 14: 219–234.

Featherstone, K., Atkinson, P., Bharadwaj, A. and Clarke, A. (2006) *Risky Relations. Family, Kinship and the New Genetics.* Oxford: Berg.

Forrest, K., Simpson, S. A., Wilson, B. J., van Teijlingen, E. R., McKee, L., Haites, N. and Matthews, E. (2003) To tell or not to tell: barriers and facilitators in family communication about genetic risk. *Clinical Genetics* 64: 317–326.

Kessler, S. (1998) Family processes in regard to genetic testing. In A. Clarke (ed.) *The Genetic Testing of Children* 113–122. Oxford: Bios Scientific Publisher.

Hallowell, N. (1999) Doing the right thing: genetic risk and responsibility. *Sociology of Health and Illness* 21: 597–621.

Hallowell, N., Foster, C., Eeles, R., Ardern-Jones, A., Murday, V. and Watson, M. (2003) Balancing autonomy and responsibility: the ethics of generating and disclosing genetic information. *Journal of Medical Ethics* 29: 74–79.

Mead, G. H. (1934) *Mind, Self, and Society: From the Standpoint of a Social Behaviourist* (Edited with Introduction by C. W. Morris). Chicago, IL: University of Chicago Press.

Pilnick, A. (2002) What 'most people' do: exploring the ethical implications of genetic counseling. *New Genetics and Society* 21: 339–350.

Sarangi, S. (2000) Activity types, discourse types and interactional hybridity: the case of genetic counselling. In S. Sarangi and M. Coulthard (eds) *Discourse and Social Life* 1–27. London: Pearson.

Sarangi, S. (2007) Other-orientation in patient-centred healthcare communication: unveiled ideology or discoursal ecology? In G. Garzone and S. Sarangi (eds) *Discourse, Ideology and Ethics in Specialised Communication* 39–71. Bern: Peter Lang.

Sarangi, S. (2010) Professional values in interaction: client-centredness, non-directiveness and other-orientation in genetic counselling. In S. Pattison, B. Hannigan, R. Pill and H. Thomas (eds) *Emerging Values in Healthcare: The Challenge for Professionals* 163–185. London: Jessica Kingsley.

Sarangi, S. (this volume) Owning responsible actions/selves: role-relational trajectories in counselling for childhood genetic testing.

Sarangi, S., Bennert, K., Howell, L. and Clarke A. (2003) 'Relatively speaking': relativisation of genetic risk in counselling for predictive testing. *Health, Risk and Society* 5: 155–169.

Sarangi, S., Brookes-Howell, L., Bennert, K. and Clarke A. (2011) Psychological and sociomoral frames in genetic counselling for predictive testing. In C. N. Candlin and S. Sarangi (eds) *Communication in Professions and Organisations* 235–257. Berlin: Mouton de Gruyter.

Skirton, H. (1998) Telling the children. In A. Clarke (ed.) *The Genetic Testing of Children* 103–111. Oxford: Bios Scientific Publishers.

Taylor, S. D. (2004) Predictive genetic decisions for Huntington's disease: context, appraisal and new moral imperatives. *Social Science & Medicine* 58: 137–149.

A version of this chapter appeared in *Journal of Applied Linguistics and Professional Practice* 9:3.

Gøril Thomassen received her PhD in Applied Linguistics from the Norwegian University of Science and Technology (NTNU) and is currently Associate Professor in the Department of Language and Literature at NTNU. Her research interests are within applied linguistics and professional discourse studies, including the discourse analysis of various forms of healthcare communication. She is now working on a project on team communication in simulated and in real clinical emergency encounters.

Srikant Sarangi is currently Professor in Humanities and Medicine and Director of the Danish Institute of Humanities and Medicine/Health (DIHM) at Aalborg University. He is also Honorary Professor at Cardiff University. His research interests are in institutional/professional discourse studies (e.g. healthcare, social work, bureaucracy, education) and applied linguistics. He is author and editor of 12 books, guest-editor of five journal special issues and has published nearly 200 journal articles and book chapters.

John-Arne Skolbekken has a PhD in health science and is Professor in the Department of Social Work and Health Science at the Norwegian University of Science and Technology (NTNU). His research interests are within modern medical risk discourse, including risk communication in such settings as advertisements for pharmaceutical products, genetic counselling and various forms of medical screening. A common theme in his research is the ethical implications of risk communication.

Appendix 1: Transcription conventions

PM   Parent male
PF   Parent Female
GC   Genetic counsellor
[ ]   Overlapping talk
-         Abrupt cut-off
=   No audible gap between the end of one turn and the beginning of
          the next
<u>Okay</u>   Marked stress
OKAY   Increased volume
((turns)) Transcriber's comment
.hh   Speaker in-breath
hh.   Speaker out-breath
okay: Lengthening the preceding sound
°okay°   Quiet speech delivery
>okay<   Talk is produced more quickly than the surrounding talk
<okay>   Talk is produced more slowly than the surrounding talk
(okay)   Transcriber doubts a word
(2)   Timed pause in seconds
(.)   Pause of less than 0.5 of a second
?   Indicates rising intonation

Appendix 2: Original transcripts in Norwegian

Example 1: 'hva slags risiko e det for at mine barn får det'

```
01 GC:   men uansett no så må jo du følges opp med ny
         koloskopi og sjå korrsn ting utvikle sæ (.) men
         det vi ska gjøre det er å se om vi kan finne noe i
         laboratoriet som kan på en måte bekrefte avkrefte
         at det er (.) en økt risiko (0.5) eh: .hh og
         eventuelt da også si noe om korr ofte vi tenke oss
         at det kan være greit for deg å bli undersøkt
02 CF:   ja [altså]
03 GC:   [men]
04 CF:   det som e viktigst for mæ no for de har jo oppdaga
         ting og æ blir jo fulgt opp
05 GC:   ja
06 CF:   det e jo kanskje ikke det som e viktigst for mæ
         <at æ blir fulgt opp e viktig> ((ler))
07 GC:   [ja ja]
08 CF:   men det som e viktigst for mæ i den sammenhengen
         her e jo mer det hv slags (.) risiko e det for at
         MINE BARN får det
09 GC:   =ja
10 CF:   = og det e jo da liksom hvordan dem ska følges opp
         det det som um [årsaken tell at]
11 GC:   [ja ja]
12 CF:   e her no
13 GC:   ja ja .hh så vi har det e flere forhold (.) eh:
         generelt æ vet ikke ka du kan om gena æ
14 CF:   litte grann
15 GC:   litte grann (.) vi har jo langs den her DNA
         tråden vår (.) som e pakka sånn bitvis i disse
         kromosomene inni cellekjernen (.) så ligg det jo
         disse her genan et gen e et område på DNA tråden
         hvor det ligg oppskrifta på viktige [proteina]
16 CF:   [ja]
17 GC:   o:g de fleste eh <altså vi arve jo jo et sett fra
         far far og et i fra mor> og de fleste e viktig i
         fra vi e et befrukta egg for at vi skal utvikle
         oss i det hele tatt (.) og så har vi andre gena
         som e mer viktig seinere i livet for vedlikehold
         (.) og viss du tenker deg et sånt tykktarmskreft
         beskyttende gen så (.) de fleste vil jo vær født
         med normale gena
```

Example 2: 'men synes du at æ bør snakk med mine barn?'

```
01 CF:  men synes du at æ bør snakk med MINE barn om det
        på nåværende tidspunkt?
02 GC:  (1,5) <.hh> .h °n-° (2) æsså <det> >.hh< (1) ng ng
        det spørs hvor >i e ha-< hvor invol- asså E DET
        noe dem har vært involvert i (1) asså æ tenke på
        med bestefar og sykdom og-
03 CF:  (0.5) ja <m> egentlig itj no sånn- dem var jo
        ganske små når e
04 GC:  (0.5) >ja<
05 CF:  (1) han dødd <så[>]
06 GC:  [>ja<] .hh nei for det at unger merke veldig ofte
        hvis noen asså en forelder e te no undersøkelse på
        sykehus også at det kan [bli en li]ten
07 CF:  [°ja°]
08 GC:  uro rundt det
09 CF:  >JA< <det> e itj i utgangspunktet nå (1) °em°
        problem på nåværende to- tidspunkt i [hvert fall]
10 GC:  [nei] nei t.hh <em> (1) det du <ska huske på>
        når det gjelder barn det er jo at (1,5) eller
        det gjeld ALLE .hh at det man forestiller seg er
        gjerne verre enn det som e [virkeligheten]
11 CF:  [jaja] det e derfor æ spør egent[°lig°]
12 GC:  [ja]
13 CF:  (0.5) (°sant ja°)
14 GC:  .hh <e>m (1) °n° så det blir litt sånn opp te deg
        <om du> forteller <det> at <du em> at vi tenke oss
        å utrede (1) dette for å sjå om det kan være noe
        risiko .hh em (1,5) <n> det tror jeg bli opp ti
        deg hva du- .hh NEI MEN det [du ska vær obs]
15 CF:  [((kremter))]
16 GC:  på er (2) e <at> e det kan <vær e> kommunikasjon
        på tvers av de an[dre (ungan)]
17 CF:  [JAJA nei] °æ skjønne [det°]
18 GC:  [>ja<] .hh <sånn at hvis> barna te søstera di for
        eksempel blir informert OG dem samsnakkes SÅ [vil
        de]t
19 CF:  [ja]
20 GC:  vær uheldig
21 CF:  .hhja
22 GC:  så hvis man setter i gang utredning så e det
        veldig greit at <e man s> kanskje innad i familien
        blir enige om kor TID man <sna[kk]e>
```

```
23 CF:   [.hhja]
24 GC:   og KA man da [si]
25 CF:   [ja]
26 GC:   ja
27 CF:   .hh men det vil jo vær veldig avhengig av (x)
         hvor-
28 GC:   >°ja°<
29 CF:   asså femogtyve år dattera E jo snart femogtyve år
30 GC:   [>ja<]
31 CF:   [.hh] <så> det e klart at <hvis> ja
32 GC:   = >ja< (3) .hh <så e>
33 CF:   (.) men hva gjør vi- hvor lang tid typisk tar det
         før man <har e> gjennomført de her undersøkelsan?
34 GC:   (1) .hh asså det tar nok en TRE måneders tid
```

Example 3: 'æ vil sjekke korr farlig e det for hu'

```
01 GC:   eh æ har fått en henvisning og egentlig så e den
         henvisninga på dæ (.) men æ ser at det e din
         datter som har fylt ut ((latter))
02 CM:   ja fordi [at de]
03 GC:   [ja]
04 CM:   e m- det hu æ ment henvisninga va tell
05 GC:   nettopp
06 CM:   æ har jo allerede fått [brystkreft]
07 GC:   [ja]
08 CM:   Det æ vil sjekke e korr farlig e det for hu
09 GC:   nettopp skjønne
10 CM:   mm
11 GC:   e:h i hvertfall så står det her at du i en alder
         av 46 år altså ung alder
12 CM:   .hh ja
13 GC:   egentlig fikk brystkreft e:h .hh og da skjønne æ jo
         at bade du og datter gjør dokk noen tanker og så
         har du fylt ut familiekart her ja
14 CM:   .hh ja
15 GC:   og der har vi tegna et kart (.) ska vi se litt på
         det vi starta med det ((snufser))
16 CM:   mm
17 GC:   eh og da i vår verden da e vi så enkel at damer e
         rundinger og menn e firkanter
18 CM:   ((latter))
19 GC:   og da finn vi dæ der 46 år (.) som sagt ung alder
         <men det går bra med dæ>
```

20 CM: ja æ e no i gang med stråling no snart ferdig med
         det så
21 GC: har du vært på noe kontroller og: (.)
22 CM: ikke enda
23 GC: ikke enda
24 CM: nei vi må jo bli ferdig med all behandlinga først
         tenker æ
25 GC: ja nettopp
26 CM: før vi teste
27 GC: men legen e optimistisk
28 CM: nei æ e no i hvert fall optimistisk æ spør ikke
         legen ((latter))
29 GC: høres bra ut
30 CM: ((latter))
31 GC: høres bra ut

Example 4: 'Viss det genet kjem fra min side'

01 CM: mm men viss at det genet kjem fra min side så har
         det jo ingenting å si for søsknene hennes som ikke
02 GC: [hh nei]
03 CD: [men du] veit ikke korr det kjem i fra
04 CM: men det <u>veit</u> vi jo [ikkje da]
05 CD: [mm]
06 GC: = nei men det-
07 CM: går det an å finn ut det da
08 GC: ja det går an å [finn ut]
09 CM: [mm]
10 GC: for det e derfor æ tenkt på å gjør det på dokk
         begge
11 CD: mm
12 CF: mm
13 GC: rett og slett
14 CM: ja for viss æ <u>har</u> [det så]
15 GC: [e:h] mens æ sitt no bare å ser familiekartet så
         ser æ jo at det <u>tre </u>døtre på andre siden her og
16 CM: mm
17 GC: ((smatter)) (1)
18 CM: det <u>e </u>det sjø
19 GC: ((snufser)) (1.5) og da <u>e</u> det kanskje ikke så dumt
         allikevel (0.5) at vi prøver å få tak i ((fars
         navn)) (1)
20 CM: mm (1)

21 GC: og viss han <u>ønske</u> det så e det nok enklere at vi
        tar blodprøve <u>der</u> da
22 CD: mm
23 GC: for [da]
24 CD: [ja]
25 GC: slår vi egentlig fire jenter [i en prøve]
26 CM: [mm]
27 GC: ikke sant (.)
28 CM: mm
29 GC: for å si noe om risiko der
30 CM: .hh ja

Example 5: 'det at den sett langt inn i tarmen'

01 CM: >eh kan æ spørr dæ om nåkka<
02 GC: ja
03 CM: altså det vil det e at den sett langt inn i tarmen
        nesten
04 GC: nesten ved tykktarmen
05 CM: ja ja altså i overgangen der ja
06 GC: ja ja
07 CM: og <u>den kan</u> la vær å blø og det etter lang tid så
        kan det gi
08 GC: ja altså du kan si at (.) eh en polypp som står
        eller og etter hvert kanskje en svulst som
        utvikler seg til i enden av tarmen vil du kunne ha
        symptoma
09 CM: mm
10 GC: [men starte det på høyre sida]
11 CM: [mm ja]
12 GC: så går det veldig veldig mange år før du får
        symptoma fordi at det som kjem fra tynntarmen e
        så tyktflytende at det vil renne forbi (.) slim og
        blod vil som regel danne sæ veldig fort slik at du
        ikke ser det eh ikke noe <u>mye </u>blod så det e <u>noen </u>
        som (.) oppdage tykktarmskreft fordi at dem blir
        blodfattig og hvis man da blir blodfattig uten
        no annen forklaring s- da SKA man ALLTID sjekke
        tarmen OM det kan vær noe som står og blør
13 CM: .hh e itj det- e itj det da NATURLIG for for <e>
        HU da som a HAR hatt (xxxx)
14 GC: °m[m°]
15 CM: [el]ler HAR [for (all)]

```
16 GC:   [mm]
17 CM:   [e enno ikkje tatt]
18 GC:   nei
19 CM:   ekke det natu- naturlig for en læge å TÆNK det da?
         visst at <hu emøm> besvim[e og]
20 GC:   [°mm°]
21 CM:   e blodfattig og har vældig lite jern i blodet sitt
         [og-]
22 GC:   [m]°m°
23 CM:   og e sånt noe at hun skal ta en sånn test?
24 GC:   ja [<(altså)>]
25 CM:   [(at hun må) sjek]k opp det <og e> i hele ta[tt?]
26 GC:   [°j]a° asså du kan si det som e (2)
         OGSÅ er en utfordring når det gjelder det med
         en sånn (1) <n> hvis man tenke en sånn familiær
         forekomst .hh det e jo det at .hh (1) DETTE TENKE
         man IKKE på HOS så UNGE [HVIS]
27 CM:   [°n.hhei°]
28 GC:   det ikke er spesiell grunn til det (3) men asså hu
         e født i
29 CM:   togoåtti
30 GC:   (.) toogåtti ja e det lenge sida hu har- hu har
         vært i kolonskopi?
31 CM:   jada og hu har fjerna <[e]>
32 GC:   [>ja<]
33 CM:   ja men e det e ska vi sjå kan det vær fire år sida
         (det no a)?
34 GC:   °mm. (1) okey°
35 CM:   (2) cirka
36 GC:    ja og no e ho blodfatt[ig og]
37 CM:   [.hh ho] e (xx) a har gått sykemeldt ho skjønner
         du (x) måna
38 GC:   (x[x)]
39 CM    [<og]> (uten at dem finn) (xxx)
```

Example 6: 'æ tenke om det kan hoppe over en generasjon'

```
01 GC:   Så det er ikke noen sterke holdepunkter at du må
         [gå hjem]
02 CM:   [<neida neida>]
03 GC:   å [si]
04 CM:   [men] æ tenke på om det kan hoppe over en
         generasjon og så te (.) liksom e:h viss- .hhja
         <skjønne du ka æ meine>
```

```
05 GC:   = ja .hh
06 CM:   .hh ja
07 GC:   [e:h]
08 CM:   [i forhold] te min datter
09 GC:   = ja men ikke ikke e:h um ikke så ung
10 CM:   nei
11 GC:   altså i og med at du har s- snart e femti år og
         ikke har funnet noe hos deg så så (.) så kan (.)
         så e æ veldig tvilsomt til at det skulle debutere
         sånn
12 CM:   mm
13 GC:   =ja
14 CM:   mm (1) men det treng jo ikke være noe til ho
         heller det e ikke det æ sei
15 GC:   [.hh nei nei]
16 CM:   for alt i verden håpe æ jo ikke det men æ like
         ikke[utviklinga]
17 GC:   [.hh nei] nei og så kan du si at det e nok en
         forskjell for dem har nok ikke sett noe hos
         henne for at (.) tykktarmen din (.) eller no har
         vel ikke du fått sett så godt etter for du har
         vel plagdes (0.5) .hh men tykktarmen den sånn
         plateepitel som vi har på
18 CM:   mm
19 GC:   alle overflata så ligger de her cellan som danne
         slimhinnan (0.5) og dem dannes nede i disse
```

Whose business is it anyway? Distributing responsibilities between family members and formal carers

Outi Jolanki

1 Introduction

This discursive study reports how Finnish working caregivers talk about care of older people, and what kind of responsibilities they attach to the positions of a family member and professional care workers. In Finland, municipalities have a legal duty to provide older people with care but Finland differs from other Nordic countries in greater reliance on family caregiving (Kröger et al. 2003). A recent study shows that among people aged 80 years old, 48 per cent receive help from children, 14 per cent receive help from a spouse and 18 per cent receive help from municipal home care even though many receive help from different sources (Vilkko et al. 2010). More recently some practical changes have taken place in distribution and provision of older people's care in Finland: those requiring extensive help and support receive more, whereas those with less 'needs' receive less formal services and care (Yeandle and Kröger 2013). In practice, they have to rely on self-help or family members or private providers for help. These changes have shifted the responsibility for older people's care from the government and local authorities more to older people themselves and family members (Jolanki et al. 2013).

In Finland, as in many other countries, integrating social and health care in home care has strengthened the medicalisation of care work and increased the need to draw boundaries between hierarchies and professions (Henriksson and Wrede 2008). Measuring outcomes of care work to improve productivity has increased attention to performing different tasks at the expense of a holistic approach to clients' situations as a whole (Mezey 2004; Phillips 2007; Tedre 2004; Wrede and Henriksson 2004). The medicalisation and 'task-oriented' care work culture has had the effect of reducing comprehensive responsibility for clients' situations and addressing instead the 'basic needs' i.e. personal medical care (Henriksson and Wrede 2008; see also Mezey 2004; Phillips 2007).

The study looks at caring relationship as a moral issue which concerns both family members and formal caregivers. The central question of the study is: how family caregivers view their responsibilities in relation to those of the professional care workers and authorities. The chapter outlines first the relations of the professional and informal caregivers and how moral arguments are used in professional decision making. Second, the chapter presents the results of the empirical analysis and discusses them in the light of previous studies and recent reorganisation of careworkers' tasks and responsibilities.

2 Professionals' and family caregivers' views of each other

The relationship between the client, family caregivers and professional care workers is essential to the wellbeing of the person cared for. The studies that have looked at the experiences from home care and institutional care show that distributing responsibilities between different actors is not an easy task. Family members and the person needing care encounter several professionals from health and social care sectors at a time when their own competence and wellbeing is jeopardised by ill health, worry and anxiety for the future.

In the case of home care, the client and family have to allow a stranger to come and take responsibility for tasks and roles that were previously the responsibility of the home owner and his/her family members (Kuronen 2007; Tedre 2004). The clients and their family members can be depicted as partners in care giving, but also as noncompliant problem-makers (Blustein 2004; Ronch 2004; Surpin and Hanley 2004; Zechner 2007). The professionals may see themselves as a 'solution team' and rely on mutual support from other professionals while, paradoxically, the client and his/ her family may represent a 'problem team' and an impediment to carrying out professional tasks effectively (Ronch 2004). The professionals can give the family members a role as helpers of the professional workers, or co-workers, or workers carrying out the tasks given by a professional care manager, or clients who need help from the professionals (Guberman and Maheu 2002; Guberman et al. 2006; Ward-Griffin and McKeever 2000). In the first option the professionals carry the responsibility for the care, while in the second option care tasks and responsibilities are shared. Alternatively, the family members can be treated as 'resources' (Guberman and Maheu 2002) whom professionals teach and train to manage personal hands-on care (Ward-Griffin and McKeever 2000), or even as 'patients' (Ward-Griffin and McKeever 2000) or 'joint-clients' (Guberman and Maheu 2002) who need professional support and help themselves. Professionals may even ally with family members to support and protect them against demands to assign more care responsibilities (Guberman et al. 2006; Mezey 2004) and be caught between organisational demands and professional ethic.

Studies on family carers show that family members categorise formal care workers in a similar fashion to how they are categorised by professionals. Care workers can be seen as partners and co-workers who share care responsibilities with family members (Sims-Gould and Martin-Matthews 2010; Soodeen et al. 2007). The clients and family members often expect care workers to do more than just provide 'instrumental care' and value the emotional support and personal relationship between the care worker and the client (Sims-Gould and Martin-Matthews 2010; Soodeen et al. 2007; Zechner 2007), while home care workers are limited in their time use and the tasks they are allowed to do (Kuronen 2007; Surpin and Hanley 2004; Tedre 2004). Care workers may become close with certain clients but it may pose problems for professionals' own strength and ability to perform their tasks (Blustein 2004). Family members may also adopt the role of 'care managers' who teach care workers what to do and how to operate in the household and with the client and contact authorities and coordinate services (Sims-Gould and Martin-Matthews 2010). Thus overall responsibility for care management and quality of the services rests with the family.

3 Morality as a topic of study in professional decision making

Modern institutions, professions, needs assessments and decisions to provide help and services for individual people require complex moral consideration of entitlements, normality, abnormality and accountability of clients (Bergmann 1998). However, modern institutional and professional discourses tend to disguise the moral aspects of decision making and professional actions and treat them as technical or practical issues (Linell and Rommetveit 1998). Guberman et al. (2006) argue that even though the values and beliefs of professional people have an important impact on how they conduct their work, they are seldom acknowledged or discussed.

Discursive studies have shown that care and family caregiving are issues that carry a heavy moral load and in which all parties involved face questions about their own and other people's rights and responsibilities

(Paoletti 2007). A study by Hellström Muhli (2010) which addressed welfare officials' assessment of client needs and rights to receive services showed that professional decision making involves deliberation of professional roles and responsibilities too. Home care can be seen as an intrusion into the daily routines of the family, but also as a right and a form of support in the everyday lives of the client and his/her family.

However, the participation of the client and their family members in decision-making processes is often minimal and the real decision-making power lies with the professionals (Olaison and Cedersund 2008). Caring professions may involve defining clients as 'failing' in their caring roles and professionals may thus transgress parental rights and responsibilities and implicitly put client competence in doubt (Roberts and Sarangi 1999). Constructing clients as failing also serves to show that professionals are required to get involved and take control (Roberts and Sarangi 1999). Hall et al. (1999) studied how professional and client roles and identities were defined and re-defined in the meetings of social workers and their clients. Here too the construct of 'failing parent' legitimated professional involvement and the 'professional knows best' logic, while clients oriented to being both cooperative 'good clients' who conceded their failure to fulfil their responsibilities (Hall et al. 1999).

The studies of language practices in social work have shown that moral categorisation and accountability are essential elements of social work through which professionals' and clients' rights, duties and authorities are defined (Hall et al. 2006; Juhila et al. 2010). In a similar fashion, Nikandar (2007) addressed decision making in older people's care in multi-professional groups of social workers, medical doctors and nurses and showed that these meetings involved defining professional and client identities. Practical decision making on home care allowances or nursing home placements involved complex ethical decisions and required professionals to define their and the family members' duties (Nikander 2007).

A theme that is rarely addressed is how family members who become caregivers of their older relatives view the distribution of responsibilities between themselves and professionals such as local officials, social and health care workers. This study focuses on mapping interviewees' experiences of negotiating responsibilities with professionals. The theme is addressed by examining episodes in which the interviewees tell about encounters with different professionals. The specific questions addressed are: How do the interviewees position themselves and professionals (care workers, authorities etc.) in their talk? How is responsibility distributed in these encounters? What meanings are given to responsibility in this context?

4 Methods and data

In this study I apply discursive psychology which was introduced in a seminal book by Potter and Wetherell (1987) and has been further developed by other researchers (e.g. Paoletti 2007; Wetherell and Edley 1999). The analysis presented here focuses on people's meaning-making activities and on how participants argue for and against different views; how they reason, explain and legitimate their own actions and decisions or those of others. The focus is thus on how language is used to make specific states of affairs look right or wrong, reprehensible or acceptable, and on arguments and positions invoked in and through talk (Wetherell 1998; Wetherell and Edley 1999).

Studies of responsibility imply an agentic view of people. In order to talk about true agency, individuals need to have the ability or opportunity to bring about change in their own conduct or in the social order (Barker and Galasiński 2001: 45). Seeing someone as responsible for their actions entails that they have had a chance to make a choice between different alternative ways to think and act. To study agency in talk, I use the concept of subject position as a methodological tool. The concept of subject position (Wetherell and Edley 1999) is a tool to analyse how the interviewees talk about themselves and other people as caregivers, family members, professionals and care workers, and what kind of actions, attributes, rights and responsibilities are attached to these positions. Therefore, positions taken in talk have normative and moral dimensions since they entail ideas about how one should behave (Wetherell and Edley 1999).

The data come from 76 semi-structured interviews, of which 70 (67 women, 3 men) were included in this study. Spousal caregivers were excluded from the analysis since their situation is different from that of parental caregivers. The data were collected as part of the project titled *Working Carers and Caring Workers – Making Paid Employment and Care Responsibilities Compatible* (WOCAWO). The interviewees were asked about the beginning of the care relationship, relationships to the person cared for and other family members and friends, service use and experiences, work, interests and hobbies and future plans. The interviews were narrative in the sense that they began with a narrative question about how the care situation began. The interviewees were then asked questions about each predefined topic, but not in a strict order. We aimed to adapt the questions to the narration of the interviewees and they were given the chance to raise and elaborate the topics they wanted to concentrate on.

The interviews were conducted in spring 2009. All of the interviewees were volunteers and informed consent of each of them was obtained prior to the interviews. It is particularly important to protect the anonymity of the participants when using small qualitative data. All personal details such as names or places were changed when the data was transcribed. The average length of the interviews was 1.5 hours. The interviews were recorded and transcribed after which the material was imported into Atlas. ti to organise and code the data. Coding was carried out on the basis of a predefined code list; relevant text fragments were indexed and marked to enable retrieval and categorisation for the analysis proper. This preliminary content analysis helped to reduce the vast dataset, in order to allow a more detailed study of talk.

For this study, I first collected the text segments that were related to questions about use of services and interviewees' experiences of social and health care services. These segments were coded with the labels 'formal services' and 'experiences of service use'. I then undertook a discourse analysis of the different positions taken and arguments used in talk. This part of the analysis focused on the positions assigned to social and health care workers and other actors representing the state or municipalities, and how the interviewees either explicitly talked about 'responsibility' or used evaluative and normative statements of what 'should' be done by social and health care workers. The detailed discourse analysis concerned those passages in which interviewees explicitly talk about social and health care services and meetings with professional people. As the interviews were carried out in Finnish, the relevant passages have been translated into English for the purposes of this study. Pseudonyms are used throughout when referring to informants.

5 Analysis

In these data, professionals are positioned as authorities, experts, co-workers, 'pieceworkers' and adversaries. These positions were partly over-lapping. The different types of relations will be examined in more detail to show how the interviewees constructed these positions, what kind of conduct was linked to different positions, what meanings were given to responsibility and how responsibilities were distributed within and between different positions.

5.1 Professionals as authorities who ally with family members

Professional social and health care workers were at times positioned as authorities who ally with family members to support them against the demands of the care. By virtue of a professional position as a doctor, nurse or the like, an actor is given an authority position. In the first extract the interviewee is Heli, a 54-year-old woman, who provides care to her mother. She is a social worker herself but works with young people. The following extract describes Heli's discussion with an occupational nurse:

Extract 1.

Heli: I feel I'm still capable of coping with my job and I've told my boss whether I think I will manage next autumn, too, and I'm also going to tell our occupational health physician about my visits here ['here' refers to sheltered housing where her mother lives]. Because my occupational health nurse told me to cut down; you should stop taking so much responsibility for your mother's care. Don't visit her in the hospital as often as you do and so on. I said well I don't know, although it is a burden and causes anxiety, I cannot give it up just like that. But I just want to pour out my fatigue and anguish to them. It's my way of trying to stay on top of it. I think it's good of them to say these things, it makes me think about it, about my personal limits, to what lengths I am willing to go. I mean now when I go I can stay just for a while instead of staying for a long time.

Here Heli positions the occupational nurse as someone who sees her as taking too much responsibility; the nurse has in fact ordered her to visit her mother less frequently and to take less responsibility for her care ('cut down', 'stop taking so much responsibility', 'Don't visit her … as often'). The occupational nurse and occupational doctor serve as recipients of her feelings of tiredness and anxiety. In this way she is positioned as an agent who uses other professionals to unload her sentiments. Yet, health care workers are also positioned as agents, who set limits and legitimate the cutting down of her caring responsibilities ('they say'), while she herself does not know her limits ('it makes me think about it, about my personal limits'). Heli constructs herself as someone who has taken her care responsibilities to the extreme, while other professionals help her to cut them down for the sake of her own wellbeing (cf. Guberman et al. 2006). To put it differently, this kind of talk suggests that the interviewee is 'caring, but is not coping' (Hall et al. 2006: 114) and therefore a call for external help is legitimate. The views of a professional authority figure are used to legitimate reducing commitment to care responsibilities or withdrawal from care giving.

Professionals were occasionally positioned as authorities who ally with family members against the 'system' (society and local authorities) and its representatives such as officials and political decision-makers. Social and health care workers were in these cases positioned as separate from the government and local authorities who were constructed as adversaries. In the following the interviewee is Raili, a woman aged 66. She helps her mother who has Alzheimer's disease. Here is her response to the question about willingness to give up caregiving:

Extract 2.

OJ: Right, well, have you ever considered stopping, not helping anymore, have you thought about that?

Raili: Well (hmmm), I mean, no, how could you, you couldn't. You just can't, and, incidentally, the doctor, Jaana Vaara, told me when I asked for advice on how I could get my mother admitted to a care home, she told me point-blank, you should tell the attending physicians that you won't go to her home anymore and won't care for her. And that's what I did and it helped a bit. And of course I've got these internal networks because of my job, perhaps that helped too, I don't know.

The question of willingness to stop giving care to a family member is potentially very sensitive. Interestingly, though, this question seemed to give the interviewees the permission to talk about their tiredness and ambiguous feelings about caregiving. Here Raili first postpones her reply ('no'), but immediately after this denies twice the idea of ever wanting to quit helping her mother. She constructs it as a matter that is totally impossible ('no, how could you', 'you couldn't'). After this opening she resumes the topic of quitting caregiving, but in a different context. She positions the doctor as someone she can ask for advice and who urged her to use the threat of quitting caregiving as a means of getting her mother admitted to institutional care. Here, as in the previous extract, 'active voicing' is used to bring credence to own talk (Potter 1996). Professionals' views are represented through quoted talk in which the speaker is ordered to act in a certain way.

Another rhetorical tool is to construct the contrast (Potter 1996) between personalised doctor who helps the family member and adversaries, i.e. anonymous doctors who are responsible for the treatment. Implicitly, this piece of talk goes to say that these anonymous professionals expect family members to take responsibility for care, and only if they refuse this position, institutional care is offered. Raili also refers to her 'networks' at the workplace (she is a city employee), which positions her as not just any family caregiver but a member of 'internal' networks. Having professional networks has been found to help managing care responsibilities because having a more equal position with social and health care professionals enables asking for extra help or being able to challenge their decisions (Bernard and Phillips 2007). In Raili's talk the known and named doctor is positioned as an authority figure, and with the help of this doctor's advice and her own professional position Raili is able to handle the anonymous care workers and the system and shift some of the responsibility for her mother's care to formal care workers.

5.2 Professionals as experts and as co-workers

Formal care workers were also positioned as experts who should take responsibility if the person cared for became so ill that he or she required extensive or medical care. The person cared for was often positioned not only as a mother/father but also as a 'person with dementia', 'patient' or 'person with Alzheimers', which goes to say that caring for them requires medical expertise and skills. The following extract comes from an interview with Noora, a woman aged 60. Noora helps her mother, who has Alzheimers' disease and lives alone. Noora lives elsewhere but during the week she works in the city where her mother lives. The extract begins from the point where Noora has described her mother's falling accident and how she had reluctantly administered her mother's medications:

Extract 3.

Noora: I took care of that but now it's been passed on, and the council home care services take care of it.

OJ: Right, home care staff visit her, then?

Noora: Yes, well it's the community care services now, the system changed in January. She fell and was taken to (hospital) to have her head stitched. Well I said that was the culminating point for me, I started to think I cannot take responsibility for her medication and her meals. This that and everything else. I felt we need help, and my mother was really ill at the time. She had a urinary tract infection, she was really ill. It was probably good that someone visited her and looked after her also during the daytime. I visited her every night during the time.

In Noora's talk her mother's falling accident marks the point when she can no longer carry the responsibility for her mother's care on her own. In many of the interviews, the onset of a serious illness or an accident was given as a signal that professional help was needed, as is the case here. Noora positions herself as having had full responsibility for everything ('medication and her meals … and everything else'), but as no longer being able to carry the responsibility alone. With her mother being 'really ill' (repeated twice) and with her being with the mother every night served to shift her mother to the realm of professional expertise and to make Noora's request for help legitimate. However, Noora does not refer to professionals' actions as only itemised medical operations, but refers to help from home care services as 'looking after' her mother, which was a commonly used expression in these data. The interviewees in this study made a clear distinction between formal care workers, who only carry out certain tasks, and those who 'take care of' and 'care about' older people (cf. Mezey 2004; Soodeen et al. 2007). In the former sense responsibility becomes partial and linked to certain tasks. In the latter sense responsibility is more exhaustive.

Noora goes on to talk about her exhaustion and her seeing an occupational psychologist to discuss her situation:

Extract 4.

OJ: Did you make the appointment yourself?

Noora: Yes, I did.

OJ: So helping her has been a bit of an ordeal for you, then?

Noora: Yes. And when my sister went (abroad), and the other one cannot be reached and she doesn't care, I felt like, is it really true that there is no one to take the garbage out, am I to be the dustman for the rest of my life? Stuff like that, you are kind of acting out, how difficult can it be to take the garbage out? But when you feel that you have to do everything alone, that was the difficulty. But now that I feel that there are many of us doing it, it's easier. Nothing has changed in the sense that I still take the garbage out every Tuesday morning and every Friday morning, exactly as I did before. But it's sort of nicer to feel that we are doing it together. Even though you don't see them, I mean the people who are working with you. There is this one person who calls me. She's the one who is responsible for running the group, a home nurse. She frequently gives me a ring.

OJ: Really, she calls you?

Noora: Yes, like, we are running out of this and that and we should buy this and that. And that we haven't yet been able to arrange weekend care, things like that.

Noora positions herself as being left alone to do everything for her mother because her sister moved abroad and the other sister is not available and 'doesn't care' for the mother's situation. Having home care services for her mother means that she is no longer alone but shares caregiving with other people ('we are doing it together'). What is noteworthy is that Noora positions home care workers as people with whom she works and does things together even though she does not see them herself. Also, she positions the nurse who is responsible for organising care as someone with whom she has frequent contact, i.e. she becomes familiar to her. She constructs their relationship as equal as her expression 'who calls me' indicates, and this named nurse as someone with whom she shares information. Listing all the things they discuss serves to show that they address Noora's mother's life situation together and do not just sort out some specific tasks.

5.3 Professionals as failing experts and technical 'pieceworkers'

The concept of 'professional people' was often mentioned in these interviews. The people depicted as professionals were constructed as experts with special skills and knowledge. By virtue of this position they were expected to conduct themselves as professionals, which means in this context to know their profession and to carry greater responsibility for older people's care than ordinary lay people. In the following extract the interviewee is Terttu, a woman aged 57, who looks after her mother. The mother lives in her own home and receives home care services. Terttu herself is a care worker but works with younger people. In the following extract she gives a long account of her experiences with home care workers:

Extract 5.

OJ: What is your experience of home care services? How is that working out? How do you get information and is the help sufficient?

Terttu: Well, there have been ups and downs. Apparently they are short-staffed, that I can understand, there are many foreign workers, workers of a foreign background, and probably some language problems too, you know, Mom told me that sometimes men with dark skin would visit her. I was surprised that Mom has readily accepted them, so that's not a problem. I'm sure all the nurses are nice but somehow I feel that they don't see the overall situation, they just drop by to give the medication. And with Mom being hard of hearing, she has some hearing left in the right ear but she doesn't know how to use a hearing aid anymore, so the situation is what it is. The nurses can have twenty minutes to spare on Mom's care in the morning, they don't see the real situation. They've got this file where they record the visits and it always says there that everything is fine and the resident or client is contented, but it looks like a mess through the eyes of next of kin. Especially when you know that Mom has always been terribly tidy and strict, the situation now, I mean now her personal hygiene is completely neglected. It feels like you always have to make a special request to get things done, even though all of them in the home care services are professional people, but still you always need to remind them. In fact I've been calling them quite often and I'm sure they sometimes think oh no, it's that Koivisto (the interviewee's last name) calling again [laughs]. I kind of expected them to have better insight into the overall situation, into what type of help Mom needs. I've had to call them constantly, asking them, could you please do this or that, we've left notes for them in the file asking could you please make sure that Mom gets her porridge in the morning, as she no longer knows how to do that either. I must say I'm a bit disappointed but I do understand that they've got loads of places to visit and a limited amount of time. But then again if you think about a situation like giving the sleeping pill, we had agreed that they would come in the evening and give it to her. We started to wonder when we phoned her at five in the afternoon and she was in a daze at that point, I thought she must have received the pill already then. I called them and learned that they had given the sleeping pill during their first evening round, or left it on the table, and of course she had gulped it down immediately, she doesn't know the difference between day and night, and it's always dark during the winter anyway. Then she'd be wide awake at two or three a.m. and would call me non-stop. A thing like that and we had to arrange it separately, like, would it be completely impossible for you to go and give the sleeping pill during the last round? Now it's working fine. But you'd imagine that trained adult people would understand what to do when the person in question has memory problems. A healthy person knows when to take the sleeping pill even if you left the bottle there. Things like that have surprised me a bit. But Mom has been really satisfied, everyone is really nice to her, there's no problem in that sense.

The central feature of this extract is that Terttu positions home care workers as 'all professional people' and 'trained adult people' whom one would 'imagine' to know how to deal with a person with dementia. In other words, since they are professionals more could be expected of them than what they accomplish. However, the reality which Terttu constructs in her depiction of her mother's everyday life is that care workers carry out specific tasks and leave some work undone unless reminded, with none of them having an 'overall view' of the situation and what kind of help her mother needs. In Terttu's narration she has become a 'care manager' who supervises and controls the work done by the professionals (cf. Sims-Gould and Martin-Matthews 2010). Detailed description and listing different problems serve as rhetorical tools that construct Terttu as a reporter of factual events and thus give credence to her arguments of negligence (Potter 1996). Also, by pointing out the frequent nature of the negligence she constructs negligence as a continuing problem and not an isolated incidence (Potter 1996). These rhetorical tools serve to further strengthen her claims regarding the severity of the problems. The family members are positioned as those who need to keep an eye on the situation to make sure that care workers do what needs to be done.

In Terttu's talk, the care workers' responsibility or, better yet, responsibilities, are reduced to carrying out specific tasks. Thus the care workers are represented to act as 'pieceworkers' (Mezey 2004: 75) and are reproached for a 'task-oriented' approach (Henriksson and Wrede 2008). In contrast, in Terttu's talk responsibility receives a broader meaning: it means looking after a person and not just carrying out specific tasks. A recurrent phenomenon in these interviews is that the interviewees bring up both the wrong attitude and lack of resources and staff as reasons for problems and negligence in older people's care. Here, Terttu softens her blame of care workers by mentioning staff shortage, language problems with non-Finnish care workers and busy schedules. These arguments serve to show that she is not being unreasonable (Potter 1996) and takes into account different perspectives to alleviate care workers' blameworthiness for the situation. Yet, at the end of the extract she returns to the subject of professionalism ('trained adult people') and renews her argument that more could be expected of them. Thus professional care workers are depicted as uncaring professionals (cf. Juhila et al. 2010) and failing experts (cf. Roberts and Sarangi 1999) who lack competence, which calls for family members' involvement. These interviews show that clients and service users can thus engage in categorising in the same way as professional people do in relation to their clients (Hall et al. 1999). Following this logic, the family members are positioned as a party that needs to monitor, control and make sure that everything is done and that care workers do their duties.

5.4 Professionals fighting over professional boundaries

One recurrent theme in the interviews is that different groups of professionals are depicted as agents who define their professional boundaries in relation to other care work professionals and seek to focus on their 'own responsibilities' according to what tasks are officially their territory. In the following extract the interviewee, Kristiina, is a woman in her forties who looks after her grandmother. The grandmother lives in service housing and has had various health problems. In the following extract, I ask Kristiina about her experiences of health care services as she has previously mentioned her grandmother's several visits to the health care centre and hospital:

Extract 6.

Kristiina: Well yes, I am familiar with it, but not with much else, and of course with sheltered housing and their services, their care services and food and so on.

OJ: Well, how do they operate, then?

Kristiina: Well, as I said, there was this one time when we were kicked out of the health centre ward, and I was taking grandma back to the sheltered housing block. I was terribly disappointed that they would keep her in the health centre ward only for twenty four hours, so I took her back to the sheltered housing block, and they said, why did you come back, she cannot cope here. I broke down in tears because they wouldn't let us stay there. So we were in a situation where the health centre did not want her and sheltered housing did not want her, so where shall I take her? I mean I don't have any options left, where can I take her? Do I really have to fight between them to figure out where granny belongs and where she can cope and where I could take her. The situation was unbelievable. I was running around in the health centre and in the sheltered housing block wearing my (work) jacket, I bet none of them will ever buy a home from us (laughter), it was just insane. Grandma was sitting in the car, and I was, like, where shall I take her. It's impossible for me to take her to my house; she cannot cope there because I'm working. The situation was totally unbelievable.

In the interviews, the family carers would occasionally position themselves as agents who need to fight with the authorities and formal care workers to receive social or health care services, benefits or other entitlements. Here Kristiina positions herself as caught between two groups of care workers who try to shift the responsibility for her grandmother's care to another party and away from themselves. She positions herself as being forced to fight to get care and find a place where the grandmother belongs. Detailed description again serves to give credence to her arguments and to emphasise the outrageous conduct of the professionals. Also, several and repeated extreme case formulations (Pomerantz 1986) ('we were kicked out', 'It was just insane', 'The situation was totally unbelievable') serve to construct the situation as incomprehensible for any 'sane' person. The severity of the professionals' unprofessional behaviour is stressed by the emotional reaction ('I was in tears'). Kristiina's reference to having to use work time to fight with professional care workers gives further evidence of the professional people's reproachable behaviour. She is positioning herself as a working person who has to jeopardise her profession ('none of them will ever buy a home from us') due to the (in)actions of other professionals.

The relation between family members and the 'system' is sometimes depicted as an ongoing 'battle', to use the expression of one of the interviewees. In this kind of talk the formal care workers and authorities are positioned as a party that acts and fulfils their duties only if pressured or not even then. When Kristiina says that the professionals do not want her grandmother ('health centre did not want her … sheltered housing did not want her') and she has to fight to find out where the grandmother belongs, she is positioning care workers as ones who have a choice, as agents. To talk about 'wanting' positions the professionals as people who can make a choice, instead of just being dictated by professional rules.

The following extract continued right after the previous extract. As the interviewer, I assumed that the grandmother lived in ordinary service housing, which may have very few services available. I asked a clarifying question about the service housing and intensive care services available:

Extract 7.

OJ: Yes, in other words sheltered housing is not what you'd call intensified service accommodation, it's just...

Kristiina: They should of course help, too, but they usually tend to plead understaffing and have no time to visit each person as often as the person would need. So I told them the next time this granny needs an ambulance, I will not call it, I want you to call it. I need something tangible in that situation to be able to say that the nurses in sheltered housing think that she can't cope at home. Then they'll have to keep here there. And the next time it happened I said I will come and accompany her to the hospital, I mean the health centre, but I will not call an ambulance. (OJ: Right.) So I waited, it was a Friday night, until the nurses called the ambulance. I mean it's not just me, they are saying it too, this is not going to work out. Only then did they agree to admit her to the health centre, it was about a week after they kicked us out.

OJ: Maybe it looks better if the call comes from a sheltered housing nurse, maybe it's the fact that you as next of kin are there that makes them somehow...

Kristiina: Well yeah, as next of kin I would sometimes try to put pressure on the service housing personnel to...

OJ: Well, what about, what is your experience, that if you go to the hospital as next of kin, or seek out care from a health care facility, that they kind of assume that you are the one who takes care of her?

Kristiina: Yes, exactly, they assume that I'm the one who takes care of her and looks after her. It's obvious. So it's a lot more effective when the nursing staff of one facility discuss with that of another facility. It's more effective somehow. I guess they think that for next of kin a loved one is naturally more important than anyone else, although it's not true. Even if you try to explain that we will not come here without a really good reason, just take a look at the person's history, there have been several operations and she takes very few medications and rarely needs to see a doctor; we will not come just for the fun of it. They don't seem to get it, and it's easier for me to plead that they [other professionals] think so too: she cannot go to her home because she cannot cope there, they cannot help her. So in a way they have given the matter a push.

Kristiina says that her only solution to make the health centre admit her grandmother was to force the service housing staff to act by refusing to cooperate and sometimes by 'putting pressure on' them. In this way, she shows again that 'extreme' actions were required. A family member is positioned as someone caught between professional care workers and their dispute over professional boundaries. Kristiina positions herself as an agent who refuses to take this position and manages to make the service housing staff cooperate with her. One of the recurrent elements in these interviews was that having an official status as a professional care worker or the like means being in a better position to apply for and negotiate services. Here, too, Kristiina positions herself, as next of kin, as a less credible agent to the health centre than service housing staff. She also suggests that professional care workers believe that family members are biased and apply for health services needlessly. According to Kristiina, her attempt to argue that her grandmother is seriously ill and help is not sought needlessly ('we will not come here without a really good reason') goes unnoticed. This piece of talk can be interpreted as telling about professional ideology; that professionals 'know best' and family members' assessments of the need for medical help are likely to be biased and subjective (cf. Hall et al. 1999; Nikander 2007). So, in her narration Kristiina is positioned as being forced to take all the responsibility and all the blame while other agents shun their responsibilities.

6 Discussion

To briefly outline the different meanings given to responsibility in this context, responsibility firstly received the meaning of legal responsibility. The interviewees brought forward that in Finland the municipalities, not the family, have legal responsibility for the care of older people. They thereby positioned themselves as not legally responsible for the care of their older relatives. Secondly, responsibility received the meaning of a practical and 'technical' matter associated with different professions. As I see it, in this kind of talk 'responsibilities' translates to carrying out itemised tasks and being accountable for nothing else but them. Thirdly, responsibility meant looking after, taking care of or caring for and about someone, which translates into the moral responsibility of fellow humans to look after one another. This meaning of responsibility was linked to both professional and kinship positions.

In the following I will summarise the different professional and family member positions and how they were linked to different understandings of morality. The professionals were positioned as authority figures who, on the basis of their professional status, made it legitimate for family members to think about their own wellbeing and reduce the hours spent on caring or give up caring. This finding is in line with previous studies on how professionals can view family members as clients who need their help (Guberman and Maheu 2002; Mezey 2004). The health of the person being cared for and professional expertise were used to demonstrate family caregivers' exhaustion, which legitimated the request for external help and use of formal care services (Hall et al. 2006). To put it differently, the interviewees positioned themselves as having and taking moral responsibility for their family members. But the professional expertise of doctors and other care workers legitimated reducing commitment to care if it threatened the caregiver's personal wellbeing and health. Hence sharing the responsibility with formal caregivers was constructed as a necessity. Professionals were also positioned as experts who could be expected to take responsibility for the care by virtue of their training and special skills (cf. Simson-Gould and Martin-Matthews 2010; Soodeen et al. 2007). By constructing the cared for as a 'patient', 'person with dementia' or the like, he/she was positioned in the realm of medical expertise which family members could not have. Again, the shift of responsibility was constructed as a necessity.

Professionals were positioned also as co-workers and people with whom a family caregiver can share caregiving tasks and who provide information and organise services (cf. Guberman and Maheu 2002; Olaison and Cedersund 2008; Sims-Gould and Martin-Matthews 2010; Ward-Griffin and McKeever 2000). Good professionals keep in touch, inform caregivers of different options available, and look after the carer and the person cared for alike. As I see it, this kind of talk is about moral responsibility, which is exhaustive and concerns conduct in general and not just in caregiving situations. In such talk, the family caregiver is positioned as an equal agent in relation to the professional and can trust that the person cared for will be looked after even if she or he is not present. Being a trustworthy professional requires not only having expert knowledge and technical skills but taking overall responsibility for the wellbeing of the client and committing emotionally to the clients' situation (Soodeen et al. 2007; Zechner 2007).

Professionals were also positioned as adversaries who sought to thwart older people from being admitted to institutional care. At times care workers were positioned as authorities who ally with family members to help them to resist these attempts. The former professionals were mostly positioned as anonymous decision-makers and the latter ones as known and trusted persons. Previous studies have suggested that for some professionals family caregivers represent a 'resource' that can be mobilised to adopt care responsibilities but for some others they represent clients whom professionals try to protect against overly burdening care responsibilities (Guberman et al. 2006; Ward-Griffin and McKeever 2000). Recent changes in the provision and targeting of public care services give reason to argue that family caregivers are seen in this way in care policy (Yeandle et al. 2012). The turn into a 'familist' direction can be seen, on the one hand, as an attempt to empower ordinary citizens and strengthen family ties, but on the other hand as an ideological choice to shift more responsibility to individual people and family (Jolanki et al. 2013; Yeandle and Kröger 2013). This discussion is beyond the scope of this study, but it can be said that in this data some of the interviewees depict their position in terms of 'shifting responsibilities' and public actors (state and municipalities as entities and municipal authorities) as seeking to evade their legal responsibilities.

Professionals were also positioned as 'failing' experts (Roberts and Sarangi 1999) and 'pieceworkers' (Mezey 2004) who carried out only specific tasks (cf. Henriksson and Wrede 2008). The recurrent expression used to describe professionals' actions in this kind of talk was 'it is not my duty'. So, responsibility becomes 'responsibilities' and is divided into the performance of some itemised and specified tasks linked to certain professions. Recent changes in the training and duties of home care workers have meant that workers need to focus on itemised tasks and efficient time use (Henriksson and Wrede 2008; Phillips 2007). Consequently, responsibility becomes a technical and itemised matter (cf. Bergmann 1998; Linell and Rommetveit 1998) as opposed to looking after people exhaustively. The findings suggest that conflicts can arise over the responsibilities of different professional groups and if these are unclear, the older care recipient and family member can be caught between different professional groups who try to decide whose duty the person and the task is. In the interviewees' talk, defining responsibility in this way means not taking responsibility.

These findings show that the professional position and being 'a professional person' is loaded with moral expectations. The findings also show that while professionals categorise clients according to their success or failure to act as competent and capable actors who fulfil their responsibilities (Hall et al. 1999; Juhila et al. 2010), non-professional people also categorise professionals as 'failing' or competent (cf. Roberts and Sarangi 1999). However, the interviewees justified the negligence of care workers by referring to lacking resources, such as understaffing and work overload, which are not in their power to control. If one does not have a choice, one cannot be seen as responsible for one's actions. The care workers were excused since their negligence was unintentional (cf. Juhila et al. 2010). The real blame and responsibility was placed on the shoulders of decision-makers and authorities, who have the power to allocate sufficient resources.

The findings indicate that expectations of service users and individual people may go against the criteria of professionalism adopted by professionals themselves (Hellström Muhli 2010) or formally defined tasks and rights (Kuronen 2007; Surpin and Hanley 2004; Tedre 2004). Ordinary people may expect professionals both to perform their tasks and to have a broader responsibility for the situation of the care recipient and even the situation of the family members (cf. Soodeen et al. 2007). Professionals were clearly also expected to take personal responsibility. Yet, according to Hellström Muhli (2010), for professionals 'to remain professional' equals not being personally involved or being too close to clients. Professionals need to balance between keeping a professional distance and becoming personally involved with clients (Blustein 2004).

7 Implications of the study

The findings indicate that the relationships between professionals and family caregivers can go either way – from allies to adversaries. As for the above discussion about dialogue and communication inherent in social life, these findings provoke a question: How do professionals view 'active' family members who make it their duty to monitor the quality of care given? One could argue that when family members see that their criteria for good quality services and care have not been met, they see it as their responsibility to monitor and control the situation. Hall et al. (2006) raise the question of client participation and power relations between clients and professionals. The analysis presented here shows that family members represented their definitions of responsibility to be at times in conflict with how professionals defined the situation. The central issue is if family caregivers are given authority and rights to participate in discussions with professionals about the quality and development of older people's care.

The findings from this data and previous studies suggest that this is not necessarily how professionals or caregivers represent the situation.

Also, the findings suggest that the recent development towards strict boundaries between professions and their responsibilities (Henriksson and Wrede 2008) may put clients and their family members in an insupportable position, if and when they are caught in between this 'territorial warfare'. These situations also go against the traditional work ethic of many care workers. Changes in professional training have brought about an emphasis on technical skills, medical expertise and measurable outcomes while care workers may be inclined to see their role more as helpers of the whole family. These trends can be assumed to erode work motivation and the image of care work. Since having enough workforce in caring professions is a major future concern, the problems of understaffing and disputes between professions in daily encounters should be addressed at a higher level of decision making. The family members' importance as caregivers of older people is likely to increase and therefore they too should be accepted as equal participants in discussions with professionals about the tasks and responsibilities of older people's care.

References

Barker, C. and Galasiński, D. (2001) *Cultural Studies and Discourse Analysis. A Dialogue on Language and Identity*. London: Sage.

Bergmann, J. R. (1998) Introduction: morality in discourse. *Research on Language and Social Interaction* 31(3–4): 279–294.

Bernard, M. and Phillips, J. (2007) Working carers of older adults: what helps and what hinders in juggling work and care? *Community, Work and Family* 10(2): 139–160.

Blustein, J. (2004) Integrating medicine and the family: toward a coherent ethic of care. In C. Levine and T. H. Murray (eds) *The Cultures of Caregiving* 127–146. Baltimore, MD: Johns Hopkins University Press.

Guberman, N. and Maheu, P. (2002) Conceptions of family caregiving: implications for professional practice. *Canadian Journal on Aging* 21(1): 25–35.

Guberman, N., Lavoie, J.-P., Pepin, J., Lauzon, S. and Montejo, M.-E. (2006) Formal service practitioners' views of family caregivers' responsibilities and difficulties. *Canadian Journal on Aging* 25(1): 43–53.

Hall, C., Sarangi, S. and Slembrouck, S. (1999) The legitimation of the client and the profession: identities and roles in social work discourse. In C. Roberts and S. Sarangi (eds) *Talk, Work and Institutional Order. Discourse in Medical, Mediation and Management Settings* 293–322. Berlin: Walter de Gruyter.

Hall, C., Slembrouck, S. and Sarangi, S. (2006) *Language Practices in Social Work. Categorization and Accountability in Child Welfare*. London & New York: Routledge.

Hellström Muhli, U. (2010) Accounts of professional and institutional tension in the context of Swedish elderly care. *Journal of Ageing Studies* 24: 47–56.

Henriksson, L. and Wrede, S. (2008) The making of medico-managerial care work culture in public home care for the elderly. In S. Wrede, L. Henriksson, H. Höst, S. Johansson and B. Dybroe (eds) *Care Work in Crisis. Reclaiming the Nordic Ethos of Care* 131–152. Malmö: Studentlitteratur.

Jolanki, O., Szebehely, M. and Kauppinen. K. (2013) Family rediscovered? Working carers of older people in Finland and Sweden. In T. Kröger and S. Yeandle (eds) *Combining Paid Work and Family Care. Policies and experiences in international perspectives* 71–87. Bristol: Policy Press.

Juhila, K., Hall, C. and Raitakari, S. (2010) Accounting for the clients' troublesome behaviour in a supported housing unit. *Journal of Social Work* 10(1): 59–79.

Kröger, T., Anttonen, A. and Sipilä, J. (2003) Social care in Finland: stronger and weaker forms of universalism. In A. Anttonen, J. Baldock and J. Sipilä (eds) *The Young, The Old and the State: Social Care Systems in Five Industrial Nations* 25–54. Cheltenham: Edward Elgar.

Kuronen, T. (2007) Vanhusten kotisiivous – hoivaa vai palvelua? [Cleaning the homes of older people – care or service?]. In M. Seppänen, A. Karisto and T. Kröger (eds) *Vanhuus ja sosiaalityö* [*Old Age and Social Work*] 139–166. Jyväskylä: PS-kustannus.

Linell, P. and Rommetveit, R. (1998) The many forms and facets of morality in dialogue: epilogue for the special issue. *Research on Language and Social Interaction* 31(3–4): 465–473.

Mezey, M. (2004) Nurses and their changing relationship to family caregivers. In C. Levine and T. H. Murray (eds) *The Cultures of Caregiving* 70–86. Baltimore, MD: Johns Hopkins University Press.

Nikander, P. (2007) Interprofessional decision making in elderly care: morality, criteria and help allocation. In I. Paoletti (ed.) *Family Caregiving for Older Disabled People. Relational and Institutional Issues* 319–332. New York: Nova Science Publishers.

Nikander, P. (2008) Constructionism and discourse analysis. In J. A. Holstein and J. F. Gubrium (eds) *Handbook of Constructionist Research* 413–428. New York and London: Guildford Press.

Olaison, A. and Cedersund, E. (2008) Home care as a family matter? Discursive positioning, storylines and decision-making in assessment talk. *Communication & Medicine* 5(2): 55–68.

Paoletti, I. (2007) The intricacy of gender, moral, relational, financial and housing issues. In I. Paoletti (ed.) *Family Caregiving for Older Disabled People. Relational and Institutional Issues* 333–357. New York: Nova Science Publishers.

Phillips, J. (2007) *Care*. Cambridge: Polity Press.

Pomerantz, A. (1986) Extreme case formulation: a way of legitimating claims. *Human Studies* 9: 219–229.

Potter, J. (1996) *Representing Reality. Discourse, Rhetoric and Social Construction*. London: Sage.

Potter, J. and Wetherell, M. (1987) *Discourse and Social Psychology: Beyond Attitudes and Behaviour*. London: Sage.

Roberts, C. and Sarangi, S. (1999) Negotiating and legitimating roles and identities. In S. Sarangi and C. Roberts (eds) *Talk, Work and Institutional Order. Discourse in Medical, Mediation and Management Settings* 227–229. Berlin: Walter de Gruyter.

Ronch J. L. (2004) Changing institutional culture: turning adversaries into partners. In C. Levine and T. H. Murray (eds) *The Cultures of Caregiving* 155–170. Baltimore, MD: Johns Hopkins University Press.

Sims-Gould, J. and Martin-Matthews, A. (2010) We share the care: family caregivers' experiences of their older relatives receiving home support services. *Health and Social Care in the Community* 18(4): 415–423.

Soodeen, R.-A., Gregory, D. and Bond Jr, J. B. (2007) Home care for older couples: 'it feels like a security blanket'. *Qualitative Health Research* 17(9): 1245–1255.

Surpin, R. and Hanley, E. (2004) The culture of home care: whose values prevail? In C. Levine and T. H. Murray (eds) *The Cultures of Caregiving* 87–99. Baltimore, MD: Johns Hopkins University Press.

Tedre, S. (2004) Likainen työ ja virallinen hoiva [Dirty work and formal caregiving]. In L. Henriksson and S. Wrede (eds) *Hyvinvointityön ammatit* [*Carework Professions*] 63–83. Helsinki: Gaudeamus.

Vilkko, A., Muuri, A. and Finne-Soveri, H. (2010) Läheisapu iäkkään ihmisen arjessa [Older people and care received from the family and the relatives]. In M. Vaarama, P. Moisio and S. Karvonen (eds) *Suomalaisten hyvinvointi 2010* [*Wellbeing of the Finns 2010*] 60–77. Helsinki: National Institute for Health and Welfare.

Ward-Griffin, C. and McKeever, P. (2000) Relationship between nurses and family caregivers: partners in care? *Advances in Nursing Science* 22: 89–103.

Wetherell, M. (1998) Positioning and interpretative repertoires: conversation analysis and post-structuralism in dialogue. *Discourse & Society* 9(3): 387–412.

Wetherell, M. and Edley, N. (1999) Negotiating hegemonic masculinity: imaginary positions and psycho-discursive practices. *Feminism and Psychology* 9(3): 335–356.

Wrede, S. and Henriksson, L. (2004) Kahden kerroksen väkeä: kotihoidon ammatillinen uusjako [Upstairs, downstairs: professional re-division of home care work]. In L. Henriksson and S. Wrede (eds) *Hyvinvointityön ammatit* [*Carework Professions*] 210–234. Helsinki: Gaudeamus.

Yeandle, S. and Kröger, T. (2013) Reconciling work and care for older parents, disabled children and partners: convergent or separate paths in three welfare systems? In T. Kröger and S. Yeandle (eds) *Combining Paid Work and Family Care. Policies and Experiences in International Perspectives* 219–239. Bristol: Policy Press.

Yeandle, S., Kröger, T. and Cass, B. (2012) Voice and choice for users and carers? Developments in patterns of care for older people in Australia, England and Finland. *Journal of European Social Policy* 22(4): 432–445.

Zechner, M. (2007) Puolisoitaan hoivaavien luottamus vanhuspalveluihin [Trust for old people's care services among spousal care givers]. In M. Seppänen, A. Karisto and T. Kröger (eds) *Vanhuus ja sosiaalityö* [*Old Age and Social Work*] 139–166. Jyväskylä: PS-kustannus.

A version of this chapter appeared in *Journal of Applied Linguistics and Professional Practice* 9:3.

Outi Jolanki received her PhD in health sciences from the University of Tampere, Finland. Currently she works as post-doctoral researcher at the School of Health Sciences, University of Tampere. Her research interests include family care, combining work and eldercare, the cultural meanings of old age and ageing, older people's housing and moving decisions and qualitative methods.

'Getting placed' in time: Responsibility talk in caseworker-client interaction

Maureen T. Matarese

1 Introduction[1]

Social work is a field with many potentially uncomfortable challenges that must be handled through face-to-face social interaction, one of which may be conveying that service is predicated upon satisfying responsibilities required by the institution. Particularly when a client is an adult, establishing requirements for how one should live his/her life may be face threatening. Responsibility talk in practitioner-client institutional interactions is often described in relation to accounting (Buttny 1993; Goffman 1971) or as constructions of client (im)morality (Hall et al. 2006; Juhila 2003; Nikander 2003; Olesen 2003). This study shows that responsibility talk extends beyond the dichotomies 'responsible/irresponsible' and 'moral/immoral'. It contributes to the literature by describing one caseworker's construction of responsibility through her interactions with three homeless clients in a New York City shelter, revealing the significant impact of the shelter, shelter policy, and personal contexts on the construction of responsibility in talk. In so doing, it extends research on institutional talk and specifically responsibility talk by considering how responsibility is constructed through a confluence of discursive choices, including deontic modality (modals of necessity and obligation), personal pronoun use, and expressions of time and space, though justifications and accounts also become important in counterbalancing statements of obligation. In addition to an analysis of these discourse features, the study explores hypothetical time and space, which I term 'imagined time' and 'imagined space', as concepts that aid in describing how the shelter caseworker positions two long-term clients and one undocumented (illegal immigrant) client when doing responsibility talk.

Ultimately, the study argues that the construction of responsibility is highly dependent on institutional and interactional contexts. Responsibility talk in this context draws on time and space as they are made meaningful by the shelter policy.

1.1 Institutional talk and responsibility

While linguistic anthropologists have chronicled how responsibility is communicated in macro-cultural contexts (e.g. the Wolof village in Irvine 1992; or Western Samoa in Duranti 1992), research on responsibility talk in institutional settings has primarily been left to sociologists and sociolinguists. For example, Goffman's influential discursive work on institutions (1961a) and their interaction orders (1983) established a framework for discursive micro-sociology and highlighted the discursive commonalities that exist across institutional settings. His work on 'offerings' (1981) and 'accounting' (1971) addressed what strategies speakers use to accept or deny responsibility (in full or in part), describing apologies, explanations, justifications, and excuses which a speaker may utilise to maintain an interlocutor's face.

Research on the construction of responsibility in institutional talk contexts has approached the issue from multiple perspectives. Scott and Lyman's (1968: 46) study of accounting practices established the groundwork for the discursive analysis of accounts, one of the primary ways that responsibility is constructed in talk, suggesting that accounts 'bridge the gap between expectation and action', often providing explanations for troublesome or untoward behaviour. In so doing, accounts may provide excuses or justifications for behaviours that deviate from those anticipated. Buttny and Morris (2001) extend that definition, suggesting that accounts may also occur in the larger context of narratives, characterised by story structure. While varying in construction, accounts highlight the position(s) or orientation(s) that interlocutors take toward their own responsibilities and others' responsibilities.

In social work interaction, the analysis of accounts has been used to understand how responsibility is constructed between married couples in counselling (Kurri and Wahlström 2005), in child protection cases (Hall et al. 2006), and in homeless shelters (Juhila 2003; Juhila et al. 2010; Matarese and Caswell 2014; Saario and Raitakari 2010). Juhila et al. (2010) describe constructions of responsibility focusing on accounting and blaming in practitioner and client talk in a Finnish supportive housing unit, revealing how practitioners control clients through both disciplinary action (in which control is required to maintain institutional rules) and caring interventions (requiring care implies that a client cannot maintain control him/herself). In each of these cases, accounting practices and responsibilities intersect with moral categorisation (the notion that accounts position interactional stakeholders in morally-relevant ways).

I have argued that institutional spaces are increasingly saturated with various forms of responsibility talk, particularly given recent proclivities toward neo-liberal, managerialist (i.e. business-oriented) organisational models for social institutions that emphasise, among other things, increased responsibility, accountability, and efficiency (Matarese 2008; Matarese and Caswell 2014). While accounts, and particularly excuses and justifications, are traditionally central to the analysis of responsibility, as they are here, studies on accounts in social work institutional settings have yet to include in their analyses attention to the ways in which allusions to policy-related time and space function in the construction and negotiation of responsibility in social work interaction. Given that social work in this context involves working with the same clients over time and given the interactional time spent discussing clients movements out of shelter space, this study extends discussions on constructing responsibility in talk by exploring how one caseworker, Ms Innis, constructs responsibility when interacting with three clients (pseudonyms are used for participant and location names to protect the confidentiality of the participants). The data reveal how institutional regulations regarding time and space shape this caseworker's construction of responsibility in talk, particularly because time and space are made meaningful by the institutional policy and context.

More specifically, the study compares the caseworker's responsibility talk with long-term stayer clients with her responsibility talk with an undocumented homeless client. Given policy mandates to place long-term clients (in shelter nine months or longer) more quickly, responsibility talk with these clients as they near the nine-month benchmark is more aggressive. This study shows how the caseworker's talk with the new undocumented client surprisingly resembles her talk with the long-term clients nearing the nine-month benchmark. She discursively treats this new undocumented client like persisting ones. 'Imagined time' and 'imagined space' (talk that speaks for the future worlds of an individual and/or posits a vision for the future actions, movements, or whereabouts of an individual) are introduced to aid in describing the projected, future non-compliance of a new undocumented client as established in the caseworker's responsibility talk.

1.2 Research Context

Clients of varying categories stayed in the large, urban shelter where research for this study took place. All clients began as short-term stayer clients. If they resided in shelter for a brief time (between a couple of days and three months) they were called 'short term'. Ms Innis' talk with short-term stayer clients was generally friendly, and devoid of responsibility-implicative language. In her meetings with short-term clients, Ms Innis maintained control of the conversation; through her role as questioner and evaluator, she also provided clients with space to talk, and established affiliation and alignment (Matarese 2008).

The city's Department of Homeless Services (DHS) utilised a nine-month benchmark to 'identify clients who may have been suitable for more intensive case management' (DHS IRB, personal communication, 24 March 2011). Those who exceeded this benchmark (called 'long-term stayers' by casework staff) received more intensive case-management and were among the first encouraged by their caseworkers to find housing quickly and leave shelter. Time was made meaningful by the policy, which emphasised the speedy and efficient placement of long-term staying (LTS) clients, as well as by casework practices and talk.

Another cohort of clients were labelled 'hard-to-place' due to the various barriers that prohibited them from more easily acquiring housing earlier in the process. Many clients who were hard-to-place became long-term stayers; however, not all long-term stayers were necessarily hard-to-place. Hard-to-place clients could include those with a drug addiction, those with co-occurring illnesses, sex offenders, violent felony offenders, arsonists, and undocumented immigrants, each enduring different obstacles to securing housing.

Undocumented clients were not necessarily long-term stayers (though they could be), but they were generally hard-to-place. 'DHS held the same expectations for undocumented clients as other shelter residents'; however, due to the illegal citizenship status of undocumented homeless clients, they faced particular challenges in accessing certain types of housing such as 'subsidized and supportive housing' (DHS IRB, personal communication, 24 March 2011). According to the caseworkers interviewed, undocumented clients often stayed in shelter for lengthy periods of time; however, those observed for this study left after a couple of months. This chapter compares a caseworker's late stage LTS talk with her talk with an undocumented client, highlighting how the caseworker discursively positions the new undocumented client like a late-stage LTS client.

2 Methodology

The study presents three cases from a linguistic ethnography of caseworker-client interaction in a New York City men's homeless shelter over a nine-month period, with attention to the construction of responsibility in talk vis-à-vis expressions of time and space with two LTS clients and one undocumented client. While exploring the broader question – how caseworkers and clients interact – the study describes how responsibility is constructed through one caseworker's talk during regularly-scheduled, one-on-one caseworker-client interactions.

The author obtained permission from the New York City DHS to conduct this study. The analyses and interpretations expressed herein represent the opinions of the author and do not reflect the opinions of the DHS or its staff. Participants for this case study included the caseworker (pseudonym: Ms Innis), two LTS clients, both of whom were men between the ages of 45 and 60 (pseudonyms: Julio and Michael), and an undocumented client (pseudonym: Luciano). All participants gave informed consent after reading the study's parameters in the language of their choice. Each meeting was audio-recorded, and the researcher took notes and transcribed as the caseworker and client spoke in order to ensure that each meeting was captured. The first excerpt in this data set had a corrupted audio file, and as such details regarding prosody cannot be included for that excerpt, though the transcript of the talk is faithful. The other excerpts were drawn from audio-recordings. The excerpts with the LTS clients were taken from meetings that occurred just before or shortly after clients became LTS clients (approaching or passing the nine-month benchmark for leaving shelter) in order to closely examine Ms Innis' construction of responsibility in talk, given those circumstances. The final excerpt was taken from the first case meeting between Ms Innis and the undocumented client, Luciano.

Data are analysed using discourse analysis, with an emphasis on understanding responsibility as it is socially constructed in talk (Thornborrow 2002). A variety of lexico-grammatical features (deontic modals, pronouns, verb tense, and lexical choice) and discourse features (accounting, justifications, pre-sequencing, pre-expansions, discourse markers, and other features) become relevant in constructing responsibility in these institutional interactions. The analysis of the three cases includes 24 individual caseworker-client meeting transcripts, which were selected based on the largest concentrations of discourse features communicating responsibility in talk. Data extracts revealing high concentrations of deontic modals and expressions of time and space were chosen to highlight the interrelationship between these linguistic features in constructing responsibility in talk. Ms Innis' incorporation of expressions of time and space helped situate that responsibility was constructed vis-à-vis the location of that client in space and time.

In the following data analysis sections, the first two excerpts are LTS clients (Julio and Michael). They illustrate the linguistic and discursive features that construct responsibility in talk, particularly given time and space constraints at the shelter. The third and final excerpt is from an interaction between Ms Innis and an undocumented client, Luciano, who is not an LTS client, but given his undocumented status, I argue that he is discursively treated as such.

3 Data analysis

3.1 Doing responsibility talk with LTS clients

Talk with LTS clients had a variety of distinctly recognisable features. With clients who began with Ms Innis and became LTS clients over time, Ms Innis' discourse shifted toward increased constructions of responsibility and increased talk *about* time *over* time (Matarese 2008). With later-stage long-term clients, Ms Innis used specific lexico-grammatical and discourse features which constructed the client's responsibilities and which were not observed in her talk with early stage LTS clients.

Ms Innis' talk with LTS clients shifted as they neared the nine-month benchmark. In describing a client's responsibilities, Ms Innis often referred to descriptions of the historical shift in shelter policy (including references to New York City Mayor, Michael Bloomberg), her interpretation of the shelter policies and plans, and how policy translated into administrative pressure on caseworkers toward the last months of a long-term client's stay.

The first example of Ms Innis' construction of responsibility comes from a meeting between herself (CM, case manager) and Julio (J). Julio had surpassed the nine-month benchmark for leaving shelter, and in response Ms Innis presented him with a list that included all the LTS clients that had been identified as priority placements for housing. This excerpt illustrates how Ms Innis constructed responsibility in her talk with an LTS client, given the shelter and policy contexts:

Excerpt 1

```
 1  CM:   the list. see this list? you're on it. you have to go.
 2         Julio, all these people highlighted have been here over 360
 3         days. as per DHS everyone who has been here for a year or
 4         more needs to go. no you have to pick a place.
 5  J:     what do you mean pick?
 6  CM:    you have to take a room. you have to take a room. This
 7         thursday. don't miss it, the 16th. see it? ((points to a
 8         calendar)). august 16th thursday? clients that's been in the
 9         shelter too many days. you've been here 417 days. they want
10         want you outta here. you've been in [other shelter]. it's a
11         lot of days to be in shelter. they want you out. so I have
12         to get the brunt of this.
13  J:     shared room.
14  CM:    shared. you have PA. they're gonna come down on me because
15         you've been in too many days. see all the people on this
16         list? I've already told them. you all are priority eligible
17         clients, more than 365 days in the shelter. all of it adds
18         up. we're all under one umbrella.
```

This excerpt includes three salient features: 1) Ms Innis' use of deontic modals, which construct responsibility; 2) justifications for those responsibility constructions; and 3) expressions of time and space, which situate his responsibility in context.

The term *deontic* comes from the Greek *deon* meaning 'duty or obligation' (Coates 1983). While this study does not consider all deontic modals (*must*, for example, does not often surface in the talk), *have to* (or *havta*), *got to* (or *gotta*), *need to*, and *supposed to* were often used by Ms Innis to express responsibility and obligation, particularly with LTS clients. Lines 1, 4, and 6 include *have to* directed toward Julio (*you*), which expresses obligation while suggesting that the speaker is not the 'authoritative source of this obligation' (Coates 1990: 56). Ms Innis also uses *need to* (line 4) to express a more general client responsibility. Those deontic modals convey Julio's obligations while ensuring that 'DHS' (and not she) is the authority ultimately holding him accountable.

Those modals displace responsibility to an external authority, much like justifications, which work toward the same end. Justifications 'involve claims in which the actor implicitly accepts responsibility, but denies the offensive character of the event in question' (Buttny 1993: 16). Ms Innis' justifications allow her to accept responsibility while displacing primary power to the administration, using them as a scapegoat (Scott and Lyman 1968). She begins with her statement 'see this list?', a pre-sequence (Schegloff 2007) that is marked because it underscores Julio's lack of compliance (Maynard 1992). Ms Innis uses a pre-sequence to pre-empt Julio's potential rejection of her argument 'you have to go'. Her justification continues through her reference to authorities whose decisions she is required to carry out. Thus, 'the list', 'these people highlighted' (line 1), and 'DHS', the authority behind the list (line 3), are used to provide rationale for the pressure she places on Julio. She likewise refers to shelter policy when she first explains the benchmark for length of stay in shelter ('clients that's been in the shelter too many days') in line 8–9 and then refers to the authority responsible for enforcing this rule, 'they' (line 9). Ms Innis' reference to her own accountability to the administration (lines 11–12) may function to appeal to her client's sympathies, as she explains that she could be penalised by 'they' for Julio's lack of compliance (lines 14–15). Her use of *have to* and *need to*, which highlights her involvement in enforcing responsibility while downplaying her authority, leads naturally into a series of justifications that distances her further from the authority figures holding both of them responsible.

These face-saving strategies (Goffman 1967) allow her to re-establish 'relational alignment' (Stokes and Hewitt 1976) after several statements that command him to 'pick a place' (line 4) and 'take a room' (line 6) – both directive statements minimally suggesting that Ms Innis has the power to assign him tasks that he is obliged to complete. Her talk highlights the balancing act required to save his face given her requirement to hold a grown male adult accountable for uncompleted tasks. Responsibility, therefore, is constructed (in part) in talk through justifications, references to responsible action (accomplished through deontic modals), and attention to her client's face wants; however, time and space also play a part in these constructions.

Ms Innis' description of responsibility is directly tied to expressions of space (where the client is obligated to go). Thus, in Ms Innis' statement 'you have to go' (line 1) *have to* is followed by *go*, expressing Julio's obligation to move from one space (the shelter) to another. Likewise, 'you have to take a room. You have to take a room' (line 6) demonstrates Julio's responsibility for acquiring a shared room, moving from the space of the shelter to a new space – independent living.

Expressions of space/time surface in Ms Innis' justifications as well. As such the adverb 'here' (line 2) is qualified by how long Julio has spent 'here' – 'over 360 days'. Similarly, invoking DHS as justification (line 3) qualifies space ('here') with a reference to time ('for a year or more').

Likewise her description of the policy ('clients that's been in the shelter too many days') specifically links his spatial habitation in the shelter with the number of days that he has lived there ('too many', '417', 'a lot'). Notably, while time alone does not constitute a reason for serving a client with a shelter violation, Ms Innis constructs the nine-month benchmark as a 'deadline' by which Julio has had to leave, perhaps as a strategy to convince him to leave more quickly (Lipsky 1980). Expressions of space and time, therefore, help orient the justifications vis-à-vis time-sensitive policy benchmarks.

3.2 Hypothetical spaces and times in constructing responsibility

While the previous excerpt illustrates the factors that construct LTS client responsibility talk, the next two highlight another analytical tier: how hypothetical spaces and times aid in constructing responsibility in two distinct client cases: Michael's and Luciano's. Michael (M) had been staying in the shelter for eight months, nearly an LTS client. He was abusing heroin methadone, and alcohol. He expressed no interest in a detoxification programme or related housing. While many discussions with Michael resembled the prior excerpt with Julio, this excerpt shows how Ms Innis incorporates hypothetical spaces into her construction of responsibility. This is one of their last interactions before Michael left shelter of his own accord:

Excerpt 2

```
 1  CM:   and if you're not the:n, (.) what's hap- then where we gonna
 2         be? you're gonna come out you're gonna leave here. (.)
 3         you're gonna go into a room. (.) I'm gonna be straight >shit
 4         ain't gonna work out< a:nd >you're gonna be back here.< (.4)
 5         it's a revolving door. I've been here two and a half years,
 6         and in my two and a half years god, TUH. I've SEEn (.) this
 7         place is like a revolving door.
 8  M:    ((laughs))
 9  CM:   six months to a year everybody goes out, (.) for six months
10         summer is nice winter they back. I can't- it's- it's- you
11         see then, why you here? (.2) I don't wanna see that with you
12         michael, so you know what you <need to do:>? you know what
13         your situation is, you you know what you're doing (.) but
14         on another ha:nd, I'm definitely telling you (.) you need to
```

15   get it together. and I'm going to:- honestly: you got till:
16   (.4) next month (.) that's it. you've been here long enough
17   and we haven't done anything. we haven't gotten you nowhere,
18   and so you gotta make that decision.

In many respects this excerpt resembles the prior excerpt. Like her interaction with Julio, Ms Innis incorporates expressions of time and space into her construction of responsibility, which centers around the deontic modals in lines 12 and 14. However, in contrast with the previous excerpt, the first several references to time and space (line 2) are part of a hypothetical narrative. The excerpt begins (line 1) with an if-then conditional statement that initiates a future talk sequence in which Ms Innis imagines Michael's future living space circumstances. Despite her repeated use of 'we' ('where we gonna be?'), her short hypothetical narrative centers on Michael, given her repeated use of the second person pronoun *you* (lines 1–4).

Narratives, which sequentially describe events that have occurred within the time frame of the story (Labov and Fanshel 1977), can function as accounts to justify or defend certain actions (Buttny 1993). This brief narrative describing Michael's future functions to justify Ms Innis' actions. Within this narrative, expressions relating to spatial changes are emphasised (lines 2–4) through verbs that signal movement from one space to another ('leave' and 'go'), nouns/adverbs ('here' and 'room'), and 'back' (suggesting movement toward a former location).

In some contexts a counsellor may use hypothetical questions to help prepare the client for future events and situations (Noordegraaf et al. 2008). Speer and Parsons (2006) suggest that hypothetical questions can also have a gatekeeping function. In such cases a psychiatrist asks the patient to suppose, or imagine, a hypothetical scenario and to discuss how he/she would react given that scenario. While Michael may be considering her initial question ('where we gonna be?'), Ms Innis answers the question herself, making it not only a hypothetical imagining and positioning of his future space and time but also a rhetorical question that only she can answer vis-à-vis her prior experience.

Ms Innis positions Michael in future space, a powerful move. Though the questioner in an institutional interaction has asymmetrical power advantages, there is an assumption that in conversation each question requires an answer (Sacks 1992), particularly given the rising intonation noted in line 2. Ms Innis does not, however, provide interactional space for Michael to answer but predicts his future herself. She demonstrates her authority not only by telling Michael what to do but *where* he will be in the future – the 'imagined spaces' (cf. Anderson [1991] on 'imagined communities'), or hypothetical future spaces, that he will occupy.

In Ms Innis' conversation with Michael, it is clear that she is looking at Michael now and envisioning him returning to the shelter in six months. She imagines his change of space, moving from his current position (in shelter) to housing and back to shelter. After this imagined positioning, Ms Innis supports her hypothetical narrative with a brief historical narrative that begins with the 'revolving door' metaphor (lines 7), which acts as a summative abstract of the situation, which she then explains in a sequential ordering of two events, both of which emphasise space ('everybody *goes out*' and 'they *back*', lines 9–10). Each of these short narratives provides an opportunity for justification. The historical narrative based on Ms Innis' experiences and observations also doubles as evidence for why Michael should reverse his ways and comply with his assigned tasks. Both narratives serve to justify the pressure that Ms Innis places on him when she tells him to 'get it together', giving him a month's deadline for complying with her requests (line 15).

The next excerpt, perhaps the most intriguing, comes from Luciano's case. Luciano was a short-term client only staying at the shelter about two and a half months. Despite his short stay, analyses of Ms Innis' talk with him revealed that her interactions with him resembled her talk with clients nearing the nine-month benchmark. In this excerpt, Ms Innis not only imagines Luciano's potential future state as a long-term stayer, but she also verbally positions him in that imagined future by using linguistic and discourse features similar to those she uses when speaking to LTS clients. While Luciano's status as an undocumented immigrant made him a 'hard-to-place' client, at the time he was neither a long-term stayer in shelter, nor would he necessarily become one.

Excerpt 3 comes from the first meeting between Luciano and Ms Innis. A Latino security guard provided Spanish-English translation between Ms Innis (who spoke only English) and Luciano (who spoke only Spanish). When Luciano arrived in the shelter, he had recently injured his foot and could not walk on it easily. His intention was to stay at the shelter between two and four months while his foot healed, then find a job 'off the books' and move out of shelter. He was not insistent on staying for four or five months but was open to guidance on the topic.

In the excerpt Ms Innis utilises similar strategies as she did with the long-term clients, including imagined space and time as she explained to the translator that Luciano could not wait for his foot to heal:

Excerpt 3

```
 1  CM:  he sits here all day, (.) but he doesn't know that as he
 2        stay here, (.) the system is changing around him (.) the
 3        system system is changing around him (.) y'used to be able
 4        to do that but not anymore (.) see? (.) and then so since
 5        his plan in his mind is to stay in a shelter for four, five,
 6        six months and then figure out what he's going to do (.)
 7        he can't do that. (.) he needs to start thinking about what
 8        he's going to do now (.) because I can't transfer him to
 9        another shelter because it's not an option anymore for us
10        (.) you have to place these clients. (.) mayor bloomberg
11        is like, bring down homelessness and not transfer them (.2)
12        got to be placed, and so that's the problem (.) so all the
13        people who's undocumented [institution name] don't have a
14        problem paying for a ticket for them to go back to their
15        family in whatever country, that's why I offered him that.
16        (.) because some people don't have the mo:ney: or the
17        connections or whatever. (.) we can take care of that. (.)
18        the problem is (.) he can't wait five months and say, >'I
19        don't want to go' if I go through the whole process and
20        then he change his mind< (.) >then he wanna stay here< (.)
21        he's not really doing nothing here (.) ask him, he's not
22        doing anything. (.)
```

This excerpt shares similarities with the others presented in this study. Ms Innis constructs responsibility by balancing obligation ('he needs to', line 7) situated in time ('four, five, six months' and 'now') and space ('a shelter') with accounts that place authority and blame with the institution, the policy, and the mayor (lines 8–12), justifying the pressure she will place on Luciano.

The excerpt also highlights the delicate balance between constructing responsibility and providing justification for enforcing those responsibilities. Ms Innis' generalised description of client practices in the shelter ('you used to be able to do that but not anymore', lines 3–4) suggests that responsible clienting now involves positive progress toward leaving shelter for permanent living. This claim of responsibility is counterbalanced by another justification, which is initiated by the discourse marker 'see', which not only conveys that what follows is 'proclaimed knowledge' (McCarthy 1994: 112), but also pragmatically expresses 'what you're saying is not right, this is how it happened' (Hale 1999: 70). The justification itself is complex, interwoven between descriptions of Luciano's responsibilities. Statements conveying the shelter rules ('can't', line 7) and deontic modal use conveying responsibility ('need to', line 7) are followed by a brief justification that restores alignment with the client by explaining that the new rules do not allow her to transfer Luciano, which redirects blame and authority to the administration (lines 8–9). Further justification is provided through her subsequent reference to shelter policy and administrative practice (lines 10–12), which again distances her from ultimate responsibility for holding him accountable. She uses expressions of space to convey the requirement to move from one space to another ('you have to place these clients' and 'got to be placed'), emphasising the verb 'place' to highlight the broad importance of placement for all clients.

This excerpt also shares similarities with Excerpt 2 between Ms Innis and Michael, as Ms Innis projects a future scenario of Luciano. Because he stated that he considered staying until his foot healed and he found a job, Ms Innis first paraphrases Luciano's plan, as she sees it (line 4–5), suggesting that she is able to envision his mental plan. Moreover, in the final lines of the excerpt Ms Innis utilises imagined time and space (lines 18–20) by speaking for Luciano's future self. Imagined time is described hypothetically; using an if–then conditional statement ('if I go through the whole process and then he change his mind') she speaks for his future self, suggesting that he will resist movement, situating his resistance in space ('go' vs 'stay here') vis-à-vis time (in 'five months'). Ms Innis uses expressions of time and space to situate Luciano's expected future violation of responsibility. Given her experience in the shelter system, her presupposition is a viable possibility. She then uses this projection as justification for emphasising Luciano's current lack of responsibility: 'he's not really doing nothing over here (.) ask him, he's not doing anything', positioning him as currently non-compliant (lines 21–22).

It is noteworthy, particularly given the similarities between her discourse with Luciano and her talk with later stage LTS clients, that Luciano is only in his first month of shelter at this time, and while Ms Innis may want to prepare him for the challenges ahead given his immigration status, her construction of responsibility in talk appears premature given his current short-term status, particularly when compared to her interactions with other short- and long-term clients. Luciano is not being discursively treated like an early-stage client. Ms Innis' multiple references to Luciano's inert behaviour at the shelter also serve as a justification for the pressure she places on him. As static behaviour is counterproductive to successfully acquiring legal and independent housing, she positions Luciano as non-compliant now and in the future.

Ms Innis' interaction with Luciano closely resembles her interactions with late stage LTS clients, emphasising 'doing nothing', characterising him as irresponsible, using deontic modals, expressions of time and space, justifications, and even positioning him as irresponsible in the future. In Michael (Excerpt 2) and Luciano's (Excerpt 3) cases, Ms Innis projects their cases into the future and speaks as if that representation were a fact. However, in contrast with Michael's case, Ms Innis not only imagines Luciano's future but also discursively treats him like a late-stage long-term stayer, imagining his future as a long-term stayer and treating him accordingly. Ms Innis transcends the real time of the meeting and the space of her office and 'creates new images of the world' (Wenger 1998: 176), seeing Luciano five or six months into the future when pressure would begin mounting as he transitioned toward becoming a long-term stayer. Though prior experience had proven to her that undocumented clients often became LTS clients, Luciano left the shelter after two and a half months.

4 Discussion

Both real and imagined time and space were central to the shelter's conversational context. Length of shelter stay was central to discussions around responsibility. Real time and space situated the clients' responsibilities vis-à-vis the nine-month benchmark and the need for spatial movement from a transitional space (shelter) to a more permanent one (independent living). Likewise, Ms Innis used imagined time and space to offer potential future scenarios to Michael and Luciano, scenarios that she had seen before with other clients, according to her statements, and wanted to avoid with Michael and Luciano if at all possible. On a macro-theoretical level, then, this study lends support to the analysis of chronotope (Bakhtin 1981), as expressions of time and space worked together to establish the 'here' and 'now' of client responsibility. Though time and space are accepted partners in social life, the policy's emphasis on time and spatial movement, as clients move from shelter space to independent living spaces, reveals the inextricable relationship between time and space and the ways in which social context impacts a caseworker's institutional talk and subsequent acts.

The rhetorical question Ms Innis used in describing Michael's future experience (Excerpt 2, line 1–2) did not provide him with interactional space to verbally speculate about his own future. Imagined time and space, hypothetical situations that illuminated how Ms Innis saw the future unfolding, arose vis-à-vis her knowledge and experience, but in writing their future *for* the clients, they may have been less likely (at that interactional moment) to write it for themselves. Perhaps asking clients to 'suppose', as Speer and Parsons (2006) suggest, may empower them to consider the future for themselves. Analyses of future hypothetical, imagined scenarios could be a very important consideration in social work interaction research, particularly given the social work field's emphasis on client-centered practice (Johnson and Yanca 2006).

Moreover, the way Ms Innis constructed imagined future conversations, client statuses, and situations through her talk also positioned her as knowledgeable. By positing an educated guess about where she thought the client would be, she could present him with options in light of the potential results. Because Ms Innis had worked with many LTS clients in the past, she could envision the range of challenges Michael would face if he did not take her advice on an apartment. Likewise, her experience with undocumented clients who became LTS clients enabled her to envision Luciano as a long-term stayer, despite his short shelter stay.

However, expressions of hypothetical, or imagined, time and space not only established Ms Innis as knowledgeable and experienced but also, in Luciano's case, functioned as a bureaucratic simplification (Lipsky 1980). Lipsky suggests that street-level bureaucrats develop simplifications, or 'mental routinizations … to deal with the complexity of work tasks', which is not surprising given the challenges of the position (1980: 83). Because street-level bureaucrats implement policy in everyday practice, often their simplifications and routines enact policy in the interactional moment. Simplifications allow the bureaucrat to generalise the application of policy to clients, carefully picking and choosing moments where deviation from the general rule is necessary, requiring individualised attention (Lipsky 1980). Because Ms Innis had encountered many undocumented clients who *became* LTS clients, and perhaps because there were few individualised options for those clients, she treated Luciano like a late-stage long-term stayer from the beginning, conceivably in the hope that her determined efforts to move him from shelter early in the case might have prohibited him from eventually becoming a long-term stayer. For both Luciano and Michael, Ms Innis' imagined scenarios project marked negative consequences of client (in)action, which provided further justification for her emphasis on client responsibility.

Without ethnographic, participant observation, the significance of her talk with the undocumented client might have gone without notice. Until context, specifically client status and time vis-à-vis the policy, are included, it is difficult to see how Ms Innis' constructions of responsibility with the undocumented client vary from her talk with LTS clients. These observations, therefore, also emphasise the importance of emic analyses that allow analytical categories to evolve out of the data.

5 Conclusion

Ms Innis' construction of responsibility in talk in this particular context had a variety of features, many of which pertained directly to the influence of the shelter context. As Buttny (1993: 162) notes, 'A number of ... contextual factors may influence the course of the social accountability episode ... but which of these contextual conditions are relevant to *this* particular situated context?' To be a successful caseworker, Ms Innis needed to gain the compliance of her clients and facilitate their movement from shelter to housing. Without client compliance, her goals could not be accomplished (Lipsky 1980). Ms Innis' construction of responsibility in this context, therefore, balanced descriptions of client obligation with justifications for enforcing those obligations. To construct responsibility, she used specific deontic modals (*have to/havta, need to, supposed to*) to convey obligation, and expressions of time and space (often used together), which situated those client responsibilities within the context of the shelter. To re-establish alignment with the client, recognising that alignment may facilitate compliance, Ms Innis distanced herself from authority through justifications and role distancing (Goffman 1961b), placing ultimate responsibility for holding clients accountable with the institutional administration. Justifications and narratives, or story-like justifications (see Excerpts 2 and 3) provided accounts that served as rationale for the pressure she placed on her clients. These justifications allowed Ms Innis to acknowledge the client's obligations while placing primary authority elsewhere.

This study has presented a dynamic amalgam of linguistic and discursive choices that together shape how responsibility is constructed in Ms Innis' talk. Several key deontic modals were used to express client obligation. Time and space, both made meaningful by the shelter policy, became relevant in Ms Innis' practice, couching responsibility in the 'here-ness' and 'now-ness' (or in the case of imagined time and space in the 'there-ness' and 'then-ness') of client life, as visualised by Ms Innis.

Perhaps this study may inspire more research examining time as a factor in institutional talk. Many street-level bureaucrats – social workers, teachers, and other front-line practitioners who serve as intermediaries between the administration and clients and who put policy into practice through their everyday work – operate within critical time constraints that shape institutional talk and practice. Similar findings might be made in education wherein teachers plea to their exhausted students, 'look, we have three weeks until this test. Whether we like it or not, the school and the state require these tests, so let's work together, so that you can each do your best.' Time (and to a lesser extent perhaps, space) is increasingly a constraint on institutional practices, particularly those that fall within the standards movement.

Because this is a case study of one caseworker and three clients from the sample, the study in no way intends to make generalisations about all the caseworkers at this shelter or how DHS policies were implemented shelter-wide. The study neither posits arguments about normative LTS client talk, nor about undocumented client talk. Rather, it seeks to make a contribution by exploring how Ms Innis constructed responsibility in a context where clients were required to physically move from one space (the shelter) to another space (independent living) preferably before the nine-month benchmark (time). This study, therefore, sheds some initial light on the complex construction of responsibility and accountability in casework. As research in this area grows, we may gain a keener understanding regarding how responsibility is constructed within and across institutional contexts.

Note

1   Particular thanks to Christine M. Jacknick, Carolus van Nijnatten, and the volume editors on their feedback on this study, to Stef Slembrouck for suggesting I consider chronotope, and to Srikant Sarangi for his recommendation that I consider space in addition to time.

References

Anderson, B. (1991) *Imagined Communities: Reflections on the Origin and Spread of Nationalism*. London: Verso.

Bakhtin, M. M. (1981) *The Dialogic Imagination: Four Essays by M.M. Bakhtin*. Austin: University of Texas Press.

Buttny, R. (1993) *Social Accountability in Communication*. London: Sage.

Buttny, R. and Morris, G. H. (2001) Accounting. In W. P. Robinson and H. Giles (eds) *The New Handbook of Language and Social Psychology* 285–302. New York: John Wiley & Sons.

Coates, J. (1983) *The Semantics of Modal Auxiliaries*. London: Croom Helm.

Coates, J. (1990) Modal meaning: the semantic-pragmatic interface. *Journal of Semantics* 7: 53–63.

Duranti, A. (1992) Intentions, self, and responsibility: an essay in Samoan ethnopragmatics. In J. Hill and J. T. Irvine (eds) *Responsibility and Evidence in Oral Discourse* 24–47. New York: Cambridge University Press.

Goffman, E. (1961a) *Asylums: Essays on the Social Situation of Mental Patients and Other Inmates*. Garden City, NY: Doubleday.

Goffman, E. (1961b) *Encounters: Two Studies in the Sociology of Interaction – Fun in Games & Role Distance*. Indianapolis, IN: Bobbs-Merrill.

Goffman, E. (1967) *Interaction Ritual: Essays in Face to Face Behavior*. Chicago, IL: Aldine.

Goffman, E. (1971) *Relations in Public: Microstudies of the Public Order*. New York: Basic Books.

Goffman, E. (1981) *Forms of Talk*. Philadelphia: University of Pennsylvania Press.

Goffman, E. (1983) The interaction order. *American Sociological Review* 48: 1–17.

Hale, S. (1999) Interpreters' treatment of discourse markers in courtroom questions. *Forensic Linguistics* 6: 57–82.

Hall, C., Slembrouck, S. and Sarangi, S. (2006) *Language Practices in Social Work: Categorisation and Accountability in Child Welfare*. London: Routledge.

Irvine, J. (1992) Insult and responsibility: verbal abuse in a Wolof village. In J. Hill and J. T. Irvine (eds) *Responsibility and Evidence in Oral Discourse* 105–134. New York: Cambridge University Press.

Johnson, L. C. and Yanca, S. J. (2006) *Social Work Practice: A Generalist Approach*. Boston, MA: Allyn and Bacon.

Juhila, K. (2003) Creating a 'bad' client: disalignment of institutional identities in social work interaction. In C. Hall, K. Juhila, N. Parton and T. Pösö (eds) *Constructing Clienthood in Social Work and Human Services: Interaction, Identities and Practices* 83–95. London: Jessica Kingsley.

Juhila, K., Hall, C. and Raitakari, S. (2010) Accounting for the clients' troublesome behaviour in a supported housing unit: blames, excuses and responsibility in professionals' talk. *Journal of Social Work* 10: 59–79.

Kurri, K. and Wahlstrom, J. (2005) Placement of responsibility and moral reasoning in couple therapy. *Journal of Family Therapy* 27(4): 352–369.

Labov, W. and Fanshel, D. (1977) *Therapeutic Discourse: Psychotherapy as Conversation*. New York: Academic Press.

Lipsky, M. (1980) *Street-Level Bureaucracy: Dilemmas of the Individual in Public Services*. New York: Russell Sage Foundation.

Matarese, M. (2008) Practice, power, policy, and participation: a linguistic ethnography of cumulative caseworker-client interactions in a New York City homeless shelter. Unpublished Doctoral Dissertation: Teachers College, Columbia University.

Matarese, M. and Caswell, D. (2014) Responsibility. In C. Hall, K. Juhila, M. Matarese and C. van Nijnatten (eds) *Analyzing Social Work Communication* 44–60. London: Routledge.

Maynard, D. (1992) On clinicians co-implicating recipients' perspective in the delivery of diagnostic news. In P. Drew and J. Heritage (eds) *Talk at Work: Interaction in Institutional Settings* 331–358. Cambridge: Cambridge University Press.

McCarthy, M. (1994) What should we teach about spoken language? *Australian Review of Applied Linguistics* 17: 104–120.

Nikander, P. (2003) The absent client: case description and decision making in interprofessional meetings. In C. Hall, K. Juhila, N. Parton and T. Pösö (eds) *Constructing Clienthood in Social Work and Human Services: Interaction, Identities and Practices* 112–128. London: Jessica Kingsley.

Noordegraaf, M., van Nijnatten, C. and Elbers, E. (2008) Future talk: discussing hypothetical situations with prospective adoptive parents. *Qualitative Social Work* 7: 310–329.

Olesen, S. P. (2003) Client, user, member as constructed in institutional interaction. In C. Hall, K. Juhila, N. Parton and T. Pösö (eds) *Constructing Clienthood in Social Work and Human Services: Interaction, Identities and Practices* 208–222. London: Jessica Kingsley.

Saario, S. and Raitakari, S. (2010) Contractual audit and mental health rehabilitation: a study of formulating effectiveness in a Finnish supported housing unit. *International Journal of Social Welfare* 19: 321–332.

Sacks, H. (1992) *Lectures on Conversation*. Oxford: Blackwell.

Schegloff, E. A. (2007) *Sequence Organization in Interaction: A Primer in Conversation Analysis, Volume 1*. Cambridge: Cambridge University Press.

Scott, M. and Lyman, S. (1968). Accounts. *American Sociological Association* 33(1): 46–62.

Speer, S. A. and Parsons, C. (2006) Gatekeeping gender: some features of the use of hypothetical questions in the psychiatric assessment of transsexual patients. *Discourse & Society* 17: 785–812.

Stokes, R. and Hewitt, J. (1976) Aligning actions. *American Sociological Review* 41: 838–849.

Thornborrow, J. (2002) *Power Talk: Language and Interaction in Institutional Discourse*. London: Longman.

Wenger, E. (1998) *Communities of Practice: Learning, Meaning and Identity*. Cambridge: Cambridge University Press.

A version of this chapter appeared in *Journal of Applied Linguistics and Professional Practice* 9:3.

Maureen Teresa Matarese is an Associate Professor in Academic Literacy and Linguistics at BMCC, City University of New York. Her work explores street-level bureaucracy in institutional interactions. She has published in *Discourse Processes* and the *Journal of Applied Linguistics and Professional Practice*, and she is a co-editor and co-author of *Analysing Social Work Communication: Discourse in Practice* through Routledge.

Appendix: Transcription conventions

underlining	emphasis on a word or part of a word
< talk >	talk within brackets is slowed speech
> talk <	talk with brackets is quickened speech
CAPS	words in capital letters are said more loudly
utterance A- utterance B (i.e. 'we nee- I need')	dash shows utterance A disrupted by utterance B (utterance B is a repair of utterance A)
(.)	one beat break between turns at talk or within a turn
(.2), (.4), etc.	longer pauses gauged by counting tenths of seconds using speaker rhythm
́	marked rise in intonation
.	downward intonation
,	continuing intonation
[other shelter]	brackets substitute a proper name with a general one
(( ))	description of vocalisations like laughter and gestures
:	elongated speech
…	ellipses indicate missing fragments of talk
?	rising intonation

Reflexivity in the institution, and how it entangles with research

Chris Bulcaen

1 Introduction[1]

Reflexivity is all around, especially in professional practices. In this chapter I wish to explore, more in the form of a discussion than actual analysis, a particular aspect of reflexivity that I would call *topicalisation of institutional context*. I refer to those moments in institutional discourse when the institution, as an actual place or as, metonymically, a set of professional practices, becomes an explicit topic of the conversation or text. These meta-forms of institutional discourse range from small discussions of institutional rules and realities in provider-client or provider-provider interaction, through programmatic and managerial discourse on institutional change, to broad societal discussion of so-called 'new realities', such as, for example, interculturalism, that should impact on institutional practice. Topicalisation of institutional context is only one of many forms of explicit contextualisation that take place in institutional discourse. The interplay of different forms of contextualisation will be taken up in the analysis of the examples (see Section 3).

My attention was drawn to this issue because of the profuse manifestations of topicalisations of institutional context in my research on a particular type of social work discourse where this reflexivity on institutional context is very prominent, namely that of shelters for battered or homeless women. Although this profusiveness has in some part to do with the nature of social work in these shelters (see Section 2), I believe that it is intrinsic to contemporary social work discourse. For instance, counsellors frequently discuss the power they have over their clients, referring to their professional status as well as to the institution as such.

As topicalisations of institutional context abound profusively, the analysis of institutional discourse has to take them into account, firstly by assuming that they are a necessary part of institutional discourse; and, secondly by analysing how they are accomplished and then reproduced within the chain of entextualisation practices (Bauman and Briggs 1990),

141

e.g. how they relate to other contextualisations. This means, for instance, that research on asymmetries in discourse (see e.g. Marková and Foppa 1991) should consider the self-reflexive discourse of practitioners. In addition, as topicalisations of institutional context are meta-forms of discourse, they point to the importance of levels of discourse and chains of reproductions (or entextualisations) of discourse in social work, which has its consequences for the data-constitution and methodology of the research. Further, the critical and ethical aims of the research (i.e. the improvement of client-provider relations) get tangled up with the self-reflexivity of social workers and managers in complex and sometimes unexpected ways, as I have myself experienced when discussing my analyses and criticisms with counsellors. I will explore this entanglement throughout the chapter. It can be argued that the recognition of self-reflexivity in social work discourse leads to a more responsible form of discourse analysis, in that it reconsiders its methodology, data constitution, theoretical assumptions, presentation of research outcome, interaction with subjects and general critical and ethical aims.

2 The institution and the research

The examples discussed in this chapter stem from an ethnograpically inspired action-research project that was commissioned by the municipal authorities of a major city in the region of Flanders, Belgium: 'Action-research on the counselling of migrant women in shelters for battered or homeless women.'[2] The municipality, in particular its integration centre, wondered whether it should not establish a refugee home for muslim women because it perceived the current state of intercultural counselling to be inadequate, or even inappropriate. On the other hand, the actual counsellors of refugee homes asked for assistance with intercultural counselling. Obviously, these questions put to the foreground the institutions themselves, so that topicalisation of institutional context was an unavoidable subject in the conversations between me, the counsellors and all other persons who were involved in the research project.

In 1996 I conducted research in four shelters.[3] A client's career in a shelter looks maximally like this: (1) Referral to a shelter by herself, friends, a welfare institution, police, etc.; (2) Intake by a counsellor, upon which the decision to stay at the institution is taken; (3) Staying in the shelter, maximally six months (most immigrant women stay less than a week); (4) During the stay: individual conversations with counsellor(s) aimed at helping in administrative, legal, pedagogical, social and emotional problems, group sessions, children's activities, daily activities, going outside the institution for work, administrative business, court, language lessons, meeting family members, etc.; (5) Leaving the institution after reaching a solution to the problem(s) or returning to the original situation without any change; (6) Continuing contacts with the shelter or referral to other residential or ambulant welfare institutions.

It is important to stress the legal definition – which is also the self-definition – of the professional activity of these institutions: they perform psychosocial counselling (*'psycho-sociale begeleiding'* in Dutch) that should be distinguished from any kind of therapy. The aim of the shelters is to give battered or homeless women (1) a place to rest and be safe, (2) an opportunity in which they can tell their story, (3) to give them advice, and (4) to work with them at reconstructing and changing their family and social life. Mental and addiction problems do not get treated in these shelters and when they occur, a client can be referred to another institution. In practice the line between psychosocial counselling and therapy is far more difficult to draw. Counsellors can be lured into therapeutic activity by the reality and needs of clients. Counsellors also receive a lot of input from theories of therapy, in particular systems and contextual (Böszörményi-Nagy 1987) therapy.[4] However, the line is consequently reviewed by the teams of social workers. In fact, being concerned with and explicitly communicating about this line is perceived by these counsellors as an essential element of professionalism – I have particularly observed this in the supervision of apprentices.

Welfare institutions that restrict their professional activities to psychosocial counselling present an interesting picture to contemporary studies of institutional practices because of the high degree of non-committal engagement of the client and because of the distinction vis-à-vis psychotherapy. Shelters for women occupy a very particular position within the opposition between the private and the public sphere, not in the least because the very coming-into-being of shelters for battered women is part of the feminist challenge to the private/public distinction of liberal societies. Although the act of going to a shelter and talking about domestic problems to professionals is perceived as an act of 'going public' – this perception certainly rings true for migrant communities who are very suspicious of shelters – the 'publicness' of domestic violence and women's homelessness still has to be fought over.

All these particular aspects of psychosocial counselling in refugee shelters for women serve to enhance the self-awareness of the counsellors.

This accounts to a certain degree for the abundance of topicalisations of institutional context in my research data.

3 Reflexivity in research

In 1996 I was fresh from school. I had been heavily influenced by linguistic and sociological analyses of social work discourse that bring to the foreground the representation and contextualisation of stories, in particular the narratives of clients, as an essential discursive practice in social work (e.g. Gunnarsson et al. 1997; Linell and Sarangi 1998). So I was on the lookout for asymmetries in discourse, whether given or accomplished, for the reproduction of clients' stories in particular ways, for chains of entextualisation that turn chaotic 'real' narratives into manageable files (cf. Silverstein and Urban 1996). I certainly was under the spell of the 'hermeneutics of suspicion' (the term was coined by Ricoeur) but was, during my research, challenged by my collaborators and counsellors to go beyond that stance because they kept confronting me with detailed accounts of clients' behaviour and their own professional procedures, i.e. the institutional 'realities'. In these accounts they assimilated much of what I said about institutional action and context.

I was challenged by the fact that nobody was really surprised by what I had to say, by my analyses that matched so well the results of other institutional analyses. Counsellors were able to translate my findings into well-known and simple adhortations – such as 'you shouldn't stick labels on people', 'there is a difference between thought and action', 'we should be aware of our power as professionals' – that took the edge off my detailed criticisms. In fact, this possibility of translation was a reason for them to appreciate the results of the research project: they 'recognised' my descriptions and criticisms. Recognition and corroboration seem to be one of the main purposes of institutional metadiscursive interaction. Such exonerating translation processes are normal for human linguistic action but I would like to stress here – again – how well these well-known and simple adhortations match academic criticisms of institutional discourse and context (see the conclusion).

3 Topicalisations of institutional context

In my analysis of counsellor-client interaction, group meetings and team meetings,[5] I found different manifestations of the topicalisation of institutional context. I have not attempted to draw up a list of all different forms of topicalisation of institutional context that occur in my data. It is more important to see when and how topicalisations arise, how they relate to other contextualisation practices and what is subsequently being done with them, e.g. how they feed back into interpretation schemas, case management and the understanding between the client and the provider/ institution. One crucial distinction that should be made is between client-provider and provider-provider interaction; another one is that between dyadic-triadic conversations and group or team interaction. I limit myself here to individual provider-client sessions and to provider-provider interaction that is directly related to the former. In this chapter I shall discuss the following manifestations:

(1) *Reflexive awareness* of institutional context by counsellors and clients;

(2) *Assymetries of contextualisation*: how the interaction by clients and counsellors during a client's stay in the institution is evaluated by counsellors;

(3) *Cross-cultural differences*: how the institutional procedures and realities (e.g. racism) are explained to immigrant women.

Before turning to some analysis, I wish to stress that the examples have been chosen in order to present some problematic aspects of counselling in shelters for battered or homeless women. These extracts and the critical analysis should not be taken to imply that the whole counselling process in the shelters that I studied is insufficient or lacking in empathy and support. These extracts particularly concern the difficult moment when counselling proceeds from the basic emotional support and listening stance of the counsellor to evaluation, advice and helping strategies that impact on the client's story and life.

3.1 Reflexive awareness

At many times during their interaction clients and counsellors express awareness of what they are/were doing/saying and why they are/were doing/saying it. This awareness always includes a contextualisation of the action that is reflected upon. The action can be contextualised within a person's 'system' or 'systems' (psychological constitution, professional identity, biography, family, culture, society) or within the immediate physical surroundings, the 'institution' (more on the difference between these two in 3.2). Reflexive moments pop up frequently in interaction and are to a great extent limited to a few sequential turns. Some forms of reflexivity are unavoidable because the regulations and customs of the shelter need to be discussed with the client.

Moments of reflexivity are appreciated by counsellors as crucial 'breakthrough' moments in the counselling process. As they reason, these reflexive moments implicate that a client thinks about her situation on a more abstract or meta-level, which opens up the way to change induced by shifts on the perceptual level. As social constructionists would say: shifts in narration and contextualisation lead to different lives (see e.g. McNamee and Gergen 1992). For the counsellor, reflexive moments are much-wanted challenges to routinised and uncritical counselling behaviour that hinders the development of effective counselling strategies. These reflexive moments are particularly reserved for team interaction, in written (files, logs) or oral (team meetings) form.

However, the reality of reflexive awareness is much more hetero-geneous than that. Reflexivity serves many purposes and forms part of various discursive practices that are not necessarily geared towards change and improvement. To name just a few practices that cast doubt on the 'innovative' quality of reflexivity:

- Routinised forms of contextualisation in order to reassure clients or colleague-counsellors, e.g. 'The children are not themselves because they are in a strange environment', 'I was in a hurry, there was so much to do, I couldn't really discuss the problem in full'. These contextualisations have a function in maintaining engagements of and to clients. They serve the coordination of the counselling process, rather than the contents and progress of that process.

- Folk abstractions, e.g. 'We have to make the best of it', 'We're all in the same boat', 'We have to adapt somewhat to the ways of the Belgians'. These also have the basic function of maintaining engagements.

- The argument of intercultural difference, e.g. 'It is difficult when you don't understand the language', 'I am/you are not used to living together with non-believers', 'My own people would not help me in this way'. These contextualisations serve many purposes: comforting, management of engagement, distancing from other clients (see Example 4), an intermediate evaluative step leading to the decision to leave the shelter.

- Reflexivity as a sign of professional activity, e.g. 'I first went over some administrative details in order to put the client at rest', 'It was my strategy to let her come to that conclusion herself'.

- Reflexivity used as a means to draw a line between the counsellors and the institution on the one hand and the client(s) on the other. This is especially true for moments in which institutional regulations and customs are discussed vis-à-vis the erratic behaviour of a client or the client group as a whole. I have recordings of many group meetings in which clients cite institutional regulations in order to denounce other clients, and counsellors discuss institutional regulations and aspirations in order to remedy the 'bad group spirit'.

If I may leave the descriptive mode for a moment, I would like to emphasise that in order to have an innovative quality for social work practice, reflexivity must be worked at and with. In my data I have observed that too little is done with reflexive moments vis-à-vis discussions among counsellors and vis-à-vis the relationship between client, file and counsellor. For example, written documents are full of contextualisations, evaluations and other reflexive thoughts, but these are never openly discussed with clients. Counsellors claim that not too much weight should be given to these written statements because case management is more guided by the overall mental, unwritten picture of the client and her problems and by the daily direct confrontation with the client than by the file and other written documents. The complexities of the case and the relation with the 'face' or 'other' is perceived to be the greatest dynamic input for counselling strategy. This claim is in itself a topicalisation of institutional context, in terms of professional activities of counsellors, that needs to be examined, as I do in Example 1, because of its deceptive, problematic nature.

Example 1

In this particular 'case' of a young, unmarried Turkish woman, the counsellor was criticised by her colleagues for insufficient and brash counselling. The young client had left after only two days (a weekend), going back to her parents, with the consent of the counsellor. Some weeks later, in an evaluation session, I used this case as an example of how interpretation schemes or scenarios are used in counselling and how they can stand in the way of understanding (for a full analysis of this 'case', see Bulcaen and Blommaert 1999). The counsellor was quite outdone by this criticism because she had had a good rapport with the client.

The scenarios were also at the heart of the discussion between the counsellors. In her file, the counsellor had categorised the client as 'a recognizable story about cultural contradiction': the client was seen as a westernised girl who came into conflict with the traditional values of her parents, especially on the issues of education and freedom. This is of course a dominant picture of migrants' children, with many dramatic and culturalist connotations. The frame of the client, however, was rather different. At one time during the intake she states, in answer to the counsellor's explicit categorisation: '*but we are muslim people, aren't we ... I am very strong in my religion. I pray. I read the Quran*', adding that her family members do not behave like Muslims should. For the client there was no question of cultural opposition but her voice lost out against the interpretation of the counsellor, as can be seen in the remainder of the intake and the 'robust story' of the file report. The client's frame certainly does explain better the quick solution because during the weekend she had managed to engage neighbours and an imam in order to call her parents to order. The colleagues of the counsellor, however, had only read her file report and naturally wondered whether it was advisable to return back so soon.

The counsellor's answer to the challenge by her colleagues consisted of a number of contextualisations: (1) The client's family system (e.g. pressure in migrant communities to keep domestic problems private and to reconcile families as quickly as possible); (2) The client's psychological disposition (e.g. dynamic, optimistic, even a little naïve); (3) Institutional reality (e.g. work load, the weekend); (4) Institutional/professional activity (e.g. not overriding the wishes of the client, even if they might be unrealistic and problematic). In a combination of (2) and (4) the counsellor stated that the client was not in the right frame of mind to be subject to extensive counselling. Through this negotiation of different contextualisations the counsellor managed to convince her colleagues. The 'problematic case' was rendered into a 'recognisable' and thus 'acceptable' one in terms of institutional procedures and realities.

When at the later evaluative session I pointed to the mismatch between the frames of the client and the counsellor, the counsellor reproached herself for not seeing the mismatch. She repeated the negotiative effort described above, and concluded with above-mentioned adhortations like 'we shouldn't categorise so quickly' and 'we have to be aware of our power in interpretation'. Her reflection did not, however, feed back into a review of the counselling strategy and interview and report techniques. When the client called some months later to say that her situation was much better by then, the counsellor's reaction was a combination of perseverance in the above-described cultural scenario (e.g. 'She's going to experience a lot of difficulties in the near future') and of an acceptance of the client's frame (e.g. 'She's strong, she can influence the family system').

3.2 Asymmetries of contextualisation

From social-psychological studies of attribution and accountability practices, we know that the behaviour of the self/in-group gets treated differently than that of an other/out-group. One general distinction is that representations of self/in-group behaviour are more contextualised with the effect of being excused and averting blame.

Attribution and accountability practices abound in social work discourse because the constant evaluation of past and recent actions, thoughts and feelings is the necessary, intermediate step between narrating/listening and advice-giving. This constant evaluation takes place at all levels of interaction, and it is also promoted as a learning strategy for clients. A crucial level is that of the reproduction by the provider of the client's story, in written (the client's file) or oral (in team meetings) form. At this level, evaluation in the form of little, routinised scenarios that categorise the client (such as 'a non-assertive woman of low intelligence', 'settles herself in the victim position', 'a clear case of a second-generation migrant who falls between traditional and western cultures') prestructures the reproduction. But evaluation is also the aim of the reproduction, after which counselling strategies and advice scenarios are developed.

Input for evaluation is not restricted to the reproduction of the client's story but also comes from the report of the interaction between the client and the provider, and from the report of the client interacting with the other clients in the institution. This input is explicitly looked after: the observation of clients is part of a counsellor's job and is needed for additional input and to triangulate the client's story. From this conception by counsellors and from what I observed one can deduct that this form of input is almost exclusively aimed at constructing a picture of the psychological and moral dispositions of a client. This input from observation can also be gathered by colleague-counsellors who are not directly involved with a certain client. In practice the reproduction by these colleague-counsellors usually takes the form of anecdotes that are attached to the original counsellor's tale. This corroborative interaction among counsellors sometimes takes the form of a chaotic and dynamic spiral denouncing of a client. Only rarely are anecdotes invoked to challenge the original counsellor's tale.

Analyses of social work discourse (e.g. Hall et al. 1997) have pointed at several problematic aspects of these reproduction and evaluation practices, such as the categorisation that takes place, the construction of robust stories, the foregrounding of the voice of the counsellor, the practice of recontextualising a client's behaviour within an institution as a client's general, individual and context-independent moral disposition. I have detected all these problematic aspects in my data and discussed them with counsellors. The point I want to make here is that counsellors themselves actively negotiate the reproduction of stories and observations. They put in little assessments and evaluations and they frame some details of a story into well-known scenarios and theoretical descriptions, as can be seen in Example 2.

Example 2

The client is an unmarried young woman who ran away from home, and is exhausted from lack of sleep and an interrogation by the police. She is not very fluent in Dutch. She has difficulty in telling a well-structured narrative and is vague about some crucial incidents. This is fairly normal and understandable behaviour for clients during an intake, but the counsellor in this case does not take this into account. She also does not notice the client's lack of proficiency in Dutch. Although the intake is formally in order (all the questions and information that belong to this speech genre get discussed), the counsellor's attitude lacks emotional bonding and consideration. She is also interrupted by phone calls at very emotional moments. After the short intake she consults with colleagues. In this conversation, which takes as long as the intake, the issue of contacting the client's parents is discussed and the following remark is made by the counsellor about her contacts with the policewoman ('X' in the extract) who brought the client to the centre:

[From the transcription of the interaction with colleagues]

mhm . yes . I I should have really . gone into it at that moment . when
. X . dropped her off here . I asked her . has there been contact with
the parents . no but we are certainly going to do that tomorrow ... but

yes . I had . her here … made her enter . and and . I haven't gone into it . I should have . said . why can't it happen now . because when that father .. but it's too late for that now

We see here how a counsellor reflects upon her behaviour. She asks herself why she didn't pay enough attention to the matter of contacting the client's parents, which is a policy of this particular shelter (a policy considered all the more necessary for young, unmarried Muslim women). She asks herself why she did not apply the fairly usual strategy of exhausting the knowledge and abilities of other professionals involved in the 'case'. Then she adds 'but yes . I had . her here … made her enter', the full meaning of which reads like: 'the client looked exhausted and forelorn so it was important to take her into the house quickly and have her rest, that was not the moment to discuss details of her story' (this meaning is corroborated by later accounts by the counsellor). This is an instance of an exonerating contextualisation in which one professional activity is selected over another, and thus foregrounded in the account (my alternative suggestion to the counsellor was to combine the two activities by letting the client in and taking the policewoman apart for a moment). The scenario of 'an exhausted woman' is used to legitimate that selection. In contrast, however, that scenario is not used to contextualise the words of the client during the intake. Her somewhat uncommunicative behaviour and her narrative difficulties are used to slant her as being economical with the truth and her share in the family conflict. Linguistic misunderstandings and failures are not sought in the communication process and its context, but in the client's character or initial, strategic intentions.

The next day the client is called by the police to have a meeting with her parents at the police station. After that conversation she goes home. In team meetings later that day and that week surprise was expressed at this quick 'solution'. The counsellor repeats the above contextualisations and adds that the intake took place during a very busy moment. The quick initiative of the police is also mentioned – it is again a reason to 'slant' the image of the client: she was apparently not very firm in her decision to break with her family. These last, usual contextualisations were accepted by the team. They expressed them again when I later criticised the interview strategy of the counsellor. My arguments and alternative suggestions were subordinated to the institutional realities of time pressure and work load.

Example 2 is just one example from my data that shows how in reports of interviews the action of a client is usually contextualised within her individual psychology (the way she answers and acts is thus indicative of her problems), while that of the counsellor is more contextualised within the identity of the profession (the presentation of information and questions is guided by professional methods and experience) and the institution (e.g. time pressure, work load, group atmosphere). We find similar practices in Example 1 and the case mentioned in Example 2 is one where contextualisations in terms of institutional realities abound in accounts at all levels, and prior to that the construction of them was even an obstacle to effective counselling. This is the assymetry in attribution that I described at the beginning of this section. Counsellors have a battery of exonerating contextualisation practices at their disposal, and their use of them is usually not challenged by colleagues.

However, during consultations among counsellors, clients' behaviour does sometimes get contextualised into the institutional setting (e.g. 'She's having difficulties coping with the children in this strange setting', 'She is being excluded from the client group because she doesn't speak the language or has "strange" habits') but this always takes the form of little informal, ad hoc and routinised formulations at the end of a discussion. Contextualising scenarios are never structurally integrated into the interpretation and evaluation of a 'case'.

Example 3

The following is an extract from a client's file in which the challenging expert voice of a psychiatrist is reproduced in such a way as to ward off the challenge [X replaces the name of the client]:

> With regard to the considerations of the personel and other clients about the behavior of X (isolates herself from the group, reacts sometimes in an exaggerated, nervous and hysterical way, sits at times in her room with a kitchen knife, etc., reacts anxiously), the psychiatrist has found nothing abnormal! At the moment of the interview C was very calm and reasonable.

The psychiatrist in this case is working in a welfare centre that is linked organisationally to the shelter, so he has a lot of experience in interviewing clients of refugee homes and is appreciated for that by the counsellors. His conclusion, which is an answer to the counsellor's questions about the mental state of the client, is overshadowed by the many and apparently inexhaustible 'considerations' of in-house participants that precede the head phrase, as well as by the ones that have already been mentioned in the file. After this particular instance of discourse representation follows a suggestive qualification in the second sentence of the context of the psychiatrist's interview that throws doubt on its objectivity and legitimacy, as compared to the wealth of evidence that the counsellors have collected. A somewhat ironic but telling detail in this extract is how the voices of other clients receive legitimation as expert witnesses.

In subsequent team meetings this reproduction practice is continued but with more vigour and detail. The assessment of the counsellor is corroborated by her colleagues. The challenging voice of the cultural broker, who had had separate conversations with the client and assessed her differently, is also marginalised in the wealth of anecdotal material about the chaotic and hysteric behaviour of the client. One obvious question – why the client should be so 'calm and reasonable' during interviews with the psychiatrist and the cultural broker – is not raised: it was just assumed that unexplainable mood swings are characteristic for this category of clients. Moreover, in this whole 'case' the voice of the client is seriously neglected as she is very quickly categorised as 'a hysterical, non-intelligent girl who is not free of guilt herself' and 'a migrant child who cannot take care of herself'. All the information that the counsellors receive – from the client, other clients, other professionals – is framed into these scenarios. The one important piece of information, given by the client and confirmed by a professional who knows the family, namely that her brother is the source of her anxieties, does not easily fit into these scenarios and gets obscured and ultimately lost. The 'solution' process is then totally geared towards quickly reconciling the girl with her family, without changing anything about the basic interaction and trust problem within the client's family system.

The point here is that counsellors in this case perform all kinds of contextualisation with relation to the discourses of the client, themselves and other experts. Evaluative scenarios and unquestioned observations contextualise the client within her psychological and moral dispositions, and prestructure the entextualisation of other, challenging voices. It is very difficult to 'break open' these frames and the contextualisation practices that go with them.

3.3 Cross-cultural differences

I have already mentioned that it is part of the intake routine to discuss the institution in terms of its rules and the agreement to them that the client has to display. Explanations of regulations are accompanied by a discussion of what the counsellors can do for clients and of what institutional life looks and feels like. A frequently cited line is: 'It can at times become difficult to live together with strangers in this strange place, but you should remember that you all have similar problems, so you can draw strength from being in a group.' This form of topicalisation of institutional context is aimed at maintaining the counsellor(s)-client(s) network and bond.

The data in my research clearly show that this part of the intake and subsequent conversations is more elaborate in intercultural counselling sessions. Independent of whether an interpreter was present or not, the institutional procedures and realities (e.g. racism) are extensively explained to immigrant women. Counsellors claim that they need to do this because of linguistic and cultural differences. They also refer to the fact that migrant women are usually not acquainted with welfare institutions. But they are also influenced by their own belief that there are many conflicts with migrant clients over regulations. This is a distorted belief because, due to language problems and intercultural differences, conflicts with migrant clients over regulations are less sorted out than with non-migrant clients, while the sorting out of conflicts is perceived as an important activity that reflects well on the moral disposition of the client.

What I want to put forward here is that these elaborate explanations also serve to maintain the counsellor-client bond by referring to the possible occurence of intercultural conflicts that might arise during the client's stay in the shelter. Topicalisation of institutional context is here part of a prevention strategy.

Example 4

In this case there is a very good understanding between the client and the counsellor. The client is very talkative and committed. In the second part of the long intake about half an hour is spent on explaining regulations and realities in the shelter. The counsellor makes the following evaluative comments about the institutional context – I quote from a paraphrased transcription:

> (1) It is the intention that you rest this first week .. although here .. too many children .. [the counsellor starts counting the children] .. this first week very little will be asked of you

(2) It's a bad group at the moment . it is just not workable at the moment . but yes I'm not going to ... despite all our efforts there are many conflicts in the group [to which the client replies that she is used to living together with others and handling conflicts]

(3) During group meetings some long-standing conflicts . we emphasise more strongly what it is not allowed for instance racism is not possible here . it is tolerated from nobody [counsellor raises her voice] . first a warning and then expulsion . intolerance is not accepted ... where am I in my explanation?

(4) The women break the regulations . they have gone out more than one time . they've been collectively warned . we are not a hotel . we don't have hard evidence

(5) This group is not an exemplary group to come into . the children shouldn't be left alone

(6) [The complaints of one particular client over the daily fee are mentioned and ridiculed]

(7) that was it . welcome to the shelter . I hope that you can find your place . it's not always easy to live together with others in a group

We have here a set of various topicalisations. One (7) is vague and a matter of the routine mentioned above; others are more concrete and informative (1, 3). What is special in this intake is that the counsellor breaks some professional rules: she talks negatively about other clients (in 6) and the group of clients (in 2, 4, 5). The client, however, takes it in good humour and doesn't get biased. Lastly, there is the emphasis on the anti-racist policy of the shelter (in 3). The good rapport between the client and the counsellor, as well as the reflexive and 'wise' stance of the client (see 2), partly account for the transgressions of the counsellor – and it must be said the whole team of counsellors was very annoyed at the erratic behaviour of the inmate group. But there is also some intercultural apprehension, evidenced by the elaborate and high-voiced turn in (3), but also by the fact that before the client's entry the counsellor had warned, orally and verbally, all inmates not to exclude or racially discriminate the client.

Exclusion and racism are all too common experiences for immigrant women in shelters for battered or homeless women. Despite having an anti-racist regulation, welfare institutions in Belgium lack anti-racist awareness and strategies. A midway solution lies in a 'prevention policy' which involves explicitly discussing the issue with an incoming migrant client so that she can brace herself for potential conflicts. Counsellors are aware that in this way they put the onus on the victim, but don't really have other explicit strategies for preventing and countering racist incidents. The client in this case takes the 'prevention policy' and transgressions in good humour, but in other conversations I have observed how these negative topicalisations of institutional context prejudge a migrant client in her attitude towards other inmates. They also match well with migrants' general intercultural anxiety about western individuals and institutions.

4 Conclusion

I hope to have given sufficient proof of the constitutive nature of contextualisations in social work discourse and of the reflexive awareness that counsellors display. Within this perspective, some taken-for-granted, self-evident critical stances of institutional analysis need to be reviewed. For instance, most topicalisations of institutional context in social work discourse concern the power that a provider has over the client, so it is wrong to start with a suspicious and critical stance regarding the discourse that we analyse and name 'asymmetrical discourse', without taking into account these reflexive moments of participants.

Methodologically, I wish to stress the importance of observing, through ethnographic research, the chain of entextualisation processes within an institution so as to capture the workings of topicalisations of institutional context. At the ethical level, and on the issue of responsibility, the researcher should take note of and observe the 'naturally occurring' reflexivity of counsellors as it forms a constitutive aspect of professionalism and as a possible ally but also as an impediment in the research.

Because of the action-oriented nature of my research project, which included many evaluative sessions with the counsellors and myself, I was able to experience how these different forms of contextualisation, especially the topicalisation of institutional context, can play an exonerating role, despite the much lauded aspects of reflexivity. We must not limit ourselves to using this intrinsic reflexivity of social work discourse in order to align social workers and managers with the 'need' for linguistic analysis. Discussion of context by participants should be studied in its own right because (1) it is an integral, constitutive part of institutional discourse, and (2) context can be negotiated in ways that contradict the purpose of reflexivity, much avowed by scholars and social work managers, i.e. to improve professional activity and relations with clients.

Notes

1   I wish to thank Jan Blommaert, Teresa Carbó and Jan-Ola Östman for their comments on a first version of this study. The study was first presented at the sixth International Pragmatics Conference in Reims, 19–24 July 1998, in a panel on Institutional Discourse, organised by Srikant Sarangi and Stef Slembrouck, and I have benefited from the panel comments made by Charles Briggs.

2   The original Dutch name was: 'Begeleiding van migrantenvrouwen en – meisjes in centra voor residentieel welzijnswerk' (VFIK Project 307). I collaborated with Jan Blommaert (coordinator of the project), Fadime Köse (Turkish interpreter) and Latifa Sadik (Moroccan Arabic and Berber interpreter). I myself, as a man and researcher, was not present at client-provider interaction moments, and in fact almost never saw clients. It was my collaborators Fadime Köse and Latifa Sadik who, in the course of their work as interpreters and cultural brokers, recorded and collected data. They acted as participant observers, but their first job was to assist counsellors and clients with translation and cultural explanation. Consequently, most recorded interaction is triadic (Wadensjö 1998) because an interpreter is present. The languages involved were Dutch, Turkish, Moroccan Arabic, French and English. I was present, as a participant observer, at interaction moments between providers themselves, such as team meetings. Some special team meetings were organised in order to discuss the research project and my analyses of the data. The outcome of the project was an accessible report (Bulcaen and Blommaert 1997), individual and group evaluative and discussion sessions, and a symposium. Following on from the project, I have been involved, for some four years, in follow-up evaluative sessions of intercultural counselling, as well as in meetings aimed at structural changes.

3   These institutions are, in order of dominance in the data: (1) a crisis centre for homeless people, where the mixed-gender clientele can stay for up to three weeks; (2) a feminist refugee home for battered women that has a secret address where women can stay for up to three months; (3) the 'female' wing of a shelter for homeless people, where women can stay as long as six months; and (4) a shelter for battered or homeless women that is located some 20 kms from the city where clients can stay for up to six months. The last two centers are of Catholic inspiration but this has no consequences for the clientele. All shelters accommodate the children of clients. I identified the four institutions because they have distinct regulations, histories, practices and principles which are frequently invoked in the metadiscursive communication with other institutions and persons, such as myself.

4   Another important aspect is that there is no specific paramedical training for psychosocial counselling. The counsellors I observed had very different backgrounds.

5   I was able to collect substantial data about the counselling of some 56
    women, most of whom were Turkish; others were of Moroccan, African
    or East-European identity. Before collecting the data the consent of clients
    and counsellors was continually asked. Only two women refused their
    conversations to be recorded. In all, the data included approximately 300
    hours of audio-taped conversations, some 240 participant observation
    reports and numerous photocopies of documents from the clients' files.
    Some 10 conversations were transcribed. According to the specifications
    of the research contract, the data were destroyed once the research report
    was finished. I was allowed to use further the bits of transcription and data
    that I cited in the research report (Bulcaen and Blommaert 1997). The
    result, however, is that I cannot present the reader with elaborate extracts
    of transcription.

References

Bauman, R. and Briggs, C. (1990) Poetics and performance as critical perspectives
on language and social life. *Annual Review of Anthropology* 19: 59–88.

Böszörményi-Nagy, I. (1987). *Foundations of Contextual Therapy: Collected
Papers of Ivan Boszormenyi-Nagy, MD*. New York: Brunner/Mazel.

Bulcaen, C. and Blommaert, J. (1997) *Begeleiding van migrantenvrouwen en
-meisjes in centra voor residentieel welzijnswerk. VFIK Project 307. Ein-
drapport.* Antwerpen: IPrA Research Center.

Bulcaen, C. and Blommaert, J. (1999) De constructie van 'klassieke gevallen': case
management in de interculturele hulpverlening. In F. Glastra (ed.) *Organisaties
en diversiteit: Naar een contextuele benadering van intercultureel management*
139–158. Utrecht: Lemma.

Gunnarsson, B.-L., Linell, P. and Nordberg, B. (eds) (1997) *The Construction of
Professional Discourse*. London: Longman.

Hall, C., Sarangi, S. and Slembrouck, S. (1997) Moral construction in social
work discourse. In Gunnarsson et al. (eds) *The Construction of Professional
Discourse* 265–291. London: Longman.

Linell, P. and Sarangi, S. (eds) (1998) *Discourse Across Professional Boundaries*.
Special Issue of *Text* 18(2): 143–315.

McNamee, S. and Gergen, K. J. (eds) (1992) *Therapy as Social Construction*.
London: Sage.

Marková, I. and Foppa, K. (eds) (1991) *Asymmetries in Dialogue*. Herfortshire:
Harvester Wheatsheaf.

Silverstein, M. and Urban, G. (eds) (1996) *Natural Histories of Discourse*. Chicago,
IL: University of Chicago Press.

Wadensjö, C. (1998) *Interpreting as Interaction*. London: Longman.

Chris Bulcaen is curriculum manager for the programme in Linguistics and Literature at Ghent University, Belgium. He holds a master in African Languages and Literature (Universiteit Gent) and an MA in Cultural Studies (Lancaster University).

Part III
Responsibility relations in the media

Political interviews and responsibility: A case study of its interactional organisation

Anita Fetzer

1 Introduction

Political interviews are investigated in a number of analytic frameworks, which, from an interdisciplinary perspective, are not mutually exclusive but rather supplementary. While the conversation-analytic approach (Clayman and Heritage 2002; Greatbatch 1998) focuses primarily on the interactional organisation and reconstruction of a communicative event thus highlighting the fact that a genre does not exist in isolation but is reconstructed in and through the process of communication, pragmatics (Fetzer 2000; Jucker 1986; Wilson 1990) and critical discourse analysis (Fairclough and Fairclough 2012) investigate the specific functions of language with regard to language production and language comprehension. Pragmatics examines the dichotomy between what is said and what is meant by focussing on genre-specific strategies, such as evasiveness, indirectness or reformulation, and critical discourse analysis explicitly accounts for the interdependencies between discourse and social context, which are further differentiated in a socio-semiotic framework accommodating verbal and nonverbal means of communication (Bell 1977). The social psychology paradigm (Bull 2003) investigates political equivocation.

Conversation analysis has been a prominent research paradigm for the investigation of political interviews. Here, turn taking is assigned the status of an organising principle, to which interactional and institutional roles are anchored. In the frame of reference, a political interview is defined by the context-sensitive employment of the turn-taking system, viz. the coparticipant-specific use of the adjacency pair question-answer: the interviewer (IR) employs the initiating format and asks questions, and the interviewee (IE) employs the responsive format and answers questions. A political interview is not only interactionally organised on the micro (or local) level but also on the more remote level of genre with its constitutive opening, closing and topical-sequence sections. Thus, in order to interactionally organise the genre of a political interview in a felicitous manner, the IR and IE need to employ the coparticipant-specific first, respectively second, part of the adjacency pair question-answer. Or, to adapt the conversational-contract outlook on communication, the IR has the exclusive right to employ the initiating format and thus may ask a question or utter a greeting, while the IE has the obligation to answer the question or respond to the greeting. Should the IR refrain from asking questions,[1] the interactional organisation of a political interview is infelicitous. The IE's obligation to answer a question does not constitute such a strong local requirement in spite of the fact that s/he has the genre-specific obligation to answer the question. This is due to the fact that the obligation can be postponed by the initiation of a clarification sequence, for instance a local question-question sequence. But are question-answer sequences and coparticipants' rights and obligations sufficient conditions for an examination of the interactional organisation of responsibility in political interviews?

In sociopragmatics, the first and second parts of the adjacency pair question-answer are not synonymous with the commonsense view of a question as a means of seeking information and the commonsense view of an answer as a means of providing information. Instead, questions and answers are employed strategically as they may fulfil a number of communicative functions in discourse. In a political interview, for instance, a wh-question[2] can be employed to elicit unknown information by saying

(1)   IR   What figure?

(2)   IR   Who comes first for you, the farmer or the consumer?

In (1), the IR requests the IE to provide specific information which may have been explicated in the preceding linguistic context or which may have been presupposed. In that setting, the IR requests the IE to spell out specific information in order to comment on it, elaborate on it and continue with a topical sequence the information is a constitutive part of. The unknown information requested in (2) does not need to be spelt out as the addressee is requested to name one of the two alternatives, viz. the farmer or the consumer, which is to be assigned the status of new information in order to be commented on.

The first part of the adjacency pair question-answer can also be employed to request the addressee to carry out a specific communicative act, for example the ratification of an other-reformulation by agreeing or disagreeing with it, as is the case in (3):

(3)   IR   Is this a commitment then?

Unlike the fairly clear-cut examples discussed above, in which the IE is requested to provide very specific information, the IR's employment of the first part of the adjacency pair question-answer in the following example

(4)   IR   Can you actually think of other alternatives?

does not generally have the communicative function of eliciting unknown information about the IE's ability to think of other alternatives. Instead, the IE is requested to provide one or more solutions to a specific problem. For these reasons, the employment of the first part of the adjacency pair question-answer in a political-interview setting requires further specifications: not only does the employment of the first part assign the IR the right to elicit unknown information, but it also puts constraints on the IE's answer which, in order to be appropriate, should consist of elaborate comments on some state of affair. Furthermore, by employing the initiating format, the IR may not only initiate specific discourse topics and elaborate on them, but s/he may also close them. But for whom does the IE provide the requested information, comments and opinions: for the IR, the audience, or for both of them?

In sociopragmatics, coparticipants perform communicative acts in an intentional and strategic manner by intending their communicative act to count as a communicative act with a particular force. In speech act theory, speech acts are not only performed intentionally and strategically, but also sincerely (Austin 1980; Searle 1969). If the sincerity condition is adapted to a dialogue frame of reference, a coparticipant's communicative intention is meant as uttered and interpreted as meant (Fetzer 2002b). While sincerity is anchored to an individual coparticipant and to their performance of a communicative act, responsibility is anchored to the set of coparticipants, in general to speaker and hearer, and to social and linguistic contexts. For this reason, responsibility is assigned a bridging function between individual coparticipants and their individual communicative intentions on the one hand, and their collective communicative intention to interactionally organise a communicative project (Linell 1998) or communicative genre (Luckmann 1995) on the other. Against this background, a conception of responsibility in discourse cannot ignore the perlocutionary effects of a communicative act regarding coparticipants, genre and social and linguistic contexts. But what consequences does this have for the examination of the examples analysed above?

In a speech-act-theoretic frame of reference, IR and IE perform different kinds of speech acts, such as requesting information, stating opinions or providing information. Since an IR requests an IE to provide specific information, it is generally assumed that the IE provides the information for the IR. But is that really the case? Does a political interview consist of an IR and an IE exchanging speech acts? If a political interview is investigated with regard to language production and language comprehension, then it does consist of an IR, who produces speech acts, and an IE, who interprets speech acts. However, there is more to the interactional organisation of a political interview than the constitutive parts of IR, IE and speech acts. Firstly, the ratified coparticipants of a political interview do not only consist of the actual language producers of IR and IE, but also of the audience,[3] in front of whom and for whom the political interview is performed (Fetzer 2006). Secondly, an investigation of natural language communication needs to adopt both micro (or bottom-up) and macro (or top-down) perspectives. This means that the individual speech acts should not be investigated in isolation but rather as constitutive parts of the whole interview. For this reason, the examination of single speech acts needs to account for the questions of whether the coparticipants' communicative contributions are coherent, and of whether the coparticipants act in accordance with the contextual constraints and requirements of the genre. But what are the actual constraints and requirements for the interactional organisation of responsibility in a political interview?

In the following, the interactional organisation of responsibility in the genre of a political interview is examined. The section, responsibility in context, examines the concept of responsibility in sociopragmatics, where it is assigned a presuppositional status indexing both the felicity conditions of dialogue and the coparticipants' rights and obligations, and it adapts the results obtained to the status of responsibility in political interviews. In order to account for the interactional organisation of responsibility, the dialogue act of a plus/minus-validity claim and the macro validity claim of a political interview are introduced. Section 3 presents a case study of how responsibility is interactionally organised in the genre and media event of a political interview. Special attention is given to the distribution and communicative functions of explicit and implicit references to the media frame, such as the TV programme and the institutional roles of IR, IE and audience, which index responsibility in that context.

2 Responsibility in context

In the research paradigms of speech act theory (Austin 1980; Searle 1969), sociopragmatics (Sarangi and Slembrouck 1996) and ethnomethodology (Garfinkel 1994), a coparticipant is assigned the status of a rational agent, who performs actions in an intentional manner. This is reflected in the ethnomethodological concept of accountability of social action, according to which coparticipants not only perform social actions but are also able to account for their actions as they know, at some level, what they say and what they mean by their utterances. The premise of accountability of social action and of one of its subsets, communicative action, is also implicit in Recanati's availability principle, which is based 'on a specific cognitive hypothesis, according to which what is said is consciously accessible' (Recanati 1989: 328). Following Sbisà (2002), the satisfaction of felicity conditions is assumed by default and, for this reason, sincerity and accountability are assumed to obtain in discourse. However, it is not only speakers who perform communicative acts intentionally but also hearers who interpret their coparticipants' contributions in an intentional manner (Grimshaw 1980). Here, the premise of rationality manifests itself on the micro level in meaningful and purposeful production and interpretation of local meaning.

The premise of intentionality of communicative action is further refined in speech act theory's felicity condition which indexes the domain of sincerity (Searle 1969). The primarily micro-oriented perspective of speech act theory has been adapted to the contextual constraints and requirements of the macro domain (Fetzer 2000; Van Dijk 1981) and to genre (Östman 1999), where sincerity is anchored to individual coparticipants and to their performance of communicative acts in context (Fetzer 2002a). Unlike felicity-condition based sincerity, responsibility is anchored to both illocution and perlocutionary effects (Mühlhäusler and Harré 1990), and is, for this reason, a dialogical notion par excellence feeding on the set of ratified coparticipants, communicative action, genre, and social and linguistic contexts. Analogously to sincerity, responsibility is assigned the status of a default and therefore is also assumed to obtain in discourse. In a political interview, for instance, an IR may perform the communicative act of requesting an IE to provide information about their hairdresser or furniture in a sincere manner as the IR may have a genuine interest in the topics. A responsible IR, however, will not perform the requests unless they are relevant to a political question which is being discussed. Against this background, the interactional organisation of responsibility can no longer be based on the coparticipant- and genre-specific employment of the turn-taking system and on the adjacency pair question-answer only, but rather needs to accommodate further discursive and contextual constraints and requirements, which are examined in the following.

2.1 Responsibility in political interviews

The conversation-analytic approach to the interactional organisation of a political interview has not only investigated the context-sensitive constraints and requirements of the turn-taking system but has also interpreted them with regard to the interactional organisation of neutralism (Clayman 1992; Greatbatch 1998), which has been extended to the domains of genre-specific style and discourse topic. In the extended frame of reference neutrality is assigned the status of an ideology (Fetzer 1999). So, are the concepts of neutralism and responsibility interrelated? From a bottom-up perspective, neutralism and responsibility are reconstructed in and through the process of communication. While a neutral IR employs a neutral discursive style, asks neutral questions in order to elicit party-political opinions and perspectives, a responsible IR will not only act in accordance with the genre's ideology of neutralism but also take into consideration the audience's information wants and the perlocutionary effects of a communicative act. Against this background, a follow-up question is not interpreted as an act of intrusion, viz. a face-threatening act (Brown and Levinson 1987) as it would be in an ordinary face-to-face interaction, but rather is looked upon as a strategic means to achieve yet more neutrality by unbiasing a non-neutral politician. The refined interpretation of a follow-up question is reflected in the fact that it is frequently supplemented by explicit references to the media frame and its presuppositions, such as the audience's information wants, and to other possible perlocutionary effects thus signifying the IR's responsible attitudes towards their communicative act and towards their fellow coparticipants (Fetzer 2006).

Blum-Kulka (1983) has specified the context-sensitive employment of the turn-taking system with regard to the leitmotif of a clear-cut division of labour. This is not only reflected in the clear-cut rights and obligations of IR and IE, but also in the institutional roles' clear-cut domains of society: the IR is a representative of the domain of mass-media, the IE represents the domain of party politics and the audience represents the general public. Furthermore, it is reflected in the clear-cut selection of discourse topics, for an IR does not select a discourse topic at random by initiating a topical sequence on, for instance, hairdressers, furniture or hobbies. Instead, they restrict their selection to the public domains of party politics, government, institution and mass-media. And should there be references to so-called private domains, they tend to be accounted for and assigned public relevance, thus signifying the IR's responsible attitude towards the communicative act and towards the coparticipants. If Blum-Kulka's notion of clear-cut rights and obligations is adapted to the interactional organisation of responsibility in the genre of a political interview, the coparticipants are assigned clear-cut responsibilities regarding their fellow coparticipants and their communicative acts in context. While an IR is primarily responsible for the felicitous interactional organisation of a political interview regarding the contextual constraints and requirements of genre and media communication, an IE is primarily responsible for the successful communication of party-politics, institutional matters and governmental affairs. From a social-control viewpoint, the clear-cut division of labour puts an IR in a position to exercise control over an IE as it is the IR's responsibility to accept or challenge the IE's moves. Thus, the context-sensitive employment of the turn-taking system can function as a control mechanism as it assigns an IR the right to initiate discourse topics, to which an IE needs to respond. The response is controlled by the IR, who can accept the response as it is, or who can reject the response thus signifying that it has not been appropriate.

It is the responsive format which prevents an IE from directly asking a question in order to initiate a discourse topic. Instead, he needs to employ a presequence, in which he *asks permission* for the right to initiate a discourse topic, to comment on it or to close it, for instance, by saying[4]

(5)   IE   One moment. **Can I ask you one question?**

Through the indexical reference *one moment* and through his question, the IE requests the IR not to carry on with his intended topical sequence, thus signifying a halt in the flow of discourse. In the meantime he initiates a negotiation-of-validity sequence about the question of whether the IR's attitudes towards the content of his questions and towards his coparticipants have been in accordance with the dialogue principle of responsibility.

Another control mechanism with regard to gaining the floor and exercising social control is the coparticipant-specific employment of interruptions, which can fulfil a number of functions in communication, such as displaying alignment in overlaps, displaying surprise or initiating a clarification sequence (Tannen 1981). In a political-interview setting, an

IE's interruption is only acceptable if it initiates a clarification sequence in order to negotiate meaning. Should interruptions be intended to fulfil other functions, an IE may suffer some kind of verbal sanction, since IE-initiated interruptions are generally interpreted as an attempt to stop the introduction of a discourse topic or to terminate an elaboration sequence, which are IR's rights. And because of this, the IE is frequently summoned by the IR, who demonstrates his responsibility by employing a rather formal term of address on those occasions, such as title and last name, as is the case in (6):

(6)   IR   but that planning **Mister Prescott** would you seek…

To demonstrate his responsibility, the IR may also request the IE to adhere to the genre-specific rights and obligations, which represents one of the strongest verbal sanctions. In (7), the IR's explication of his right to ask a question in order to elaborate on a discourse topic (*I have the right to say*) is supported by the formal term of address of title and last name:

(7)   IR   no, **I have the right to say this is an interview** and I'm sure you
            will recognise it because you understand the nature of political
            interviews, **Mister Heseltine**, as well as I do

IR-initiated interruptions are generally looked upon as a corrective mechanism which signifies that the IE's response is inappropriate because of length as in (7), or clarity and relevance as in (6). For this reason, IR-initiated interruptions are intrinsically linked to the interactional organisation of responsibility which indexes the media-frame specific constraint of the audience's information wants and the genre's ideology of neutralism.

The research paradigms of conversation analysis, critical discourse analysis and sociopragmatics have contributed immensely to the investigation of the face-to-face interaction between IR and IE. However, the interactional organisation of responsibility cannot be based on the face-to-face interaction between IR and IE only, but also needs to accommodate the fact that a political interview is a public event in and through which a public discussion is presented to and for a public audience through printed and/or audio-visual media (Bell and Garret 1998; Clayman and Whalen 1988/89; Fairclough 1998; Fetzer and Weizman 2006; Heritage et al. 1988; Lauerbach and Fetzer 2007).

The following section introduces a sociopragmatic framework which accounts for the dynamics of natural-language communication and for multiple frame interactions. Special reference is given to the question of how responsibility is accounted for.

2.2 The dialogue act of a *plus/minus-validity claim*

Natural-language communication is a dynamic endeavour in which (minimally) two coparticipants cooperate and collaborate in order to negotiate and construct meaning in context. To account for the prerequisites of cooperation, collaboration and negotiation of meaning, dialogue is anchored to the Gricean *logic and conversation* and its overarching cooperative principle: 'Make your conversational contribution such as is required, at the stage at which it occurs, by the accepted purpose or direction of the talk exchange in which you are engaged' (Grice 1975: 45). To capture the dynamics of discourse and its inherent dyadic constellation, a conversational contribution is contextualised and defined by its constitutive references to context. The resulting dialogue act of a plus/minus-validity claim[5] is anchored to a tripartite system of objective, social and subjective worlds (Fetzer 2002a, 2002b), which are referred to in an explicit and implicit manner. The objective world is determined by the dichotomy of true/false, and its references can only be realised explicitly, such as *food is the essential emphasis*. Since the dialogue principle of responsibility is presupposed in discourse and its interactional organisation is generally done in an implicit manner by acting in accordance with the felicity conditions, the objective world is of no immediate relevance. The *subjective world* is determined by the premise of sincerity; that is, speaker's communicative intention meant as uttered and interpreted as meant. References to the subjective world are generally realised implicitly. Sincerity is a fundamental felicity condition and therefore is also a necessary condition for the interactional organisation of responsibility. The *social world* is determined by the paradigm of appropriateness and its references can be realised explicitly and implicitly, such as *I'm not asking you whether that leak did come from the treasury* or *this sounds quite plausible*. For this reason, it is of immediate relevance to the interactional organisation of responsibility. To be felicitous, a plus/minus-validity claim needs to contain references to the three worlds, and all of the references need to be ratified in discourse. As a consequence of that, implicit and explicit references to responsibility are also ratified.

In communication, coparticipants postulate, ratify and negotiate the communicative status of validity claims in context by accepting them and assigning them the status of a plus-validity claim, and by rejecting them and assigning them the status of a minus-validity claim. Communication is thus conceived of in a (minimally) three-move sequence, namely (1) a speaker postulates a validity claim in context, (2) the hearer ratifies the postulated claim through (3) an acceptance or through a rejection. In case of acceptance, s/he assigns the validity claim the status of a plus-validity claim and attributes it to the coparticipants' discourse common ground (Fetzer 2002a). In case of rejection, the validity claim is assigned the status of a minus-validity claim. Unlike the clear-cut three-move sequence of postulation, ratification and acceptance, a rejection initiates a negotiation-of-validity sequence, in which the non-accepted claims and non-accepted presuppositions are spelt out to be negotiated. Only after the status quo has been re-established, that is after an agreement about what claim or presupposition is accepted and what claim or presupposition is not accepted has been reached, felicitous communication is possible. But what relevance does the validity-claim framework have for the interactional organisation of responsibility?

In dialogue, responsibility represents a fundamental dialogue principle which has been assigned a presuppositional status. Adapting Sbisà's claim that the satisfaction of felicity conditions is assumed by default (Sbisà 2002) to a dialogue framework, the dialogue principle of responsibility is also assumed by default. Analogously to speech act theory's felicity conditions, dialogue principles are generally not made explicit when entering a conversation by saying for instance *what I am saying now is meant sincerely and of course I do take responsibility for my words and actions*. Rather, their validity is presupposed to obtain. So, if coparticipants act in accordance with the felicity conditions of dialogue, they assign the dialogue principle of responsibility the status of a plus-validity claim and attribute it to their discourse common ground. For this reason, responsibility does not need to be mentioned any further. An explicit reference to responsibility in dialogue signifies that the fundamental dialogue principle is no longer assumed to obtain by default and for this reason has been assigned the status of a minus-validity claim which needs to be negotiated.

In the following, the macro validity claim of a political interview is introduced and examined with respect to the interactional organisation of responsibility.

2.3 The macro validity claim of a *political interview*

The dialogue act of a plus/minus-validity claim accounts for the micro domain from a bottom-up perspective. Because of its inherent dynamic structure, it can also account for the macro domain by adopting a top-down perspective. While the former systematises a validity claim's contextual references, the latter specifies the contextual references of a validity claim and assigns them the status of a macro validity claim's constraints.

A prototypical political interview represents a dyadic event, in which the communicative status of validity claims is negotiated. Adopting conversation-analytic terminology, a political interview is interactionally organised by the IR's and IE's postulation of validity claims, by their ratification through an acceptance or rejection, and by the negotiation of validity claims in context. Can the macro-validity-claim frame of reference provide us with more insights with respect to the interactional organisation of responsibility? If the investigation of a political interview is restricted to the face-to-face interaction between IR, IE and a face-to-face audience, the validity-claim outlook may refine some of the results obtained in the conversation-analytic and sociopragmatic paradigms by, e.g. systematising some of the contextual references. But a political interview does not only consist of the interactional organisation of the face-to-face interaction between IR and IE. Rather, the interactional organisation of the face-to-face interaction is at the same time an interactional organisation of a media event. For this reason, an extended frame of reference is required, which differentiates between the first-frame interaction between IR and IE, and an interaction between the first frame and the media frame, as is illustrated by Figure 1.

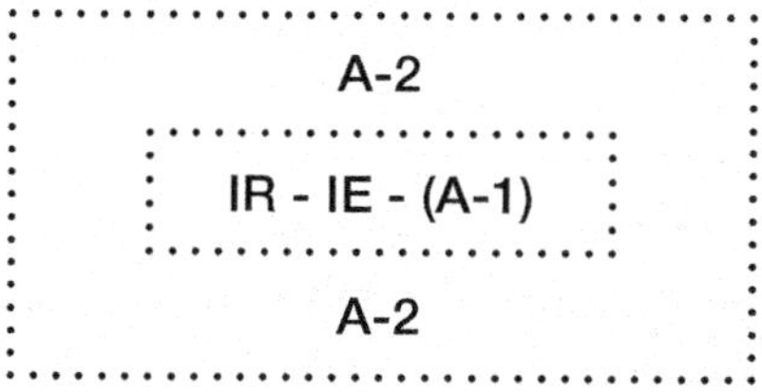

A-2

IR - IE - (A-1)

A-2

Figure 1

The negotiation of validity claims in a political interview is not only based on the first-frame coparticipants of IR, IE and a possible first-frame audience (A-1) and on their presuppositions, but also on the second-frame audience (A-2), metaphorically speaking, the audience at home in front of their television sets, radios, computers, newspapers or magazines, and on media-specific presuppositions, such as transmission, channel or medium. So how are the refined contextual constraints and requirements of a political interview accounted for in the framework of the macro validity claim of a political interview, and what specifications are required for the three worlds?

The objective world and its premise of truth do not require any specification because a true proposition is true in any context. For this reason, micro truth is true in macro contexts. The subjective-world premise of sincerity requires specification. Not only does a coparticipant's micro intention anchored to a micro validity claim need to be sincere, but their macro intention anchored to a macro validity claim also needs to be sincere. The premises of micro and macro sincerity are reflected in the coparticipants acting in accordance with the genre- and media-specific rights, obligations and responsibilities. The social world's premise of appropriateness requires specification with respect to the adjacency pair question-answer, i.e. the IR asks questions, which the IE answers. The audience does not have the right to employ the answer format but may have the right to ask questions, for instance in panel interviews. There is no self-selection with regard to the employment of the turn-taking system, but IR-selection. The social world requires further specification with respect to neutral face wants: there are constraints with regard to references to negative and positive face, such as avoidance of ingroup markers, e.g. *mate* or *buddy*, and avoidance of very formal politeness formulae, such as *would you mind if I asked you to answer my question* or *would you be so kind as to be more precise*.[6] The participation format requires specification insofar as all coparticipants are assigned a ratified status. The linguistic realisation and interpretation of the coparticipants' communicative intentions is also constrained by the genre's leitmotif of neutralism, namely rational and public debate. This is also reflected in the coparticipants' public and political information wants. Against this background, follow-up questions are generally not interpreted as acts of intrusion, but, as has been demonstrated above, as strategic devices to secure the discourse common ground between the first- and media-frame coparticipants.

The macro validity claim of a political interview is interactionally organised by the genre-specific negotiation of validity claims in context based on the fundamental pragmatic premises of cooperation and intentionality. From a bottom-up perspective, the dialogue act accommodates the premises by anchoring them to the coparticipants and to their communicative acts. It is at the locus of negotiating the communicative status of a validity claim, where the connectedness between the micro and macro domains manifests itself and where it needs to be accounted for. So, how is responsibility negotiated in the context of a political interview?

2.4 Negotiating responsibility in political interviews

Mundane everyday communication does not generally take place in front of an audience who is assigned the status of a ratified coparticipant (Goffman 1986; Levinson 1988), and who is obliged to ratify the validity claims, but not allowed to participate in the process of negotiating their communicative status. Moreover, the second-frame audience's ratification of the first-frame validity claims is a necessary condition for the macro validity claim of a political interview to be felicitous. Due to media-specific constraints, the second-frame audience is not in a position to directly negotiate the communicative status of validity claims with the first-frame coparticipants but may discuss them directly with other members. In general, the negotiation of validity claims requires the explication of one or more of their presuppositions. While presuppositions are explicated for the first-frame coparticipants in an ordinary face-to-face interaction, they are explicated for both the first- and second-frame coparticipants in a political interview thus guiding the audience in their process of inferring the IR's and IE's communicative intentions. The dual frame of reference is of importance for the non-acceptance of a validity claim. While a plus-validity claim is attributed to the coparticipants' discourse common ground, a minus-validity claim signifies a halt in the flow of discourse. From a sequential-organisation viewpoint, it initiates a negotiation-of-validity sequence, in which the appropriateness of the communicative act, the appropriateness of its linguistic realisation, and the validity of its presuppositions are at stake. For instance, the ratification of

(8)   IR   put bluntly you have something of a credibility problem

requires the reconstruction of the underlying validity claims and their pre-suppositions with regard to the questions of what communicative act is being performed (a request for information or a challenge), of what social and institutional positions the coparticipants are assigned to (politician or journalist; IR or IE), of what sequential status the claim has (initiating or responsive; part of the opening, closing or topical sequence), and of how explicit its linguistic realisation is. Only then is it possible to ratify the claims by assigning them the status of a plus- or a minus-validity claim.

As has already surfaced in the analysis of the dynamics of negotiating validity claims in context, the ratification of a validity claim is connected with its contextualisation. Should a coparticipant accept the claim as postulated, he accepts it by saying, for example,

(9)   IE   that's only natural isn't it

and thereby assign it the status of a plus-validity claim. Should he reject the claim, he will assign it the status of a minus-validity claim by saying, for instance,

(10) IE   well that's an unfair charge

A non-acceptance initiates a negotiation-of-validity sequence, in which the coparticipants explicate what is not being accepted, such as the appropriateness of the explicit realisation *credibility problem* or of the contextual reference *you*, that can be interpreted as expressing individual or collective reference. But do acceptances and non-acceptances only differ with regard to the initiation of a negotiation-of-validity sequence?

There is another crucial difference between an acceptance and a non-acceptance: the former does not only represent the acceptance of the linguistic realisation of the coparticipant's communicative intention, but also of the appropriateness of the communicative act, of its presuppositions and of the coparticipants' rights, obligations and responsibilities. The non-acceptance of a validity claim does not realise the rejection of the claim and of its presuppositions, but rather the non-acceptance of the appropriateness of the linguistic realisation and/or the non-acceptance of the communicative act's appropriateness, because, as a general rule, presuppositions need to be made explicit before it is possible to reject them (Harnish 1991). Naturally, this also holds for the concept of responsibility, which is generally done in and through the process of communication and therefore represented implicitly. In a negotiation-of-validity sequence, the concept of responsibility and its relevance to the 'current purpose of the exchange' (Grice 1975: 45) needs to be made explicit before it can be negotiated. The fact that presuppositions cannot be rejected unless they have been made explicit does not only hold for the micro domain, but also for the macro domain and its specified values. So how is responsibility referred to?

In an ordinary face-to-face communication, responsibility is anchored to the set of ratified coparticipants, to their communicative acts and to linguistic and social contexts. In a political-interview setting, responsibility does not only hold for the set of IR, IE, communicative action and linguistic and social contexts, but also for the first-frame set interacting with the media-frame. The extended domain of validity also holds for the presupposed discourse common ground, which does not only need to obtain for the first-frame interaction but also for the media-frame interaction.

Against this background, the media frame and its presuppositions are of crucial importance to the interactional organisation of responsibility. This is reflected in the IR's and IE's references to media-frame presuppositions *viewers* and *programme* in (11) and (12), which support the speaker's implicit challenges while signifying their responsibilities:

(11) IR   but I think **the viewers** will be very interested

(12) IE   I've agreed to come on **this programme** not to discuss these issues, to discuss important factors about ideas

In (11), the IR makes manifest his responsibility towards the second-frame audience and their information wants. That is, the IR himself might be satisfied with the IE's response but his responsibility towards the second-frame audience makes a further challenge necessary. Unlike the IR, the IE employs a reference to the media frame in a negative context *(not discuss these issues)* in (12) and signifies that the IR has performed an irresponsible communicative act by discussing topics which have not been agreed upon.

In the following negotiation-of-validity sequence, the communicative function of explicating presuppositions is further refined by the accommodation of a longer stretch of discourse:

(13) IR   .... you're saying sympathy action won't be permitted?
      IE   No. Well, you've got to distinguish the question of proof here. I mean ...
      IR   [How can they]
      IE   [Now what point] I made
      IR   except by asking the employer. And the employer says no no, don't worry about that dispute. We're a separate company. We're not going to be led by the nose by some ....
      IE   Well, in that case the court would have to decide whether that was a genuine view or whether it wasn't if ...

In (13), the IR reformulates the IE's contribution by saying *you're saying sympathy action won't be permitted* (line 1) and requests him to ratify the reformulation. The IE does not accept the reformulation, which is reflected in the negative operator *no* (line 2) and the negative discourse marker *well* (line 2). Instead, he recontextualises the reformulation by making explicit the presuppositions of sympathy action to both IR and second-frame audience, namely that sympathy action is not such a clear-cut matter at all since *you've got to distinguish the question of proof here* (line 2). Here, the pronoun *you* expresses generic meaning, which entails the second-frame audience, and therefore functions as a reference to the media frame. There is an instance of simultaneous talk (lines 3 and 4), which manifests the IE's attempt to interrupt the IR in order to close the discourse topic, which is, however, not successful. The IR does not accept the IE's recontextualisation and requests him to provide further evidence, viz. *how can they* (line 3), while continuing with his argumentation to secure the discourse common ground between the first- and the second-frame coparticipants in lines 5–7: *except by asking the employer. And the employer says no no, don't worry about that dispute. We're a separate company. We're not going to be led by the nose by some ....* Again, the IE recontextualises the IR's contribution by reframing the argumentation with an explicit reference to the institutional domain of legislation: *well in that case the court would have to decide* (lines 8–9).

Negotiating validity claims in political interviews is a rather complex endeavour and cannot be reduced to the analysis of the first-frame encounter, the actual interview, but requires the accommodation of interfacing first and second frames and of interfacing objective, subjective and social worlds. As a result of the dual orientation, the first-frame coparticipants do not only postulate their validity claims for their direct communication partners, but also, if not mainly, for the second-frame audience. For this reason, the first-frame coparticipants' main responsibilities are anchored to the interfaces of first and second frames. This is supported by the genre-specific employment of back-channel behaviour (Heritage 1985), third-turn receipts (Clayman 1992) and relevant nonverbal behaviour, such as gaze.

The following section examines linguistic evidence for the dual orientation of a political interview as communicative genre and media event, and gives particular attention to their impact on the interactional organisation of responsibility.

3 The linguistic representation of media references: A case study

In discourse studies, the contextual constraints and requirements of a communicative genre are assigned the status of maxims or guidelines. Since they do not have a normative status, they can be exploited in order to get in a conversational implicature and express pragmatic meaning which goes beyond the linguistic-surface meaning (Grice 1975; Levinson

1983). Yet is it possible to infringe on the maxims at any stage of an interview? Undoubtedly, there exist more marked and less marked political interviews.[7] While an unmarked interview adheres to the genre-specific constraints and requirements, a marked interview is defined by sequential deviation. It needs to be pointed out, however, that there cannot be complete deviation because the macro validity claim of a political interview is an interactionally organised event and can only be instantiated with an appropriate opening sequence, which, by definition, is both process and product of the genre-specific employment of social and linguistic codes. Naturally, the instantiation of the opening sequence needs to be anchored to the macro- and micro premise of sincerity. So how are political interviews instantiated, how are the media frame and its presuppositions represented linguistically and what relevance does this have for the interactional organisation of responsibility?

From a linguistic-representation viewpoint, references to the media frame can be represented in the explicit and implicit modes, such as

(14) IE   I don't want to give you or the green lobby groups who are watching **this programme** erm the message that it is simple

The IE explicates the mediated status of political interviews by indexing the media frame with *this programme*, thus implicating the ambivalent nature of the medium and its constraints on length, which do not allow the IE to be as explicit as he would like to be. This signifies the IE's responsible attitude towards both IR and some singled-out members of the second-frame audience, viz. *the green lobby groups*. Implicit references to the media frame are represented by generic terms indexing the public domain, such as *the public* or thanking the IE in the closing section. But are the coparticipants free to employ any mode of linguistic representation, or are there marked and unmarked instances?

In the following, references to the media frame are systematised with regard to their distribution and communicative function.

3.1 Media references in the opening section

In the political interviews investigated, the frequency of explicit references to the media frame TV and to its presuppositions, such as, audience or programme, is distinctively higher in the opening and closing sections than in the central or topical-sequence section of the encounter, and it is distinctively higher in the opening section of the political interview than in any other section. An unmarked political interview is thus defined by explicit and implicit media-frame references in the opening section, as illustrated by the following three examples:

(15) IR   Good afternoon and welcome to **on the record**. In **today's programme** mad cow disease and the minister of agriculture, John Gummer, argues his case that your beef is safe in his hands. Then Labour's answer to the poll tax. What is it? Would you like it? **On the record** puts the roof tax to the test. Put bluntly, you have something of a credibility problem.

In (15), the media frame is explicitly referred to in the opening section by *good afternoon and welcome to on the record* (line 1). Here, the second-frame audience is addressed explicitly, which is supported by the IR's direct gaze. Additionally, there are references to media-specific presuppositions, such as the programme-specific presupposition *on the record* (lines 1, 4) and the media presupposition *programme* (line 1).

In (16), the second-frame audience has already been referred to in the opening section of the interview. In spite of that, there is another reference to the media-specific presuppositions in the opening section of the internal first-frame interaction, namely *programme* (line 6):

(16) IR   Michael Heseltine, not so long ago **on this programme** you said that you would not run against the prime minister ….

In (15) and (16), the terms of address represent instances of a public discursive style: the IE is explicitly referred to by his title *minister of agriculture* and by his first and last names (*Michael Heseltine, John Gummer*). Since IR and IE know who the other is, the explicit references are redundant in the first-frame interaction. The marked information management status, or infringing on the Gricean maxim of quantity, assigns them the function of implicit references to the media frame. But what communicative functions do the explicit and implicit references to the media frame fulfil? In the framework of the dialogue act of a plus/minus-validity claim, they realise specific validity claims and are, if ratified, assigned the status of a plus- or a minus-validity claim. Should they be accepted, they are assigned the status of a plus-validity claim and attributed to the discourse common ground. Thus, references to the media frame in the opening section of the interview contribute to the initiation of the macro validity claim. If they are accepted, they are assigned the status of plus-validity claims. Regarding the interactional organisation of responsibility this means that the IR's responsibilities towards the second-frame audience are accepted and assigned a presuppositional status. Once the media frame has been established, it does not require any further explication. Because of that, there are hardly any explicit references to the media frame in the topical-sequence section of the interview, where *professional politics* (Fairclough 1998) is discussed. This may be one of the reasons why the central part of the interview is often perceived and interpreted – from a social-reality viewpoint – as a single-frame interaction.

The following example also displays explicit references to the media frame in the opening section, namely *first full length interview* and the name of the programme *on the record*. Additionally, there are the implicitly realised references to the media frame *shadow secretary of state for employment* and *Tony Blair*:

(17) IR   Today in his **first full length interview** as the shadow secretary of state for employment Tony Blair goes **on the record**. ... Now the policy that you have drawn up ...

Explicit references to the media frame are required for the instantiation of a televised political interview. Once accepted, an explicit reference to the media frame infringes on the Gricean maxim of quantity and therefore expresses more than the actual reference to the media frame. So, are there any media references in the closing section?

3.2 Media references in the closing section

The closing section of an interview consists of the initiation of the closing frame and the actual closing of the encounter. In the data analysed, the closing frame is generally initiated by the IR's explicit reference to the closing section, such as

(18) IR   one final question

(19) IR   let me put this final thought to you

While explicit references to the second-frame audience are a necessary condition in the opening section, this does not seem to be the case for the closing section, where there are only implicit references to the second-frame audience:

(20) IR   **Minister**, we will see how **the public** judges you. Thank you very much

In (20), the reference *public* does not directly refer to the media-frame audience, but to a less determinate general public which entails the second-frame audience. And it is the 'public' who evaluates the politician's performance.

In the following examples, the IR does not employ the first-person singular pronoun *I* to close the interaction. Instead, he uses the first-person plural form *we/us*, which, from a linguistic-meaning viewpoint, indexes the set of IR and second-frame audience. With the implicit media reference, he signifies a responsible attitude towards his fellow coparticipants:

(21) IR   **We**'ll see what happens next **secretary of state**, thank you.

(22) IR   **Mister Lamont**, thank you for being so straight with **us**.

(23) IR   **We** look forward to seeing how you decide to make it better. **Jack Cunningham**, thank you.

In all of the closing sections investigated, the IR does not only employ the media-specific address terms of title, first name and last name, e.g. *secretary of state*, *Mister Lamont* or *Jack Cunningham*, but also the conventionalised appreciation device *thank you*. This represents a rather formal and public mode of closing an interaction and therefore is assigned the status of an implicit reference to the media frame. In the data investigated, the IR's expression of appreciation is generally intensified by the adverbial *very much*, by a brief characterisation of the IE's performance or by other routine formulae, such as *good to talk to you*, signifying a responsible attitude towards the coparticipant's face wants, as is the case in (24), (25) and (26):

(24) IR   Good to talk to you. Thank you, **Michael Heseltine**

(25) IR   **Mister Prescott**, thank you very much

(26) IR   **Minister**, thank you very much

The terms of address employed in the data investigated are assigned the status of public discursive style because explicit references to the communication partner's title, first name and last name are redundant in the closing section of a mundane everyday communication. Furthermore, the terms of address employed in the opening and closing sections are identical, which may indicate that the social identities of the coparticipants have remained unharmed.

Unmarked political interviews are defined as structurally less complex from a linguistic-representation viewpoint, as more frequent from a discourse-distribution viewpoint and as less salient and easier to process from a cognitive viewpoint. In marked interviews, the illusion that a political interview is a single-frame interaction can no longer be sustained as there are not only explicit references to the media frame and its presuppositions, but also lengthy and controversial processes of negotiating the status quo.

3.3 Media references in the topical-sequence section

Unmarked political interviews are defined by references to the media frame in the opening and closing sections, and marked interviews exploit the already accepted references by making them explicit in the central section of the interview. The illusion of an independent single-frame interaction is challenged and the second-frame audience is gradually made aware of the genre's complex interactive structures and manipulative strategies. In the following, explicit and implicit media-frame references in the topical-sequence section are differentiated with regard to their communicative functions, which do not only depend on their linguistic meaning but also on their source.

3.3.1 IR's references to the media frame

IR's references to the media frame do not generally initiate a negotiation-of-validity sequence but rather intensify the pragmatic force of the validity claim, as is the case with the following examples:

(27) IR   Erm **I would not seek to portray you** other other than you
          would like.

(28) IR   You say it should. But I notice, and **so will the viewers notice,**
          the absence of a pledge that waiting lists will come down.

Explicit and implicit references to the media frame have a number of different communicative functions. In (27), the IR employs the implicit reference to the media frame *I would not seek to portray you other* to refute the challenge of manipulation, thus indicating his responsible attitude towards the media frame. If the IR's reference to the media frame is not taken up by the IE, it is accepted and does not need to be negotiated. In (28), the IR employs the explicit reference to the second-frame audience *and so will the viewers notice* in order to boost the pragmatic force of challenging the IE for not having been precise enough. Through the explicit reference to the second-frame audience the IR signifies that the IE has not attended to their information wants in an appropriate manner and thus has acted irresponsibly.

3.3.2 IE's references to the media frame

IE's references to the media frame have a different communicative function. They are used to provide a reason for opting out (Grice 1975) and they are used to challenge the IR. In (29), the IE explicitly refers to the second-frame audience in his argumentation about the complexity of environmental matters (lines 4 and 5). In that context, the reference to the second-frame audience is used to opt out of the Gricean CP, thus supporting the IE's presentation of self as a responsible politician who is fully aware of the complexities of the matter and therefore is unable to give a brief and unambiguous answer at that stage of the interview:

(29) IE   And I believe the government should respond to that, and Chris
             Patten does too, so does the prime minister and therefore there
             would have to be some price to pay. It will not be costless and it
             will not be painless. And therefore by setting this target I don't
             want to give <u>you</u> or <u>the green lobby groups,</u> **who are watching
             this programme** erm the message that it is simple. It is not
             simple.

The following excerpt is also an instance of opting out. Again, the IE presents himself as a responsible politician who cannot – due to the inappropriateness of the public media context – comply with the IR's request to provide specific information. This is due to the fact that the IE is only in a position to *speculate* but not to provide precise information. That is to say, speculating in the framework of the genre of a political interview is interpreted as infringing on the maxim of quality as well as on the public's information wants, and therefore is looked upon as an irresponsible act. And because of that, the IR is implicitly criticised for having asked such an irresponsible question in the first place:

(30) IE   It would be very foolish of me **to speculate on this programme** as to what in fact might be in the white paper or indeed what the chancellor of the exchequer might wish to say

In (31), the IE's reference to the media frame (*why I can't possibly start telling you publicly*) also signifies his opting out. Again, he indicates that the IR's question has been inappropriate because such a question can only be answered in a non-mediated context (*I discuss that with Norman* – the chancellor of the exchequer). The media-frame reference supports the IE's presentation of self as a responsible politician, and at the same time it indicates that the IR has not acted in a responsible manner:

(31) IE   … and I know you'll understand **why I can't possibly start telling you publicly** what I believe the proper figure is. I discuss that with Norman …

In (32), the IE employs the implicit media-frame reference *the press*:

(32) IE   Well, if I had said that, then that would have been perfectly reasonable. What I said was …. but, of course, if **the press** reports you in a way which is not true and there was only one report of that

The criticism of the press is an instance of indirectly criticising the IR for not having displayed a more critical attitude towards the selection of media information. Again, the IR is implicitly blamed for having neglected his responsibilities towards his fellow coparticipants.

In the following excerpt, the communicative function of media references is investigated in a longer stretch of talk:

(33) IE   Well certainly, we we've kept spending ahead of inflation every year since we've been in and I have no intention of erm slowing down at the expense to the service at the present stage. Erm I think **my friends on the television** were trying to help me - erm **the film** an hour ago - were trying to help me in the negotiations

with ... I think **the public** want both the union and ourselves not to have a rerun like that or anything like it but you got onto my pay-roll costs the biggest single item of cost in the health service and **if I just get myself some brownie points** with you know **my appearing on television** saying I'll pay whatever Roger Poole wants ...

IR   I've never heard it said before. Erm let me go on to something which the **voters** will be very interested in ...

In (33), the IE uses a number of explicit references to the media frame and to its presuppositions. In line 3, he refers to his *friends on the television* who employ the media-specific strategy of showing a *film* (line 4), which adopts his viewpoint and thereby indirectly supports his policies. He also comments on how the media can be exploited by making explicit positive aspects (line 8) of *appearing on television* (line 9), and at the same time he demonstrates that he is a responsible politician, who does not exploit the media in order to leave a good impression on the viewers. In response, the IR implicitly refers to the second-frame audience by *the voters* (line 12) in order to intensify the relevance of his intention to elaborate on the current discourse topic. While both IR and IE refer to the media frame and its presuppositions, only the IE employs media references to support his argumentation. The IR uses the media-frame references in the context of challenges, where they boost the pragmatic force thus implicating that the IE has not only displayed an irresponsible attitude towards the IR but also towards the second-frame audience.

In (34), the IR employs the implicit reference to second-frame audience *many people* to support his intended elaboration on the discourse topic, which the IE does not want to discuss any further. The IE explicitly refutes the IR's argumentation by saying *for many people this is not an issue*. He blames the IR for acting in an irresponsible manner because of fabricating *some sort of story*:

(34) IR   Let me, let me, I understand what you're saying and, of course, we must discuss these things, **but for many people this is an issue**

IE   No, no no. For many people this is not an issue. You're trying to make it an issue because you hope then that you will get **some sort of story** because I've moved a subclause somewhere. That there is a significance which I shall not intend ....

The following example stems from the same interview. It is an extremely controversial interview with numerous frame breaks, which is also referred to as confrontation (Schegloff 1989). Not only are there explicit references to the media frame but also deviations from the turn-taking system, the coparticipants' rights, responsibilities and obligations, and their discursive styles:

(35) IE   I've agreed to **come on this programme** not to discuss these issues, to discuss important factors about ideas, about the direction of policies, about where we should go in the nineteen nineties. That's what I agreed to do and if you ever .....

IE   **Jonathan, you are wasting your time**

IR   right

IE   and what **viewers** happen to be **watching. You are wasting their time as well** so let us now continue with the agreement that we had to discuss issues

.....

IE   Now use words in order to try to **leave an impression.** Now can we just understand clearly **the basis on which I came on this programme** that we were going to talk about issues. I will talk about issues because they are very important

.....

IE   No but you and now you are going to get the last word in which you leave an impression **in front of your viewers**

IR   No, I have the right to say **this is an interview** and I'm sure you will recognise it **because you understand the nature of political interviews**, Mister Heseltine as well as I do

.....

IE   One moment. **Can I just ask you one question?**

IR   Well of course.

.....

IR   I'm not going **to weary you or the viewers**

IE   Is it, is it, now wait a minute, here we are you're dodging, so **you won't weary the viewers**

IR   It's a it's a

IE   **you've been wearying them for the last ten minutes**

IR   It's a, **I don't think they've been weary for the last ten minutes at all,** ...

IE   But I think **the viewers will be very interested** in that

IR   **I suspect they will be and I hope they are** because these things are always interesting. Now because **we don't want to waste any more time** you very much

IE   LAUGHTER

IR   want to talk about policies ...

In this sequence, both IR and IE employ references to the media frame and to its presuppositions. The IE explicates the presuppositions and is extremely outspoken about the unspoken background assumption that discourse topics have been agreed upon before going on record, e.g. *I've agreed to **come on this programme** not to discuss these issues, to discuss important factors about ideas, about the direction of policies, about where we should go in the nineteen nineties. That's what I agreed to do and if you ever* (lines 1–3). The media-specific presuppositions are further explicated in lines 10–11, where the IE refers to their conversational contract in *the basis on which I came on this programme* (line 11). He also refers to the IR's rights, obligations and responsibilities with regard to the media frame. In line 5, he criticises the IR for neither being efficient nor informative thus signifying that the IR has acted in an irresponsible manner by not adhering to the genre-specific information wants. This is supported by the IE's summoning of the IR with his first name *Jonathan* in line 5 which implicates that the IR is responsible for the attempted manipulation of the IE himself and of the audience. After the very explicit challenge, the IE requests the IR to stop the attempted manipulation by saying *you are wasting your time* (line 5). Not only is the first-frame coparticipants' time wasted but also the audience's time, namely the *viewers happen to be watching ....wasting their time as well* (line 7). The IE goes even further, he also implicates that the programme in question does not have a regular audience, but only some viewers that *happen* to be watching. The challenge is further reinforced in lines 24–33, where the communicative status of the presuppositions is negotiated. In line 24, the IR refutes the IE's challenge by saying *I'm not going to weary you* *or the viewers*, which is echoed by the IE in lines 25 and 27 by saying *so you won't weary the viewers* with an ironic intonation contour. The IE does not only challenge the IR, but also portrays him as insecure, if not irresponsible and insincere, which is reflected in the proposition *you're dodging* (line 25). The game of challenges and refutations continues and the force of the arguments gets fiercer and fiercer. It culminates in the evaluation of the IR as *you've been wearying them for the last ten minutes* (line 28). Naturally, the IR refutes the challenge in a direct manner to save his face by saying *I don't think they've been weary for the last ten minutes at all* (line 29). There are more references to the IR's attempted manipulation, e.g. *now use words in order to try to leave an impression* (line 10). And the IE specifies the actual addressees of the manipulation, namely the second-frame audience, by continuing *leave an impression in front of your viewers* (lines 10 and 16). The negotiation of the media-specific presuppositions and the implicit power struggle does not stop until the IR explicates his genre-specific right to initiate and close a discourse topic in the lines 17–19, where he requests the IE to adhere to the macro validity claim's linguistic and social codes: *no, I have the right to say this is an interview and I'm sure you will recognise it because you understand the nature of political interviews, Mister Heseltine, as well as I do*. This expression of responsibility and manifestation of power anchored to the coparticipants' genre-specific rights and obligations functions as a *regulative device*. For this reason, the IE is obliged to accept it and to act in accordance with the requirement. But he does not yet give in and requests permission to change the genre-specific rights and obligations in order to gain the floor: *one moment. Can I just ask you one question?* (line 21), which the IR accepts by saying *well of course* (line 22). Both communicative contributions display plus-language (Fetzer 2000): the IE' hesitation device *one moment*, which indicates a dispreferred second, and the IR's negative discourse marker *well*, which fulfils a similar function. The negotiation of the genre- and media-specific presuppositions continues and is not resolved until the IR implicitly accepts the IE's formulation of *wasting time* (line 32) by adopting it. The IE accepts that with laughter (line 34) – yet another deviation from the genre-specific linguistic and social codes.

A necessary component of marked political interviews are *critical situations*, which result from frame breaks, and which contain references to the media frame in the topical-sequence section, challenging the validity of genre-specific constraints and requirements. The linguistic context of the media-frame references contains a considerably higher frequency of discourse markers, hedges and interpersonal markers, such as *you know*, *erm* and *I think*, which fulfil an important role in the process of negotiating the communicative status of a validity claim. Critical situations are interactionally organised by the explication of one or more presuppositions of a validity claim which have already been accepted. And it is the deviation from the accepted standard, which requires their re-negotiation. From a sequential-organisation viewpoint, a negotiation-of-validity sequence consists of minimally five moves, since presuppositions need to be made explicit before they are rejected. However, challenging presuppositions is not restricted to micro-presuppositions. Macro-presuppositions can also be challenged. Generally, explicit references to first- and second-frame presuppositions function as inference triggers for the first- and the second-frame coparticipants as they conversationally implicate that the IR's or IE's communicative performance has not adhered to the conversational contract and therefore is considered to be inappropriate. While the explication of micro presuppositions initiates a negotiation-of-validity sequence with respect to the coparticipants' rights and responsibilities, the explication of macro presuppositions has the communicative function of a regulative device, which makes their responsibilities manifest.

4 Conclusion

The dynamics of the interactional organisation of responsibility in the genre and media event of a political interview has been investigated in a sociopragmatic framework based on the dialogue act of a plus/minus validity claim which allows for the accommodation of both bottom-up and top-down perspectives. While the former explicates the process and result of the negotiation of local meaning, the latter specifies the contextual values of the macro validity claim of a political interview with regard to the first-frame interaction between IR and IE with the media frame and its media-specific presuppositions. In the dialogical setting, political interviews are defined by the coparticipants' postulation, ratification, acceptance, rejection and negotiation of validity claims in context, and they are defined by the second-frame audience's ratification, acceptance and rejection of the first-frame validity claims. The coparticipants negotiate the communicative status of a validity claim with regard to its immediate contextual references by mapping them onto the specified values of the macro validity claim. If a validity claim is accepted, it is assigned the status of a plus-validity claim; if it is rejected, it is assigned the status of a minus-validity claim.

The dialogue act of a plus/minus-validity claim is anchored to an interactive tripartite system of objective, subjective and social worlds. The social world accommodates a political interview's genre-specific constraints and requirements: the adjacency pair question-answer, ratified coparticipants with neutral face wants and political and public information wants, and a neutral and objective presentation and interpretation of communicative intentions. Political interviews represent a subset of media communication and therefore require the accommodation of the interaction between the first-frame coparticipants [IR, IE, (A-1)] with the media frame and its media-specific presuppositions. While all of the coparticipants ratify validity claims, only the first-frame coparticipants are in a position to directly negotiate their communicative status. The negotiation of validity is carried out in front of and for the second-frame audience who is thus guided in their calculation of first-frame communicative intentions. The resulting dual frame of reference provides for a presentation of the encounter as two independent, yet interdependent events, in which the explication of second-frame references in the topical-sequence section generally goes hand in hand with deviations from the genre-specific discursive styles, discursive roles, discourse topics and allocation of turns.

Unlike the individual-oriented notion of sincerity, the concept of responsibility is anchored to the set of coparticipants, to communicative action, and to linguistic and social contexts on the one hand, and to genre on the other. For this reason, responsibility represents a dialogue principle par excellence. In the framework of validity claims, it is anchored to the social world. It manifests itself in the coparticipants' attitudes towards validity claim, linguistic and social contexts, fellow coparticipants and genre. While responsibility in non-mediated discourse is anchored to the set of constitutive first-frame coparticipants, communicative action, linguistic and social contexts, and genre, responsibility in media discourse is anchored to a further frame, thus extending the first-frame coparticipants' responsibilities towards the second-frame audience. For this reason, the negotiation of validity and the corresponding explication of presuppositions does not only secure the discourse common ground for the first-frame coparticipants but also, if not mainly, for the second-frame audience. The IR's responsibilities manifest themselves in an appropriate attitude towards IE and second-frame audience with regard to their political, party-political and public information wants and neutral face wants. The IR is also responsible for the interactional organisation of the genre and media event of a political interview by ensuring that the negotiation of validity claims adheres to the genre- and media-specific modes. The IE's main responsibilities manifest themselves in an appropriate attitude towards the second-frame audience with regard to their particular information wants. Naturally, the IE is also responsible for the interactional organisation of the actual interview by adhering to the genre- and media-specific modes. The second-frame audience's responsibilities manifest themselves in the ratification of first-frame validity claims by adhering to the genre- and media-specific modes.

In the framework of validity claims, references to the constitutive systems and presuppositions represent validity claims which are negotiated in discourse. Explicit references to the media frame are obligatory in the opening section and have the function of establishing the media frame. They index the first-frame's responsibilities regarding the interactional organisation of the political interview, and they index the first-frame's responsibilities towards the second-frame audience. Once accepted, media-frame references are assigned a presuppositional status and are generally not explicated any further. If references to the media frame are employed in the topical-sequence or closing sections, they generally trigger a process of inferencing to retrieve a conversational implicature whose meaning depends strongly on the source of the message. If employed by the IR, a reference to the media frame generally boosts the pragmatic force of the validity claim and signifies the IR's responsibilities towards the second-frame audience's information wants. If employed by the IE, it is generally used as an argument for opting out, viz. for not complying with the IR's request to provide specific information. In other words, IE's references to the media frame re-frame local sequences by shifting responsibilities in context.

Notes

1 Political interviews can deviate from the coparticipant-specific employment of the initiating and responsive formats. The deviations from a prototypical political interview are, however, only local phenomena because it is a necessary condition for the coparticipants to adhere to the subjective-world premise of sincerity in order to felicitously organise the genre of a political interview as a whole (Fetzer 2000).

2 All examples are adopted from a corpus of 14 dyadic political interviews recorded between May and July 1990 from the BBC1-programme *on the record*. Since the goal of the analysis is the investigation of linguistic realisation of references to the media frame, the transcription mode employed follows orthographical standards.

3 The ratified coparticipant of audience does not need to be a constitutive part of the first-frame interaction, but it must be a constitutive part of the media-frame interaction between the first frame and the second frame (Fetzer 2000).

4 The pronominal references in the analysis of the data are based on natural gender.

5 The definition of a plus/minus-validity claim (Fetzer 2000) is informed by Habermas's (1987) *theory of communicative action*.

6 This does not mean that formulaic language is not used in a political interview. However, if that type of language is used, it generally signifies *irony* or *sarcasm*.

7 The differentiation between a marked and an unmarked (or prototypical) political interview is based on the *functional-grammar* concept of markedness (Givón 1993: 178), which is adapted to a discursive frame of reference: the marked format is defined as *structurally more complex, less frequent from a discourse-distribution viewpoint, more salient from a cognitive-complexity viewpoint* and *thus harder to process*. The unmarked format is structurally less complex, more frequent from a discourse-distribution viewpoint, less salient from a cognitive-complexity viewpoint and thus easier to process. As a consequence, an unmarked political interview adheres to the genre's constraints and requirements by not being structurally more complex, i.e. by not adding additional sequences to the standard negotiation of presuppositions or by not having longer opening or closing sections. An unmarked political interview is also more frequent and therefore less salient regarding cognitive complexity.

References

Austin, J. L. (1980) *How to Do Things with Words*. Oxford: Oxford University Press.

Bell, P. (1977) M Watkins, The damnation of Demidenk - interview or inquisition? Towards a pragmatic interpretation of genre. *Social Semiotics* 7: 31–45.

Bell, A. and Garret, P. (eds) (1998) *Approaches to Media Discourse*. Oxford: Blackwell.

Blum-Kulka, S. (1983) The dynamics of political interviews. *Text* 3(2): 131–153.

Bull, P. (2003) *The Microanalysis of Political Communication: Claptrap and Ambiguity*. London: Routledge.

Brown, P. and Levinson, S. (1987) *Politeness. Some Universals in Language Usage*. Cambridge: Cambridge University Press.

Clayman, S. (1992) Footing and achievement of neutrality: the case of news interview discourse. In P. Drew and J. Heritage (eds) *Talk at Work* 163–198. Cambridge: Cambridge University Press.

Clayman, S. and Heritage, J. (2002). *The News Interview.* Cambridge: Cambridge University Press.

Clayman, S. and Whalen, J. (1988/89) When the medium becomes the message: the case of the Rather-Bush encounter. *Research on Language and Social Interaction* 22: 241–272.

Fairclough, N. (1998) Political discourse in the media: an analytical framework. In A. Bell and P. Garrett (eds) *Approaches to Media Discourse* 142–162. Oxford: Blackwell.

Fairclough, I. and Fairclough, N. (2012) *Political Discure Analysis.* Oxford: Routledge.

Fetzer, A. (1999) Challenging the unspoken: exploiting the ideology in and of political interviews. In J. Verschueren (ed.) *Language and Ideology: Selected Papers from the 6th International Pragmatics Conference* 98–113. Antwerp: International Pragmatics Association.

Fetzer, A. (2000) Negotiating validity claims in political interviews. *Text* 20(4): 1–46.

Fetzer, A. (2002a) Communicative intentions in context. In A. Fetzer and C. Meierkord (eds) *Rethinking Sequentiality: Linguistics Meets Conversational Interaction* 37–69. Amsterdam: John Benjamins.

Fetzer, A. (2002b) 'Put bluntly, you have something of a credibility problem': sincerity and credibility in political interviews. In P. Chilton and C. Schäffner (eds) *Politics as Talk and Text: Analytic Approaches to Political Discourse* 173–201. Amsterdam: John Benjamins.

Fetzer, A. (2006) 'Minister, we will see how the public judges you': media references in political interviews. *Journal of Pragmatics* 38(2): 180–195.

Fetzer, A. and Weizman, E. (2006) Political discourse as mediated and public discourse. *Journal of Pragmatics* 38(2): 143–153.

Garfinkel, H. (1994) *Studies in Ethnomethodology.* Cambridge: Polity.

Givón, T. (1993) *English Grammar: A Function-Based Introduction.* Amsterdam: Benjamins.

Goffman, E. (1986) *Frame Analysis.* New York: Harper & Row.

Greatbatch, D. (1998) Conversation analysis: neutralism in British news interviews. In A. Bell and P. Garrett (eds) *Approaches to Media Discourse* 163–185. Oxford: Blackwell.

Grice, H. P. (1975) Logic and conversation. In P. Cole and J. L. Morgan (eds) *Syntax and Semantics* 41–58. New York: Academic Press.

Grimshaw, A. D. (1980) Mishearings, misunderstandings, and other nonsuccesses in talk: a plea for redress of speaker-oriented bias. *Sociological Inquiry* 50: 31–74.

Habermas, J. (1987) *Theorie des kommunikativen Handelns.* Frankfurt/Main: Suhrkamp.

Harnish, R. (1991) Logical form and implicature. In S. Davis (ed.) *Pragmatics: A Reader* 316–364. Oxford: Oxford University Press.

Heritage, J. (1985) Analysing news interviews: aspects of the production of talk for an overhearing audience. In T. Van Dijk (ed.) *Handbook of Discourse Analysis III* 95–117. London: Academic Press.

Heritage, J., Clayman, S. and Zimmerman, D. (1988) Discourse and message analysis: the micro-structure of mass media messages. In R. Hawkins, S. Pingree and J. Weiman (eds) *Advancing Communication Science: Merging Mass and Interpersonal Processes* 77–109. Beverly Hills, CA: Sage.

Jucker, A. (1986) *News Interviews: A Pragmalinguistic Analysis.* Amsterdam: Benjamins.

Lauerbach, G. and Fetzer, A. (2007) Introduction. In A. Fetzer and G. Lauerbach (eds) *Political Discourse in the Media: Cross-Cultural Perspectives* 3–30. Amsterdam: John Benjamins.

Levinson, S. (1983) *Pragmatics.* Cambridge: Cambridge University Press.

Levinson, S. (1988) Putting linguistics on a proper footing: explorations in Goffman's concepts of participation. In P. Drew and A. Wootton (eds) *Erving Goffman. Exploring the Interaction Order* 161–227. Cambridge: Cambridge University Press.

Linell, P. (1998) *Approaching Dialogue.* Amsterdam: Benjamins.

Luckmann, T. (1995) Interaction planning and intersubjective adjustment of perspectives by communicative genres. In E. Goody (ed.) *Social Intelligence and Interaction: Expressions and Implications of the Social Bias in Human Intelligence* 175–188. Cambridge: Cambridge University Press.

Mühlhäusler, P. and Harré, R. (1990) *Pronouns and People: The Linguistic Construction of Social and Personal Identity.* Oxford: Blackwell.

Östman, J.-O. (1999) Coherence through understanding through discourse patterns: focus on news reports. In W. Bublitz, U. Lenk and E. Ventola (eds) *Coherence in Spoken and Written Discourse* 77–100. Amsterdam: John Benjamins.

Recanati, F. (1989) The pragmatics of what is said. *Mind & Language* 4(4): 295–329.

Sarangi, S. and Slembrouck, S. (1996) *Language, Bureaucracy & Social Control.* London: Longman.

Sbisà, M. (2002) Speech acts in context. *Language and Communication* 22(4): 421–436.

Schegloff, E. (1989) From interview to confrontation. *Research on Language and Social Action* 22: 215–240.

Searle, J. (1969) *Speech Acts.* Cambridge: Cambridge University Press.

Tannen, D. (1981) The machine-gun question: an example of conversational style. *Journal of Pragmatics* 5: 383–397.

Van Dijk, T. (1981) *Studies in the Pragmatics of Discourse.* The Hague: Mouton.

Wilson, J. (1990) *Politically Speaking.* Oxford: Oxford University Press.

Anita Fetzer is a full professor of Applied Linguistics at the University of Augsburg, Germany. Her research interests focus on pragmatics, discourse analysis and functional grammar. She has had a series of articles published on context, political discourse, discourse relations, and the communicative act of rejection. Her most recent publications are *The Pragmatics of Political Discourse* (2013), *Contexts and Context: Parts Meets Whole* (2011, with Etsuko Oishi), and *Context and Appropriateness* (2007). She is editor of the book series *Pragmatics & Beyond: New Series* (John Benjamins). She is a member of several editorial boards, including *Pragmatics & Cognition, Journal of Language and Politics* (John Benjamins), *Research on Language and Social Interaction* (Taylor and Francis), *Text & Talk* (de Gruyter) and *Studies in Pragmatics* (Elsevier), and she is an elected member of the Consultation Board of the International Pragmatics Association.

Roles, dramaturgy and responsibility in Swedish TV-debates

Christian Svensson Limsjö

1 Introduction

> Ten live programs this spring, with lively debates,
> engaging topics, colourful guests,
> victims and decision makers

The quotation above is from the home page of the Swedish TV-programme *Svar Direkt*.[1] In this chapter I will focus on TV-debate programmes which deal with current topics of societal relevance and where both official representatives and representatives of the public participate.[2] In and through the media different societal groups, and the relations between them, are represented and construed in different ways. But journalists also represent themselves and thereby construe their own role or voice in the debate. This study will discuss the different voices that can be heard in mediated debate programmes and the ways in which the set-up is accomplished. How are societal problems and other issues portrayed in these programmes? How are these 'lively debates' and 'engaging topics' enacted? What kind of participation is possible for the 'colourful guests', 'the victims' and the 'decision makers'? Since these particular debates also deal with current, social and political topics, including potential problems, a natural concern for the producers is to examine who might be responsible for the event or phenomenon discussed. The purpose of this study, therefore, is to examine the possible roles and identities of the guests within the dramaturgy of the show and relate that to the distribution of responsibility and the guests' societal roles.

1.1 Media and politics – some preliminaries

A central presumption of this chapter is that our opinions and our knowledge are to a great extent maintained and transformed discursively, i.e.

through communication between people. A very important part of this communication is carried out and mediated by the mass media. Several scholars (e.g. Corner and Pels 2003; Dahlgren 2009) have underlined the social and political influence of the media, and TV as a natural part of most people's everyday life is particularly important in this respect. This mediation (of politics), however, cannot be regarded as a simple and unproblematic transmission of knowledge, meaning and understanding. Rather, it is obvious that all mediation must involve different kinds of selections and perspectives. The mass media (and its owners, editors, journalists etc.) have great influence on what are regarded as important topics and how to present them, on who gets access to the media and how they are allowed to participate. The mass media, therefore, can be regarded both as an *arena* for and as an active *actor* in (political) public debate, i.e. the mass media do not only mediate political and moral understandings but contribute to the formulation of them. The latter also implies that the mass media have a responsibility for how social and political topics and groups are portrayed (e.g. how responsibility for societal problems is distributed and described in different media genres).

1.2 Dramaturgy and identity in interaction

Denzin (2003), among others, has pointed to performance theories, especially dramaturgy, as useful tools in the analysis of contemporary cultural narratives. The common element in all dramaturgies is the use of theatrical metaphors to understand human behaviour. Dramaturgy, here, is understood precisely as a way of describing human behaviour, rather than as a closed theoretical position. Although the labels (used to describe the elements of theatrical performance) vary from theorist to theorist, they always tend to include the actors and their roles, the setting, the performative act itself and the effect of the performance (Krause and Goering 1995). In this chapter, Goffman's dramaturgical social theory (1982 [1959]) is part of the backdrop for my investigation. According to Goffman, everyday social interaction can be viewed as performances enacted by actors, i.e. people perform in different roles on different stages or settings. Two aspects are vital for Goffman; first, the possible roles (and the way they can be enacted) are to a large extent defined and framed by the given situation (stage/setting) and, second, no actor can keep the appearance of his/her role without the assistance of co-actors and an audience. According to Goffman, participants are constantly involved in self-presentation and impression management, both truly interactional activities. In presenting oneself, in preserving one's face, a person has to agree to help others present themselves and preserve their faces. Since everyone, according to Goffman, is keen not to get his or her face threatened (or one's role or self-presentation questioned), tactical teamwork arises where all participants together confirm their own and others' roles.

The dramaturgical view of the actor suggests that individuals are social rather than psychological constructs. Consequently, any role that people play is a shared interactive phenomenon that only emerges in conduct with others. Therefore, the concept of identity is here considered as an interactive phenomenon, i.e. identity is something that has to be displayed, communicated and interpersonally established. Identity, in this sense, is, according to Hydén (2001: 215), 'not something neatly delimited, but a way of establishing continuity and responsibility for actions ... in a temporal and spatial context'. This implies a view of identity as an interactive resource, i.e. as something that can be actively used by participants when they talk about their personal, professional or political identity. This also means that participants in interaction can ascribe to or emphasise different aspects of their own or others' identities in different settings and activities. An important inference from this is that identity has to be understood in relation to its context(s). As Hydén (2001: 216) points out, the very distribution of responsibility is important: 'Central to the relation between agent and action is the responsibility for the action. By assuming or ascribing various identities to persons, it is possible to negotiate responsibility for actions'.

One powerful way to establish identity in interaction is to use social categorisations such as *politician, victim, expert* etc. Identity in this sense may be established by describing others or oneself as being of a certain type. Sacks (1992) refers to this as *membership categorisation.*[3] He points out that any person can be labelled in many correct ways, but that the chosen identification carries massive implications for the meaning we attach to people and their behaviour. According to Sacks, we generally tend both to speak and hear as if a connection between a certain type of person and certain types of action exists, and vice versa. This is what Sacks called *category-bound activities*. Participants can utilise this in categorising each other. Categorisation can be made directly and explicitly by invoking a social category, like *politician* or *victim*. From this categorisation, certain types of behaviour are inferred, i.e. it is heard as if they are connected to a person of this sort. Similarly, but implicitly, certain types of actions or behaviours can be made relevant in the interaction, indicating that the agent of these actions belongs to a certain social category.

1.3 TV-debates as staged interaction

TV-debates can be characterised as *staged interactions*. Therefore, theories of dramaturgy and identity as an interactive phenomenon provide a logical foundation for an analysis of these debates. TV-debates constitute a specific form of mediated (institutional) discourse. Like other institutional conversations, conversations in the mass media can be characterised as a socially recognised activity, having specific purposes that are decided in advance, as building on routinised ways of achieving these purposes, and as having a distinct distribution of roles (asymmetrical and complementary), where at least one party has his/her role as part of a profession (Linell 1998). What distinguishes conversations in the mass media from other kinds of institutional interactions is that they are *staged*, i.e. they are prepared for performance by having a pre-planned agenda, often maintained by a more or less detailed script. Further, they are intended to be seen/heard by an anonymous (and temporally and spatially separated) audience (cf. Nylund 2000).[4] Thus, conversations in the mass media are not random social gatherings, but prepared and planned encounters with guests selected specifically (for the purpose). These staged performances, however, must be discursively maintained and enacted. In the TV-debates, the topics and the identities of the guests are (re)presented and negotiated interactionally throughout the debates.

1.4 Method and research questions

In dramaturgical terms, this study puts focus on two categories: the actors and the performative act. First, I have examined what in performance theory (Krause and Goering 1995) is referred to as *the performative act*, i.e. the presentation itself. Krause and Goering (1995: 191) say: 'The dimensions of the performative act include the topic … and the ways in which that topic is transformed into a narrative (i.e. how it is introduced, how the story is told and how closure is achieved)'. From an interactional point of view, all social encounters are sequentialised phenomena, and Goffman (1974) has especially emphasised the importance of introductions and closures in order to understand the character of a particular activity. In contrast to everyday life encounters, it is also significant for mass-mediated encounters that one party alone (the journalist) presents and identifies the topic, and the guests often follow an agenda (Clayman 1991). The producers of these TV-debates have a difficult task to accomplish. Within limited time frames they shall produce interesting discussions that attract an audience. To understand the presentation of the topic, I have therefore analysed how the producers do this, how they transform these debates into narratives, i.e. how the debates are introduced, how the stories are told and how closure is achieved.

Second, and as part of the performative act, I have examined *the actors and their roles*. This means that I have, in more detail, explored participants' identities and roles, inspired by Goffman's (1982 [1959]) notion of *impression management*. In these debates the guests' utterances can be assumed to contain self-presentations of how they want to be viewed, but above all, the producers contribute to an official impression management where they portray themselves and the guests in preferred ways. A previous study of these debates (Svensson 2001) shows that the producers (mainly the hosts) to a large extent control the interaction. The hosts talk the most (quantitative dominance): on an average, the host occupies 27 per cent and the guests occupy 2.5 per cent each of the total interactional space on an issue. Further, guests almost never ask questions. Hosts ask questions, thereby calling for responses and answers (interactional dominance). The hosts also control the agenda, i.e. the right to decide what is to be talked about, in what way and when (topical and strategic dominance). The guests, therefore, have few possibilities to influence the interaction. Further, the most common speaker constellation is the host speaking to one guest at a time, and guests seldom talk directly to each other. The debates can therefore be characterised as dyadically organised interviews where the interviewer confronts different parties one by one. In that respect it is not a real multiparty conversation or a debate where different participants speak freely to each other. Since the hosts/producers control the interaction so heavily, I will here concentrate on how they present and treat guests and just briefly mention how the guests present themselves and how they try to oppose agendas and/or roles.

A point of departure in the analysis of actors is that the interactive identity work can be understood in terms of roles. The explicit and implicit characterisation of *identities* can for example in different ways actualise the participants' social roles. A *social role* is a role socially recognised also outside the specific activity. A social role is related to the person's social position or status (e.g. a profession – an academic, a journalist – is a social role). In categorising identities, different *activity roles* are established. An activity role is the specific role a person is given or takes on in a specific activity, as for example in a TV-debate. A politician (social role) can act in other roles than that of the politician; he or she can for example be interviewed about his or her personal experience of an accident (in the activity role as eye witness).[5]

In this chapter I will, in Sacks' (1992) terms, explore membership categorisation, i.e. how social identity is attributed, explicitly and implicitly, in these debates. What categorisations are used to describe the guests; what actions and behaviours are they ascribed; and how are their utterances responded to by the host? Further, I am interested in how representatives of different societal sectors are portrayed and portray themselves in these debates, i.e. how participants' identities, seen as activity roles (the roles or identities they are attributed by the host/producers within the dramaturgy), and the communicative responsibilities attached to them, can be related to the guests' social roles (i.e. their occupations and official status) and the distribution of societal responsibility. The latter will be addressed in the discussion.

1.5 Data

The data consist of a sample of regular debate or discussion programmes from Swedish TV channels, from the years 1997–1999. The programmes were all transmitted live at the time. The programmes consist of one to three different issues or topics per programme. One issue lasts about 15 to 20 minutes. The issues are the primary units of analysis. From a larger corpus (including 53 issues) that has been used for overarching and comparative analysis, I have selected a smaller number of issues (16) for transcription and closer analysis.

The programmes have been chosen in order to match certain criteria; the programmes should be group discussions including a visual studio audience, they should deal with topics of current, societal relevance and their active participants should consist of (apart from media personnel) both official representatives (politicians, authorities etc.) and (what are sometimes construed as) 'ordinary' citizens. According to these definitions three different programmes matched: *Svar Direkt/Debattakuten* and *Nattöppet* (both broadcast by the Swedish public-service company) and *Svart eller Vitt* (broadcast by the commercial channel TV 4).

2 Results – The performative act and its roles

My analyses show that all topics build on a certain dramaturgy and consist of a few different phases or segments. Schematically these recurrent segments can be described as below. Except i), ii) and viii), these do not always appear in the same sequential order, although the order below is the predominant one.

Phase	Function	Discourse type**
*Introductions		
i) Headline	attract viewers	monological
ii) The topic (problem) is introduced by the host	set agenda	text and presentation
*Exchange of views		
iii) The existence of the problem is exemplified by a victim	exemplify problem	dialogical story telling
iv) The existence of the problem is verified by an expert	verify problem	fact seeking investigation
v) The problem is debated (by people with different opinions)	show different opinions	debate
vi) Responsible people defend themselves against criticism	challenge power	scrutinising examination
*Wrapping up		
vii) The problem is reintroduced by the host	round off, conclude	monological presentation
viii) The issue (topic) ends	close the topic	monological statement

** Discourse type here refers to a way of characterising forms of talk, e.g. advising, promotional talk, interrogation, troubles telling, etc. (cf. Sarangi 2000).

Below I will comment on the intricacies of these different phases.

2.1 Introductions

This phase consists of headlines and introductions by the hosts, where we get to know what the topic is and who will participate.

i) Headline

Topics are usually first presented in graphics or with a voice-over. This I call the headline of the topic. These headlines have two major functions: to catch the audience's attention and to present the topic and the reason why it is worth debating. The headlines focus on four different aspects in the presentation of the topic.

> a)   The topic is presented as a problem that involves risks (e.g. 'Democracy – a branch in crisis?').
>
> b)   The topic is described as involving conflict (e.g. 'Work and shut up! otherwise you are fired, fewer and fewer dare to say their opinion at work').
>
> c)   The topic is presented as new/current (e.g. 'Is the new prostitution law a gold mine for pimps?').
>
> d)   The topic is defined as extensive and frequent (e.g. '100,000 Swedes are affected by drugs at work, is it time for compulsory drug tests?').[6]

These headlines partly frame the ensuing debate by focusing on a certain aspect or understanding of the topic. One topic builds on an investigation which shows that confidence in the police has declined. However, nothing in the debate indicates that the investigation shows why there is a decline in confidence. (The guests in the studio are citizens who have not been helped when they called the police, a journalist with the police force as specialty, representatives of different sections of the police, representatives of the government and other political parties, etc.) The topic starts with a voice-over:

(1) *Svar Direkt, 16/10-1997; VO = Voice-over*[7]

1 VO: what do you do when the police do not do their job, do you take the law in your own hands or report the police to the police?

The headline is designed as a question and may therefore appear as in some sense a neutral question. But as Clayman and Heritage (2002) show, questions often establish an agenda, i.e. what the topic is supposed to be about and, consequently, what kind of answer is invited. According to Clayman and Heritage, questions furthermore often contain presuppositions (about the participants and the topic) and preferences, i.e. they are designed in a way that invites a certain kind of answer. Following this, one could say that the headline in example 1 establishes a specific agenda, namely that 'the police do not do their job'. Alternative headlines could have been 'what do you do when the police do not have the time to do their job?' or 'what do you do when confidence in the police declines?'. By choosing the headline in (1) the police are portrayed as not doing what they ought to. At the same time a dilemma for the public ('you') is implied; are they forced to take action on their own, or can you report the police to the police?

ii) The topic (defined as a problem) is introduced

After the headline, every topic analysed starts with an introduction by the host where he or she addresses the viewers and defines the problem, i.e. the topic for discussion. The hosts typically explain what the problem is and its potential consequences. Further, they often emphasise that the topics are current problems, troubling many people and including risks and conflicts (cf. the headline). In this way the host further focuses on a certain aspect of the topic. In the next example, also from the topic about the police, the introduction by the host is shown (the first thing after the voice-over in Example 1).

(2) *Svar Direkt, 16/10-1997; H = Host*

1 H: yes, that the police should function in a country, that is of course tremendously important, it is also one of the cornerstones of democracy, and what has happened in Sweden in the last, uh, in recent times, is actually that confidence in the police has declined, there are even investigations and official reports on that, and that is very strange and the police have had an extraordinarily high confidence rate and been placed high up on the lists that have been made, uh, we have been able to read the most dramatic headlines precisely about the confidence in the police

After this introduction follow pictures of headlines from newspapers, which are all about cases where the police did not have time to help citizens in need of assistance. At the same time, we hear an old record playing a famous Swedish children's song 'Here is the police man, standing in the middle of the street'.

In Example 2 the host points to the importance of a functioning police, but says that confidence in the police has been declining recently (i.e. it is a current problem), which is verified by a (vague) reference to 'investigations and official reports'. The problem is supposed to concern the whole of Sweden and is therefore extensive. A conflict is also implied, between the police and those who do not have confidence in them. Thereafter headlines from newspapers (also signalling that the topic is current) are used to illustrate that the police do not do their job, which further underline the existence and relevance of the problem. Newspapers are then used as independent sources. The music in the background is also, at least implicitly, contributing to the perception of the police. One way to interpret the old recording is that not only is the song old, but that it was a long time ago since the police actually 'stood in the middle of the street'. The music tells us (in a mocking way) about the old times when things were rather different (and better). Through the host's introduction, the newspaper headlines and the music, the police is portrayed as a failure and as almost ridiculous.

2.2 Exchange of opinions

In this extensive phase the actual debate takes place. This is where guests are presented and treated in specific, and different, ways.

iii) The problem is exemplified

What usually happens after the introduction is that the host turns to people who have personal experience of the problem and asks them to tell their stories of how they have been affected by the problem defined. In Example 3, from the topic about the police, this is what happens after we have been shown the headlines from newspapers claiming police failure to help citizens in need of assistance. The host turns to a 'break-in victim':

(3) *Svar Direkt, 16/10-1997; H = Host, PB = Patrik Brandt, Break-in victim*[8]

1 H: yes, Patrik Brandt is sitting here, you are actually behind one of these headlines, one could say

2 PB: yes, that is right

3 H: yes, can you tell us

4 PB: uh, I came home after work one day and found that my, there (had?) been a break-in in my apartment, and then naturally I call the police and I expect to get help, but instead they tell me that the police are reorganising themselves and-

5 H: did they tell you that?

6 PB: they told me that, yes

7 H: so, you called and said here is a break-in and I'm worried and then, yeah, yeah, what did they say?

8 PB: that they were reorganising themselves, they had no personnel that could assist me, that is what they told me

9 H: that was nice

10 PB: yes, very

11 H: and what did you say?

12 PB: yes, I was so shocked I hung up, then I called them back and said if you don't come here now I will call GT,[9] and then I get the answer 'yes do that, it is excellent that this becomes public'

13 H: still they are not prepared to come?

14 PB: no, they had no personnel

15 H: what, what happened inside of you then (PB: yes, I was (xx) in plain Swedish) because it, it sounds, there was actually a serious break-in, in your home

What is typical here is how the host emphasises the authenticity of the problem by presenting someone who has actually experienced the problem they are discussing. It is also typical that the host asks for a story on how the victim has been affected personally. In this way the latter effectively illustrates the problem; just by being in the studio he can prove the existence of the problem, and therefore it later becomes nearly impossible to contest its relevance.

Example 3 above is one example of the identity one might call *the narrating victim*. Excerpt 4 is another example of a person portrayed this way. At the beginning of a topic about insurance companies which ignore the law, the first guest is presented as follows:

(4) *Svar Direkt, 19/3-1997; H = Host, MR = Marika Rydstedt*

1 H: Marika Rydstedt, why don't you tell us what happened to you
2 MR: I had a car accident in nineteen-hundred-and-eighty, was hit from
behind and got a whiplash injury, then I have-
3 H: a so called whiplash-
4 MR: whiplash
5 H: whiplash injury, so basically you are in pain, yes
6 MR: and I was aching for some months and in eighty-five then, it
gradually became worse and worse over the years, so for twelve
years now I have had a more or less severe ache
7 H: mm, in eighty-five it started to get worse you said, what did you
do then, then you saw a doctor again
8 MR: then I saw a doctor
9 H: and what happened a couple of years ahead?
10 MR: then I saw a doctor the second time in eighty-eight (P: and) and
then there was a doctor who asked if I had been in a car accident
11 H: so he was actually the one who asked you?
12 MR: yes
13 H: had you yourself really at first not connected this with the car
accident
14 MR: no ...

Explicitly, guests in this phase are presented as people with direct (negative) experience of a problem. The host presents these persons in relation to their experience and not in relation to their professional knowledge (whatever that is). It is also typical that we as viewers are not always told what their occupations are (neither by the host, nor by the label shown on the screen). In contrast to other guests, it is not unusual that these persons are presented only by their name ('Marika Rydstedt') and with no title. When they are presented with a label it is as often defining an experience (cf. example 3 above: 'break-in victim') as a professional title.

Another characteristic feature is that these guests, and their stories, are very rarely (if ever) questioned. Instead they are encouraged to elaborate on their telling of their experience, and the host often asks relevant follow-up questions, as in Example 4: 'and what happened a couple of years ahead?' (turn 9). Very often the host also acts as a co-narrator, suggesting interpretations or points that should be made. In example 4 the host points out the consequences of the injury: 'whiplash injury, so basically you are in pain, yes' (turn 5).[10] Perhaps even more important is the fact that the host takes measures to emphasise that it was the doctor who raised the idea that her pain might be connected to the car accident ('so he actually asked you?', turn 11), a thought that she herself had not even considered. This person is portrayed as someone who does not try to secure advantages, or to exploit terms of insurance. Instead, she has been in pain for twelve years, not complaining, and now when a doctor made her think of the possible cause she is only claiming her rights.

These guests are presented as having personal experience of the problems, which means that they know what they are talking about. The image of persons just sharing the truth is further emphasised by the fact that they are not questioned by the host. They are further described as victims of adverse events, caused by others, and not receiving the help or compensation they are entitled to. Implicitly they are portrayed as being perfectly innocent, they just 'came home from work' or were 'hit from behind', i.e. they are not responsible for the situation they ended up in. They are described as not demanding or claiming impossible things, despite being maltreated. It is also unusual that these persons criticise anyone or demand that something should be changed (and they are not asked questions on how to solve the problem). Implicitly they are therefore portrayed as honest people who are not complaining, nagging or cheating, but just asking for the help that is due to them. These persons also usually portray themselves as ordinary, decent, hard working and responsible citizens. This is naturally related to the fact that their stories must be trustworthy. It then becomes important to them not to be seen as demanding and difficult persons. But they are also implicitly portrayed as weak (in need of help and not able to solve this on their own), and therefore also as ordinary in some sense. Implicitly we are encouraged to pity them or to be compassionate about their fate.

iv) The problem is verified

The next move from the host is usually to elaborate this personal experience by asking an expert how this (the problem now established) could (negatively) affect things in a larger perspective. On the topic of the lack of trust in the police (already cited) the host turns to a journalist.

(5) *Svar Direkt, 16/10-1997; H = Host, MS = Marie Söderqvist, Editor of Svenska Dagbladet*[11]

1 H: let us hear, Marie Söderqvist, you have spent a lot, you are an editor
        at Svenska Dagbladet, you have rather thoroughly analysed this

trust in the police and what do you think will happen if these are the kinds of stories we will get more and more of?

2 MS: I believe it is very dangerous and SIFO[12] releases these societal barometers and they have just recently released one where they measure confidence (H: mm) in different institutions and concerning the police, who in one way still have a relatively high confidence rate compared to local (H: but they have been placed number one) yes, exactly, but if you compare with local politicians and the tabloid press and stuff like that they have a high confidence rate, but it has declined dramatically, and then they have among other things asked how, how many believe that we have enough policemen to prevent crime and it is actually only twenty seven percent who answer that they think that the police are able to prevent crime, and that is actually rather dramatic that there are so few who think so, and of course that is very dangerous for a society, cause it is in some way the foundations, it is the ground structure in a society that the system of justice and the police function

3 H: but if people then feel that it doesn't matter, they don't care about us, what do they do instead?

4 MS: well, the risk is that we get vigilance committees and stuff like that, which we have seen examples of, where people themselves try to take the law in their own hands

What is typical here is how the host emphasises the importance of the problem by presenting someone who has expert knowledge on the topic. It is also typical that he asks for an explanation on how this problem can affect things on a higher level. By turning to this kind of expert the host has verified the importance or seriousness of the problem and made it a societal issue, rather than just a personal experience.

Excerpt 5 above is one example of the identity I refer to as *the explaining expert*. In Excerpt 6, which is from a topic called 'Democracy – a branch in crisis?', we can see a similar example.

(6) *Nattöppet, 20/3-1997; H = Host, LN = Lars Nord, Manager, The Institute of Democracy*

1 H: you, Lars Nord, you represent The Institute of Democracy and the image we get from these three politicians who are here now, that the political mission is actually inhuman, do you believe that in the long run one can consider that a threat to democracy itself ?

2 LN: yes, but the other side of this is that we have asked people what they think about political missions and a large majority actually think that we should place particularly high demands on representatives of the people compared to other citizens and then there is of course a risk in the long run that the ones who stay in this line of business, they are kamikaze pilots and masochists and that is of course not a particularly good mix /several laughs/ instead they should be representatives of other categories

3 H: but, I think this sounds serious, it, it means that if this development continues, we will have totally wrong people governing us

4 LN: yes, and a representative democracy cannot have the wrong people as representatives, that should be obvious

As shown in Examples 5 and 6 (turn 1 in both cases), it is typical that the host makes sure to present these persons' expertise ('you are editor at Svenska Dagbladet, you have rather thoroughly analysed this'; 'you represent The Institute of Democracy') and thereby legitimising them as authorities on the respective subjects. The guests in this phase are presented in relation to their professions and in relation to abstract knowledge. They are always introduced with their full names and professional titles shown on the screen (this is also often pointed out by the host verbally). They are not presented as having a personal stake in the matter, but as being in the possession of facts.

The host also often asks these guests questions. The questions are, however, not face-threatening in style but rather search for an (elaborate) explanation (cf. Example 5, turn 3: 'what do they do instead'). Typically the host takes it for granted that the utterance of the expert is true; he does not question it, as is shown in Example 6, where the expert talks about risks with politicians who cannot cope with their missions. The host takes for granted that the utterance of the expert is correct ('it means'; turn 3) and draws a rather far-reaching conclusion from this. These guests also often express their propositions with certainty, and they are not afraid of criticising others or of demanding changes.

Since the guests in this phase are cast as having professional expertise, and not any personal interest in the matter, they are implicitly portrayed not only as persons suited to explain these matters, but also as doing so in a neutral way (this is partly guaranteed by their jobs and positions as journalists, researchers etc.). Their expertise and knowledge should make us understand that they should be taken seriously. They have done research, talked to people, etc., therefore they know 'how it is'.[13] These persons also always make sure to legitimise their own role as an expert by accounting for why they are suited to present explanations. They are not questioned by the host; instead, their utterances are regarded as insightful and important. Implicitly, therefore, they are presented as encyclopedia pools, from which to borrow.

v) The problem is debated

After this the host usually opens up the floor for more of a debate, though he controls it rather strictly. Different opinions are now being aired. In all topics there are persons with different opinions about the problem that they express or are asked to express. Example 7 is from a topic about where to store nuclear waste and whether nuclear waste should be a local or a national issue.

(7) *Nattöppet, 20/3-1997; H = Host, IB = Irma Björk, Local Politician, Malå (s)*[14]*, ÅE = Åsa Ehnberg, Midwife, Malå*

1 H: Irma, this autumn you will have a referendum in Malå, about whether you want SKB[15] to continue investigating the preconditions in, in your area (IB: yes) do you think this is good, do you think the referendum is good, that you deal with the question in this way?

2 IB: yes, since the local government, when we made this decision, we already decided that when the examination was done we should have a referendum and therefore I think it is our obligation to keep that promise to the citizens of Malå

3 H: but, I mean, one thing is that it is your obligation, but do you think, I mean this question has become very much of a local issue and very little of a national issue so to speak, do you think that is good?

4 IB: yes, I do

5 H: you think they do a good job, you are satisfied so to speak?

6 IB: yeah

7 H: do you think SKB is doing a good job at your place?

8 IB: yes, they do

9 H: do you share her opinion?

10 ÅE: no, I don't, I don't think it is something that should be decided by the citizens of Malå

11 H: and why not?

12 ÅE: it is simply too big a question

In this phase the host lets people express their opinions, thereby showing that there are different opinions and that they are all being aired in the debate. These persons are often encouraged to express their opinions on a specific topic or they are encouraged to answer an earlier opinion or evaluation. In Example 7, we can see how the host clarifies the issue at stake, the possible opinions and who holds them. This is done by first asking one guest for a specific opinion (whether a referendum is good or not; turn 1) and then asking another guest for an opposite opinion ('do you share her opinion'; turn 9). In this way, the host can display a conflict between these two guests without giving up his neutrality (cf. Greatbatch 1998). An important task for the host is to clarify the opinions and play them out against each other, to create conflict. One way to do this is to always look for or demand a simple yes or no answer, thereby clarifying the antagonists' standpoints. Therefore, in Example 7, the opinion that the referendum is an obligation (turn 2) is treated as the 'wrong' opinion; it becomes a technicality that conceals the question of good or bad.

Excerpt 7 above is one example of an identity I call *the claims-making opinion holder*. Another example, concerning the lack of trust in the police, can be seen in Excerpt 8, where a police inspector is presented as critical of both a reform and the minister of justice.

(8) *Svar Direkt, 16/10-1997; H = Host, LO = Lars-Göran Oertel, Police inspector*

1 H: mm, Lars-Göran Oertel, you, you are stationed in one of these areas and are rather critical of the system with a local police, you have written to the minister of justice, now you have her right in front of you

2 LO: I am not critical of the local police and how they work as such, but I mean that, that the public experience that the police do not come when you call them, you don't get the help you need in emergency situations, the crimes are not investigated and so on, that is actually the result of a number of reorganisations and it started with the local police system, when the reform was introduced in ninety-four, it should also be made clear that these policemen have a lot of other tasks they did not have before and that is the basis more generally in this new organisation of the police and when you don't get new resources you take, this reform becomes an organisation within the organisation so to speak and you take resources from traditional activities, that is ordinary police duties, the ones that go out with

blue lights, the ones that come to people in emergency situations, you take resources from criminal departments that investigate
3 H: it becomes then as in these examples, simply put the public suffers?
4 LO: it is obvious that we do not have the same possibilities to assist the public when they need us in emergency situations and the like and fewer crimes get investigated
5 H: what, what are you saying, that it simply does not work with this new organisation?
6 LO: no, not, not concerning these matters
7 H: and why is that, because you have too little money or because it is
8 LO: no, because you take, you take resources from other ...

As we have seen, guests in this phase are presented in relation to a specific opinion. They are presented as opinion holders with interesting and, above all, mutually opposed opinions. Unlike neutral experts, these guests are presented as having a direct personal relation to the topic, in the sense that they are expected to belong to either the 'yes' or the 'no' side. They are portrayed as opinion holders, rather than as victims or experts. Often we see both their names and professions on the screen. The host, however, does not always present these persons with (name and) profession, but rather in relation to what they think about a particular issue. The important thing here is these persons' opinions, and therefore there are no obvious connections to their experiences or occupations.

It often happens that the host asks for a clarification of opinions. Some are merely asked to say yes or no and do so. Others are asked to explain why they have a certain opinion. The latter is seen in Example 7: 'and why not?' (turn 11). It is of course important, not only for the host (and the audience) but for the guests themselves, that their opinions are clarified. Therefore, it also happens that the host does not just clarify an opinion, but he collaborates in expressing it. This is seen in Example 8, where the host's questions consist of suggestions of how his opinion should be interpreted: 'it becomes then as in these examples, simply put the public suffers?' (turn 3). It also happens that the host questions the guests' opinions. This is not very common, however, perhaps due to the fact that the opinions are often known and expected. When opinions or statements are questioned it usually concerns another type of guest, the defending accountable person, which I will comment on below.

Since guests in this phase are presented as opinion holders, they are implicitly portrayed as persons with a conviction, persons committed to a cause and being involved. By clarifying opinions, emphasising differences and negative opinions (criticisms, accusations etc.), by playing out guests against each other, the host implicitly casts these persons as mutually opposed, angry and conflictual.

vi) The 'problem' is defended as not being a problem

In all topics, often towards the end, there are also people who are presented as involved in decision making or the measures that should follow from the problem. Usually these persons are restricted to comment on what has been said earlier on the show. We can see this in the next example concerning the topic about nuclear waste where the host confronts a member of parliament.

(9) *Nattöppet, 20/3-1997; H = Host, OJ = Olof Johansson, Member of Parliament*

1 H: but I mean you (OJ: xx) may I say so, you were actually secretary of
      the environment when this process started and now you are critical
      of the process, have you so to speak changed your mind?
2 OJ: critical, I am, I have to tolerate democratic decisions like everyone
      else, that is, my suggestion was not voted for …

A typical feature here is that the host points out that this person was involved in making the decision. It is also typical that the host questions these persons, requiring them to explain decisions and to defend themselves. Often the host also focuses on changes of mind, in search for regrets or excuses and confession of mistakes. By turning to these persons the host shows that he, as a representative of the studio audience and the viewers, does not fear power but challenges it.

Excerpt 9 above is one example of the identity that I refer to as *the defending accountable person*. In Example 10, concerning the topic about nuclear waste, several recurrent strategies are found.

(10) *Nattöppet, 20/3-1997; H = Host, SB = Sinikka Bohlin, Vice-chairman, The Committee of Agriculture(s)*[16]

1 H: but Sinikka, couldn't one say that this is an extremely big issue in
      the sense that it concerns an eternally long time perspective, couldn't
      one be allowed to think that you are somewhat unusually generous
      when it comes to distributing power in this particular issue?

2 SB: no, I think that if we at anytime have found a good way, what we call
       responsibility of production, if someone produces something, in this
       case electric power, they shall also deal with the waste
3 H: yes, but, that is one thing, that is one thing,
4 SB: but of course it is a national issue, it is not a (local issue?)
5 H: another thing, Sinikka, that is one thing (SB: yes) another thing is
       of course how you give directives, how that should be handled, is it
       reasonable that a small northern community should make decisions
       that you seemingly don't want to handle?
6 SB: yes, now this is a governmental issue, but of course we deal with this
       in the parliament too, but to me it is important that they, the place
       that possibly sometime will become the place where we will make
       this long storage, I think they must be part of the process as citizens
       since I and my children and grandchildren will live there, to me both
       parts in this process are important
7 H: we should also say that the committee of agriculture, you handle this
       issue, otherwise this might sound strange (SB: yes, thanks)

In this phase the host's questions or propositions will often suggest that
these persons have influence over decision making in some way. Their
professions, tasks and official status in relation to the problem are obviously
considered important by the producers, and they are always presented with
their names and professions on the screen label (and often verbally by the
host). In Example 9 we see this in turn 1: 'you were actually secretary of
environment when this process started'. The fact that their professions are
not always explicitly stated by the host might be because many of them are
famous politicians, of whom the viewers are expected to have knowledge
anyway. In Example 10 the host forgets this verbal presentation, and
mentions it only in turn 7: 'the committee of agriculture, you handle this
question'.

In contrast to other guests, these persons are not asked to relate a
personal story nor to explain the facts or express an opinion. The host
asks these guests to account for decisions, and demands explanations or
solutions. The host might also question their decisions and utterances,
thereby provoking defence. In Example 10, we can see how the host asks
for an account of a decision: 'couldn't one be allowed to think that you
are somewhat unusually generous when it comes to distributing power
on this particular issue?' (turn 1). We can also see how this decision is
questioned and how the politician is requested to explain her actions, also

signalling that she has the possibility to change the decision: 'that is one thing … another thing is of course how you give directives, how it should be handled, is it reasonable that a small northern community should make decisions that you seemingly don't want to handle?' (turn 3 and 5).[17] This question also contains a provoking statement ('you seemingly don't want to handle'), inviting a counter-statement.

It is characteristic of these persons, in contrast to experts, that they often claim not to be experts or know something. In Example 10, the local politician emphasises that she is not directly responsible: 'this is governmental' (turn 6).[18] It is also typical that they defend themselves by pointing out the complexity of the issue. Very often they also agree with criticism (at the same time as they explain why they are not personally involved). A typical feature is also that these persons claim to be open-minded, willing to listen, working on the problem or are prepared to change things.

Since these guests are described as involved in making decisions, they are implicitly portrayed as potentially responsible for the existence and solution of the problem. By requiring accounts, demanding explanations, focusing on changes of mind, regrets or excuses, etc., the host implicitly portrays them as potentially guilty of mistakes. They are portrayed as the ones to be questioned, as not trustworthy.

2.3 Wrapping up

vii) The problem is reiterated

Towards the end of a topic the host always returns to his or her perspective. This is done either by stating the same questions or propositions that have been repeated throughout the topic or by giving the last word to someone who has earlier demonstrated agreement with this very perspective.

In the topic about the police, the same expert (cf. Example 5) whom the host has used to verify the crisis within the police is now given the opportunity to restate this crisis once again:

(11) *Svar Direkt, 16/10-1997; H = Host, MS = Marie Söderqvist, Editor Svenska Dagbladet*

1 H: (xx) Marie, now we have very little time left, now you will have the last word here

2 MS: it is incredible to sit here saying that, that this is not a crisis, I mean in nineteen-hundred-and-fifty they solved ninety percent of all crimes related to violence, today they solve half of all crimes related to violence and you can keep on presenting statistics like that forever, the police are not capable of doing their job

viii) The topic ends

Usually the topics do not have a proper conclusion, they are cut off in the middle of the discussion. It is only in the case of a few topics that the host draws his or her own (brief) conclusions and thanks the guests for their participation.

These closures give the impression that we as viewers have taken part in a debate that goes on (which it of course does in some sense) although we stop watching. The gist of these topics is therefore that the problem is still there and therefore was worth discussing (and that we can have more debates on the same or other topics).

3 Roles and responsibility

What this analysis has shown is that the dramaturgy (the performative act) of these programmes rests on certain recurrent segments, often in a certain order, where guests are spoken to and presented in different ways. The topic (defined as a problem) is first introduced in headlines and by the host. Thereafter, the problem is exemplified by a victim, verified by an expert, debated by people with different opinions and defended by someone held accountable. Finally, before the rather abrupt closure, the problem is reiterated by the host. The topics are usually portrayed as something you can be for or against, often in dramatic terms. The focus is always on negative aspects, risks and threats. Very often the producers also rather obviously advocate a perspective that favours certain groups, e.g. the victimised citizens against the police who allegedly 'do not do their job'.

3.1 Activity roles and teamwork

As for the participants in the TV-debates, there are four main identities possible for the guests, according to how they are introduced and treated.

From the producer's point of view, guests are attributed certain identities, and thereby they are addressed in different *activity roles*, which have certain functions in the debates. These roles can be summarised as follows.

Guests can be addressed in *Example roles* (i.e. guests are portrayed as having personal experience of the problem at issue, and their role is to act as an example of a negative event by *telling a story* of how they as individuals have been affected). The guests can also be addressed in *Expert roles* (i.e. guests are portrayed as having professional knowledge about the topic, and their role is to *explain or verify* the significance and seriousness of the problem). Further, the guests can be addressed in *Opinion roles* (i.e. guests are portrayed as holding a certain opinion on a topic, and their role is to *claim or express* that opinion in relation to another opinion/guest). Finally, the guests can be addressed in *Accountable roles* (i.e. guests are portrayed as having influence over decision making, and their role is to *defend or account for* why the problem exists and what they are going to do about it).[19] The roles also have interesting relations to each other. For example, those being addressed in *Example roles* are automatically positioned in an antagonistic relation to those who want to mitigate the seriousness of the problem (e.g. guests addressed in *Accountable roles*).

It should, however, be pointed out that certain guests are presented and treated differently during one and the same topic. In the topic called 'Democracy – a branch in crisis?' the politician Birger Schlaug is at first presented in the following way:

(12) *Nattöppet, 20/3, 1997; H = Host*

1 H: but really, now we have talked to two local politicians, but you Birger, you belong to, if one may say so, you belong-, you belong to the actual bigwigs so to speak, a leading figure in a parliament party, but you have also written a newspaper article in which you really have expressed some kind of agony, almost, in relation to the political mission

In Excerpt 12 Birger Schlaug is presented as belonging to the 'actual bigwigs' but above all he is presented as someone who has expressed 'some kind of agony', i.e. someone who has suffered from the roughness of being a politician. In that respect he is being addressed in an example role. A few minutes later, on the same topic, Birger Schlaug appears again:

(13) *Nattöppet, 20/3, 1997; H = Host, BS = Birger Schlaug, mouthpiece (mp)*[20]

1 P: one moment, you can comment, but first I will let Birger comment on this

2 BS: often you hear that politicians have lost power that someone has taken their power away, but it is important just as Björn says

3 P: well, it seems like it

4 BS: yes, exactly, but it is important just as Björn says that politicians, the political majority, most politicians, have accepted to turn the power over step by step, that is very important

5 P: but how can you do that?

In Excerpt 13 Birger Schlaug is first given the word freely. He expresses an opinion ('it is important just as Björn says') and he speaks generally about politicians who have lost power. One could therefore say that he on his own initiative acts as someone with an opinion on how the problem discussed should be understood and maybe be solved (the Opinion role). The host however, through his question (turn 5), clarifies ('but how can you do that?') that Schlaug is one of the politicians that are being criticised. In that way the host questions Schlaug and demands an explanation of his actions, rather than of politicians' actions in general. He is then addressed in an Accountable role.

In accordance with the example above it is important to point out that these roles are not given or static. The role one is addressed (or act) in can sometimes change during the topic and everyone can act in the *Opinion role*. However, guests are usually only addressed in one specific role. The *Example role* is kept for those with personal experience of the problem, the *Expert role* is kept for those with professional knowledge about the problem and the *Accountable role* is kept for those who have something to do with decisions or circumstances concerning the problem.

There are of course also possibilities to oppose the ways one is portrayed and described and thereby the identity one is attributed and the role one is addressed in.

That opposition is not always successful as shown in Example 14.

The example concerns an issue on a photo exhibition called *Ecce Homo* (showing homosexual people in religious/biblical situations). The host talks about whether it is suitable or not to show the exhibition. After three 'ordinary' exhibition visitors the host turns to someone he calls a 'catholic vicar':

(14) *Debattakuten, 15/10, 1998; H: Host, JN: Joseph Maria Nilsson, Priest Catholic Church*

1 H: no, yes, some of the reactions you can get, one could ask a catholic vicar here, what do you say?

2 JN: I, I think it is remarkable that one, when one, as Elisabeth Olsson[21] actually has done with these pictures, demands understanding and acceptance of a certain group, uh, of course of homosexuals (H: mm), at the same time offends other people when she is aware that this offends very many, does not stop, nor withdraw
        [6 lines omitted]

3 H: are you offended?

4 JN: not me personally, but I-

5 H: yeah, yeah, now you really have to be somewhat honest, are you offended or not (JN: <u>well, for me</u>) <u>one cannot</u>, you are actually both a priest and a person

6 JN: yes, yes, for me personally these pictures don't matter because it does not change my view of Christ, it doesn't, but I feel for those people who are offended they-

7 H: no, but now you really can't be like that, we shall not be as I am but as I preach, priests have done that all the time

8 JN: well but you know, people who understand, I haven't seen, it is the first time I see these pictures here, except the scenario from the Holy Communion that has been shown on Aktuellt[22] et cetera (H: mm), uh, but what, I don't think it is about the pictures in themselves but about offending or not, is one group (H: mm), do they have the right to offend, is it the mass media or who decides (H: mm) who is allowed to offend, neo-nazis can't open their mouths to say what they want because then it is persecution of minority groups for example, but somebody else who comes in the name of sexuality, they have the right to say exactly what they want and offend, step on other people's view of God which is something intimate, which is the innermost in a person

9 H: (she/they?) have offended a sacredness so to speak, passed a limit of sacredness in you?

10 JN: yes, yes /some people applaud/

In this sequence the host turns to a 'catholic vicar' who considers the exhibition to be unsuitable because it offends people (one could say that he acts in the Opinion role). The host does not question this; however, on several occasions he questions if this person is honest when saying he is not personally offended. The host repeatedly seeks this guest's personal opinion ('are you offended?') and succeeds finally to get an admittance of this, despite recurring denials. Here it is rather obvious that the host tries to present this guest as an example person, i.e. as someone who has suffered personally, and he succeeds in the end.

This perhaps shows that whatever role one is trying to act in one does so in relation to how one is presented and in relation to the questions one is asked. The kind of opposition expressed in Example 14 above is also very rare in my data. This is related both to the influence of the producers (they choose the topic, perspective, guests, how and when they should be addressed) and to the fact that the host controls the interaction. Most guests therefore act in their assigned roles. These debates are staged performances or stories which are enacted in front of an audience. Those who participate do so within the frame of pre-planned roles. The participants are therefore expected to hold on to their given roles since they are part of the dramaturgy. In this sense the programme can be considered *teamwork*. This can be compared to Goffman's (1982 [1959]) idea that since everyone is keen not to lose face, a tactical cooperation arises quite naturally where all confirm their own and others' roles. The guests are also invited for a reason and with certain expectations; they are invited because they have a certain opinion or because something has happened to them. There are, seemingly, few reasons why they should not act in their role.

Those who oppose and refuse this role attribution are most often the ones addressed in Accountable roles. What they oppose, however, is the degree of responsibility while they can hardly deny their actual decisions or social status (which the host emphasises). Their alternative would be not to participate, a choice through which they would risk looking even more responsible (guilty) and perhaps also like cowards. By participating they can be said to accept their role of having to defend their responsibility. What they still oppose is often the way the topic is presented or perspectivised (indirectly putting them in an unfavourable position).

Since the guests have to relate to a given perspective on the topic, which is presented at the start, it is natural that guests who do not share this perspective say that they would like to broaden, extend or nuance what has been put forward so far. This is shown in the next example. The headline, in the form of a voice-over, of the topic is: 'The Department of Transportation wants to stop mopeds and motorcycles'. The perspective put forward by the producers is that the Department of Transportation wants to forbid mopeds and motorcycles, something which the host repeats on numerous occasions during the discussion of the topic. When we enter Example 15 the representative of the Department of Transportation has just presented numbers of casualties in traffic, something that has been questioned by another guest.

(15) *Svar Direkt, 28/8 1997; H = Host, CT = Claes Tingvall, Head of the Department of Transportation*

1 CT: you can always twist and turn these kinds of figures, of course not for the purpose of manipulation but to illustrate different things / some are laughing?/ uh, it is like this, I mean if you look at so to speak one and the same age group then evidently it is so that di-, the risk-, differences become somewhat smaller, uh, but no matter how you twist and turn this, it is vehicles that are far, far more dangerous to ride, at least on your own, right, it is completely true that cars hurt others and so on, but on your own, but mostly what we are talking about, that in the future it will be possible to do so much more for those who walk, ride bicycles, drive cars, but it is very difficult to do anything with mc:s, it, it is just telling it as it is really, then I still believe that nobody wants to talk about prohibition or something like that

2 H: mm, but still what you say is really as close to prohibition as one can get

In Example 15 we see how a guest tries to nuance the perspective which the host, with the aid from other guests, has presented earlier, i.e. that the Department of Transportation wants to stop or prohibit mopeds and motorcycles. In the guest's last sentence (turn 1) it is revealed that he, during several occasions in the show, has said that he is against a prohibition of mopeds and motorcycles ('I still believe that nobody wants to talk about prohibition'). The conclusion of the host is despite this that what the guest says is as 'close to prohibition as one can get' (turn 2). This shows that one way for the host to control the interaction and maintain the perspective is to use so called *formulations* (Fairclough 1992), i.e. to sum up or interpret what others say in order to return to the agenda.[23] The formulation is also aimed at the audience and the conclusion or interpretation made by the host invites the audience to share his or her interpretation. It is evidently not only difficult to resist the role of being an accountable person but also difficult to resist *what* you are responsible for.

3.2 Role responsibility and societal responsibility

The distribution of activity roles, and the communicative limitations and expectations attached to them, naturally affect who is discursively construed as socially responsible. Although these activity roles are not entirely static, they have an important relation to the participants' societal roles (i.e. the kind of societal groups they represent in terms of occupation and official status).

The *Example role* is usually played by ordinary citizens, private persons (e.g. cab drivers, craftsmen, gas station workers etc.); the *Expert role* is played by well-educated people (journalists, academics); the *Opinion role* is usually played by well-educated people, but not always; and the *Accountable role* is usually played by politicians and other authorities.

This recurrent distribution of roles (to representatives of different societal categories) also indicates a cultural understanding of how to handle, and conceive of, issues of societal responsibility. Ordinary people are affected by the problems, but not responsible for coming up with solutions to them. They are only responsible for sharing their story and their experience. Different kinds of experts and opinion holders (academics, journalists etc.) are responsible for sharing their knowledge and presenting alternative solutions, but not for the actual solution. Politicians and others in decision-making roles are responsible for explaining the reason for the problem and for taking measures.

The hosts (producers) also present themselves, directly or indirectly, in certain ways. By portraying the topics as important, authentic and in need of a solution (and as something that would otherwise not be discussed), they portray themselves as needed and as people who can offer a possibility to solve the problem in question. In other words, they make available a discussion space. The hosts also often take the perspective of the public by turning to the camera, speaking of 'us' and 'we'. This is further emphasised by the fact that they take their point of departure in ordinary citizens' stories, trust them and use them to challenge the power elites. In this way they are portrayed as responsible for scrutinising power and sorting out (ordinary people's) problems.

Consequently, we encounter a debate where different individuals and their personal experiences are construed as affected by the power elites and their decisions. The general perspective is that individuals are subjected to different problems by society and its institutions, without being able to influence them on their own. The ordinary citizen is therefore portrayed as a passive victim of a system he or she cannot influence. Citizens can only be helped by authorities changing decisions (on the initiative of media producers).

Interestingly enough, discussion and debate programmes on TV have in recent years been mentioned as a potential new democratic forum where the public can make their voices heard and challenge power in face to face conversation (see for example Leurdijk 1997; Livingstone and Lunt 1994). In relation to this one could ask in what sense it is fruitful for democracy that the mass media constantly reproduces a stereotypical image of an unfair society where power dominates passive and vulnerable people (that can only be helped by the media)? One could further ask if this view of and treatment of ordinary citizens encourages political engagement and participation? What other function is there for the citizen – as a narrating victim – than to act in the Example role? To me it seems clear that if the TV-debates are to fill a democratic function, the producers (the mass media) must take their social responsibility and not oversimplify societal problems and the relations between different social groups.

4 Epilogue on responsibility

There are naturally factual circumstances related to responsibility. Politicians and other power elites usually do have more responsibility for societal or political issues than do ordinary citizens. However, responsibility is not just something that people have or possess, it is something that is discursively and interactionally constructed; through communication, responsibility for actions is constantly negotiated. And as a TV-audience we seldom have knowledge of the actors' prior concrete deeds or utterances regarding a specific topic; we have to make our judgement on the basis of the things said and done in the studio (on the screen).[24]

Further, each and every participant could of course be said to be responsible for their own acts and utterances in the TV-debates – how they present themselves (how they express their responsibility). However, since the producers of these TV-debates so heavily control the interaction it is obvious that the guests' self presentations must be understood in relation to (among other things) the producers' framing of the topic (in headlines and host introductions), the verbal and visual presentation of the guests, the kind of questions and follow-up questions the guests are asked and the sequential order in which this is done.

In this respect the TV-debates are clearly not just neutral places for the exchanging of ideas, but they also contribute to *how* these ideas and persons should be understood (which implicitly contributes to the ideological reproduction of how to view societal responsibility). How responsibility is discursively construed (and further down the line, how different segments of the audience interpret this) in different media arenas or media texts therefore ought to be an important future field of research.

Notes

1   See http://www.svt.se (retrieved on 16 October 1997). *Svar Direkt* translates approximately as *Responding Directly*.
2   The data for this study were collected in the context of the research programme *Discourse in Society: On whose conditions?* (Samtal i samhället: På vems villkor?), supported by The Bank of Sweden Tercentenary Foundation (RJ, Dnr. 95-5123:01).
3   See also Potter (1996). His notion of *category entitlement* is specifically used to describe categorisation in terms of authority.
4   Note that there are many different kinds of conversations in the mass media with different features (see, for example, Dahlgren 1995: 54; Hutchby 2006; Tolson 2006). In this study, TV-debates are seen as one specific kind of mass-mediated conversation.
5   Cf. the notion of *role* in Thomas (1986) and in Weizman (2009).
6   These aspects can be related to general notions of news values in the media; deviance (positive, but often negative), conflict, timeliness/novelty, social significance/importance (cf. Allan (2004), McManus (1994) regarding TV-news or Harcup and O'Neill (2001) regarding news papers).
7   The transcripts have been translated from Swedish into English by the author. The original transcripts and a guide to transcription symbols can be found in the Appendices.
8   The identification of the guests presented before the examples is how they were presented by the labels shown on the TV-screen.
9   GT is a Swedish newspaper.
10 These kinds of utterances have been called *cooperative formulations* by Nylund (2000:160). On formulations, see also Clayman and Heritage (2002); Fairclough (1992); Heritage (1985).
11 Svenska Dagbladet is a Swedish newspaper.
12 SIFO is a Swedish opinion poll institute.
13 Note that the expert in example 6 refers to 'we' (have asked people; line 4). The 'we' might be used by professionals in institutional interaction in an excluding way to mark collegial authority or collective knowledge which is not available to the lay person (Silverman 1987).

14   The (s) indicates that the person represents the political party Socialdemo-
     kraterna (The social democrats).
15   SKB stands for Svensk Kärnbränslehantering Aktiebolag, the company
     assigned by the government to investigate the storage of nuclear waste.
16   The (s) indicates that the person represents the political party Socialdemo-
     kraterna (The social democrats).
17   This is what Nylund (2000: 158) would call a *counter question*, i.e. a follow-
     up question construed as an objection to or challenge of earlier responses.
18   People acting in this role very often use 'we' in an inclusive way (e.g. the
     party) as a way of avoiding personal responsibility (cf. note 14).
19   Similar roles can be found also in other types of media texts, audiovisual as
     well as written (see for example Fairclough 1995). What is interesting is how
     these roles are articulated together in specific media texts and how they are
     related to different societal groups.
20   The (mp) indicates the political party Miljöpartiet (The environmental party).
     'Mouthpiece' is the party term used to describe one of the two party leaders.
21   The artist behind the exhibition.
22   One of the most well known Swedish newscasts, broadcast in public service.
23   Fairclough (1992: 157) says that a formulation is when someone describes,
     explains, characterises, clarifies, translates or concludes someone else's
     utterance or a whole debate.
24   Of course, this is even more true when extensive editing or hidden cameras
     are used (cf. Economou and Svensson Limsjö 2006).

References

Allan, S. (2004) *News Culture*. Maidenhead: Open University Press.
Clayman, S. (1991) News Interview openings: aspects of sequential organisation.
     In P. Scannell (ed.) *Broadcast Talk* 48–75. London: Sage.
Clayman, S. and Heritage, J. (2002) *The News Interview: Journalists and Public
     Figures on the Air*. Cambridge: Cambridge University Press.
Corner, J. and Pels, D. (2003) *Media and the Restyling of Politics: Consumerism,
     Celebrity and Cynicism*. London: Sage.
Dahlgren, P. (2009) *Media and Political Engagement: Citizens, Communication
     and Democracy*. New York: Cambridge University Press.
Dahlgren, P. (1995) *Television and the Public Sphere*. London: Sage.
Denzin, N. (2003) *Performance Ethnograhpy: Critical Pedagogy and the Politics
     of Culture*. Thousand Oaks, CA: Sage.
Economou, K. and Svensson Limsjö, C. (2006) Hidden camera speaks louder than
     words. In M. Ekström, Å. Kroon and M. Nylund (eds) *News from the Interview
     Society* 121–144. Göteborg: Nordicom.

Fairclough, N. (1992) *Discourse and Social Change*. Oxford: Polity Press.

Fairclough, N. (1995) *Media Discourse*. London: Edward Arnold.

Goffman, E. (1974) *Frame Analysis. An Essay on the Organization of Experience*. Cambridge, MA: Harvard University Press.

Goffman, E. (1982 [1959]) *The Presentation of Self in Everyday Life*. Harmondsworth: Penguin Books.

Greatbatch, D. (1998) Neutralism in British news interviews. In A. Bell and P. Garrett (eds) *Approaches to Media Discourse* 163–185. Blackwell: Oxford.

Harcup, T. and O'Neill, D. (2001) What is news? Galtung and Ruge revisited. *Journalism Studies* 2: 261–280.

Heritage, J. (1985) Analyzing news interviews: aspects of the production of talk for an overhearing audience. In T. van Dijk (ed.) *Handbook of Discourse Analysis Vol 3: Discourse and Dialogue* 95–117. London: Academic Press.

Hutchby, I. (2006) *Media Talk: Conversation Analysis and the Study of Broadcasting*. Maidenhead: Open University Press.

Hydén, L. C. (2001) Who!? Identity in institutional contexts. In M. Seltzer, C. Kullberg, S. P. Olesen and I. Rostila (eds) *Listening to the Welfare State* 213–240. Aldershot: Ashgate.

Krause, A. and Goering, E. (1995) Local talk in the global village: an intercultural comparison of American and German talk shows. *Journal of Popular Culture* 29: 189–207.

Leurdijk, A. (1997) Common sense versus political discourse: debating racism and multicultural society in Dutch talk shows. *European Journal of Communication* 12: 147–168.

Linell, P. (1998) *Approaching Dialogue*. Amsterdam. John Benjamins.

Livingstone, S. and Lunt, P. (1994) *Talk on Television: Audience Participation and Public Debate*. London: Routledge.

McManus, J. (1994) *Market-Driven Journalism. Let the Citizen Beware?* Thousand Oaks, CA: Sage.

Nylund, M. (2000) *Iscensatt interaktion – strukturer och strategier i politiska mediesamtal* [Staged interaction – structures and strategies in political media interactions]. University of Helsinki: Department of Communication.

Potter, J. (1996) *Representing Reality: Discourse, Rhetoric and Social Construction*. London: Sage.

Sacks, H. (1992) *Lectures on Conversation*. Vol. 1 and 2. Oxford: Blackwell.

Sarangi, S. (2000) Activity types, discourse types and interactional hybridity: the case of genetic counselling. In S. Sarangi and M. Coulthard (eds) *Discourse and Social Life* 1–27. Harlow: Longman.

Silverman, D. (1987) *Communication and Medical Practice*. London: Sage.

Svensson, C. (2001) *Samtal, deltagande och demokrati i svenska TV-debattprogram* [Dialogue, participation and democracy in Swedish TV-debates]. Linköping Studies in arts and Science 227. Linköping University.

Thomas, J. (1986) The dynamics of discourse: a pragmatic analysis of confrontational interaction. Unpublished PhD Thesis, Lancaster University.

Tolson, A. (2006) *Media Talk: Spoken Discourse on TV and Radio*. Edinburgh: Edinburgh University Press.

Weizman, E. (2009) *Positioning in Media Dialogue: Negotiating Roles in the News Interview*. Amsterdam: Johan Benjamins.

Christian Svensson Limsjö is Senior Lecturer in Media and Communication Studies at the Department for Studies of Social Change and Culture, Linköping University, Sweden. His main research interests are in media and journalism and its relation to democracy and the public sphere.

Appendix 1: Transcription symbols

P	Indicates speaker identity
<u>anyhow</u>	Underlining indicates overlapping talk
(P: anyhow)	Parentheses followed by speaker identity indicate something said in another person's turn
, ?	Commas and question marks are used to indicate non-terminal and rising intonation respectively
anyhow-	Word followed by line indicates a sudden interruption
(xx)	Parentheses with xx indicate that the transcriber was unable to hear what was said
(anyhow?)	Parentheses with a word followed by a question mark indicate that the transcriber was not sure of what was said
P?	Indicates that the transcriber was not sure of speaker identity
[…]	Dots within brackets indicate that words have been left out
/laughs/	Indicate speaker's non-verbal behaviour
/P laughs/	Indicate a specific person's, other than the speaker, non-verbal behaviour
/several laughs/	Indicate several persons' non-verbal behaviour

Appendix 2: Original examples in Swedish

Example 1. Svar Direkt, 16/10, 1997, VO: Voiceover

1 VO: vad gör man när polisen inte sköter sitt jobb, tar lagen i egna
händer eller polisanmäler polisen?

Example 2. Svar Direkt, 16/10, 1997, P: Programledare

1 P: ja, att polisen ska fungera i ett land, det är naturligtvis oerhört
viktigt, det är en utav demokratins hörnpelare också, och vad
som har hänt i Sverige dom sista, äh, den sista tiden, det är alltså
att förtroendet för polisen har minskat, det finns till och med
undersökningar och utredningar på det och det är väldigt märkligt
och polisen har haft ett utomordentligt högt förtroende och legat
högt upp på dom listerna som har gjorts, äh, vi har kunnat läsa
dom mest dramatiska rubriker just om förtroendet för polisen

Example 3. Svar Direkt, 16/10, 1997, P: Programledare, PB. Patrik
Brandt, Inbrottsoffer

1 P: ja, Patrik Brandt sitter här, du är faktiskt bakom en av de här
rubrikerna kan man säga
2 PB: ja, det stämmer det
3 P: ja, kan du berätta
4 PB: äh, jag kom hem efter jobbet en dag och fann att min, jag (hade?)
haft inbrott i min lägenhet och då ringer jag naturligtvis till polisen
och jag väntar mig och få hjälp men istället får jag höra att polisen
håller på och omorganiserar och-
7 P: sa dom det till dig?
8 PB: dom sa det till mig ja
9 P: så du ringde och sa här är inbrott och jag är orolig och så, ja, ja,
vad sa dom?
10 PB: att dom höll på å omorganisera, dom hade ingen personal som
kunde komma å hjälpa
11   mig, det var det jag fick höra
12 P: det var ju hyggligt
13 PB: ja, väldigt
14 P: å vad sa du?

15 PB: ja, jag blev så chockad så jag la på, sen ringde jag upp igen å sa det
         att ni får komma hit nu annars så ska jag ringa till GT, å då får jag
         svaret att 'ja, gör det, det är jättebra att det här kommer ut'
18 P: fortfarande så är dom inte beredda å komma?
19 PB: nej, dom hade ingen personal
20 P: vad, vad hände i dig själv alltså (PB: ja, jag blev (xx) på rak
         svenska) för det, det här låter, det var ett rejält inbrott i ditt hem
         alltså

Example 4. Svar Direkt, 19/3, 1997, P: Programledare, MR: Marika
Rydstedt

1 P: Marika Rydstedt, du kan väl berätta vad du har råkat ut för
2 MR: jag råka ut för en trafikolycka nittonhundraåtti, vart påkörd
         bakifrån och fick en whiplashskada, sen har jag-
3 P: en så kallad pisksnärt-
4 MR: pisksnärt
5 P: pisksnärtskada, så du har ont helt enkelt ja
6 MR: och hade väl värk då i några månader och då åttifem då börja det
         successivt och bli värre och värre med åren, så i tolv år har jag gått
         med mer eller mindre svårare värk
7 P: mm, åttifem börja det bli värre sa du, vad gjorde du då, då gick du
         till läkare igen
8 MR: då sökte jag upp läkare
9 P: och vad hände några år framåt där?
10 MR: sen sökte jag andra gången åttiåtta (P: och) och då var det en läkare
         som frågade om jag hade varit med i en trafikolycka
11 P: så det var han som fråga dig alltså?
12 MR: ja
13 P: hade du själv egentligen inte först förknippat det med, med
         trafikolyckan?
14 MR: nä [...]

Example 5. Svar Direkt, 16/10, 1997, P: Programledare, M: Marie
Söderqvist, ledarskribent Svenska dagbladet

1 P: ska vi höra, Marie Söderqvist du har ägnat mycket, du är
         ledarskribent på Svenska Dagbladet, du har analyserat rätt mycket
         utav det här med förtroendet för polisen och vad tror du händer
         om, om det är såna här berättelser mer och mer som vi får?

2 MS: jag tror att det är jättefarligt, och SIFO kommer ju ut med en sån
        här samhällsbarometer och dom har precis i dagarna kommit ut
        med en där dom mäter förtroendet (P: hm) för olika institutioner
        och från polisen då som i och för sig fortfarande har relativt högt
        förtroende om man jämför med kommunal (P: men dom har legat
        i topp) ja, just det men om man jämför med kommunalpolitiker å
        kvällspress å sånt här så har dom väldigt högt förtroende, men dom
        har sjunkit dramatiskt, å så har dom bland annat frågat hur, hur
        många det är som tror att det räcker med poliser för att förhindra
        brott och det är alltså bara tjugosju procent som svarar att dom tror
        att polisen klarar av å förhindra brott, å det är ju ganska dramatiskt
        att det är så få som gör det, å det är klart att det är väldigt farligt
        för ett samhälle, för det är ju ändå på nåt sätt grunderna, det är
        alltså grundstrukturer i ett samhälle att rättsväsendet och polisen
        fungerar
3 P: men om människor så här känner då att det spelar ingen roll, de
        bryr sig inte om det, vad gör de istället?
4 MS: ja, risken finns ju med såna här medborgargarden ä sänt som det ju
        finns lite exempel på, där man då själv går ut å försöker ta lagen i
        egna händer

Example 6. Nattöppet 20/3, 1997, P: Programledare, LN: Lars Nord,
Föreståndare Demokratiinstitutet

1 P: du, Lars Nord, du representerar ju Demokratiinstitutet och den
        bild som vi får av de tre politiker som finns här nu, att det politiska
        uppdraget egentligen är omänskligt, tycker du att man kan se det
        på sikt så att säga som ett hot mot själva demokratin?
2 LN: ja, men den andra sidan av saken är också att vi har då frågat
        människor vad man tycker om de här politiska uppdragen och
        de allra flesta tycker ju att man ska ställa särskilt stora krav på
        förtroendevalda jämfört med andra medborgare och då finns det
        naturligtvis en risk i förlängningen att de som blir kvar i den här
        verksamheten det är typ kamikazepiloter och masochister och
        det är ingen särskilt bra blandning (skratt) utan de bör ju vara
        representativa för andra kategorier
3 P: men alltså jag tycker det här låter allvarligt det, det innebär ju
        att om utvecklingen fortsätter så kommer vi att ha alldeles fel
        människor som styr oss
4 LN: ja och en representativ demokrati kan ju inte ha fel människor som
        representerar det säger sig ju självt

Example 7. Nattöppet 20/3, 1997, P: Programledare, IB: Irma Björk, Kommunalpolitiker, Malå (s), ÅE: Åsa Ehnberg, Barnmorska, Malå)

1 P: Irma, till hösten då ska ni i Malå folkomrösta om ni vill att SKB ska fortsätta och undersöka förutsättningarna uppe i, i er kommun (IB: ja) tycker du att det är bra det här, tycker du det är bra att ni folkomröstar, att ni hanterar den här frågan på det här sättet?

2 IB: ja, eftersom fullmäktige då vi tog det hära beslutet om förstudie, då tog vi ju redan då ett beslut om att då förstudien och granskning var klar så skulle vi ha en folkomröstning och då tycker jag att det är vår skyldighet att hålla det löftet till Malåborna

3 P: men alltså en sak är att det är er skyldighet, men tycker du, alltså den här frågan har ju blivit väldigt mycket en kommunal fråga och väldigt lite en riksfråga om man uttrycker sig så, tycker du att det är bra?

4 IB: jo, tycker jag

5 P: du tycker att de sköter sig bra, du är nöjd så att säga?

6 IB: jodå

7 P: tycker du att SKB sköter sig bra uppe hos er?

8 IB: jo då det gör dom

9 P: delar du hennes uppfattning?

10 ÅE: nej, det gör jag inte, jag tycker inte att det här är nånting som ska bestämmas av medborgarna i Malå

11 P: varför inte det då?

12 ÅE: det är för stor fråga helt enkelt […]

Example 8. Svar Direkt, 16/10, 1997, P: Programledare, LO: Lars-Göran Oertel, polisinspektör

1 P: Hm, Lars-Göran Oertel, du, du finns i ett sånt här område och är rätt kritisk mot närpolissystemet, har skrivit till justitieministern, nu har du henne alldeles framför dig

2 LO: jag är inte kritisk mot närpolisen och hur dom jobbar i sig utan jag menar att, det här som allmänheten upplever att polisen kommer inte när man ringer, man får inte den hjälp man behöver i akuta situationer och brotten blir inte utredda å så vidare, det beror alltså på en massa omorganisationer å det började med närpolisen, när man införde den reformen som man gjorde nittifyra, då ska man ha klart för sig att närpoliserna dom har ju en massa andra sysslor som de inte hade förut och det ska då utgöra basen i den här nya polisorganisationen totalt sett då va och då, då är det ju så att får

man inga nya resurser då tar man, närpolisen blir ju alltså grovt uttryckt en organisation i organisationen och man tar resurserna då från traditionell verksamhet, det är alltså ordningspolistjänst, såna som åker ut med blåljus, dom som kommer till folk i akuta situationer, man tar resurser från kriminalavdelningar som utreder

3 P: det blir då såna här exempel, tredje man får sitta emellan helt enkelt

4 LO: det säger sig självt då att vi har inte samma beredskap att rycka ut till allmänheten när dom behöver oss i akuta situationer å så vidare å det blir färre brott utredda

5 P: vad, vad är det du säger, att det fungerar då helt enkelt inte med den här nya organisationen?

6 LO: nej, inte, inte när det gäller den biten

7 P: och varför då, för att det är för lite pengar eller att det är

8 LO: nej, därför att man tar, man tar då resurser ifrån andra [...]

Example 9. Nattöppet, 20/3 1997, P: Programledare, OJ: Olof Johansson, Riksdagsman

1 P: men alltså ni (OJ: xx) får jag säga det, du var ju miljöminister när den här processen drog igång och, och nu är du kritisk till processen, har du, har du så att säga ångrat dig

2 OJ: kritisk, jag är, jag måste ju tolerera demokratiska beslut likaväl som alla andra, det vill säga jag blev nedröstad om kommunalt veto [...]

Example 10. Nattöppet, 20/3 1997, P: Programledare, SB: Sinikka Bohlin, v. ordf. jordbruksutskottet (s)

1 P: men du Sinikka, man kan väl ändå säga att det här är en extremt stor fråga så till vida det handlar om ett så oändligt långt tidsperspektiv, kan man inte få tycka att ni är lite ovanligt generös när det gäller att sprida makt i just den här frågan?

2 SB: nej, jag tycker om vi nån gång har hittat en bra väg, det som vi kallar producentansvaret, om någon producerar något, i det här fallet el, ska också ta hand om avfallet

3 P: jamen, det är ju en sak, det är ju en sak

4 SB: men visst är det en nationell fråga, det är ingen (kommunal fråga?)

5 P: en annan sak, Sinikka, det är ju en sak (SB:ja) en annan sak är naturligtvis hur ni ger direktiven, hur det ska skötas, är det rimligt att en liten norrlandskommun ska sitta och fatta beslut som ni i princip inte vill ta i har man en känsla av?

6 SB: ja, det ligger ju hos regeringen, men vi är naturligtvis inblandade
        i riksdagen också, men för mig tycker att det ändå är viktigt att
        dom, det stället som eventuellt nån gång blir det här stället (där?)
        vi ska göra den här långa förvaringen, jag tycker dom ska vara
        med i processen som medborgare eftersom jag och mina barn och
        barnbarn ska bo där, för mig är det viktigt båda delarna i den här
        processen

7 P: vi ska säga också att jordbruksutskottet, ni hanterar den här frågan,
        annars kanske det ser lite konstigt ut (SB: ja, tack)

Example 11. Svar Direkt, 16/10 1997, P: Programledare, MS: Marie
Söderqvist, Ledarskribent SvD

1 P: (xx) Marie, nu har vi väldigt kort tid på oss, vänta nu, nu ska du få
        sista ordet här

2 MS: det är otroligt och sitta och säga att, att det inte är kris, jag menar
        nittonhundrafemti så löste man nitti procent av alla våldsbrott,
        idag löser man hälften av alla våldsbrott och så kan man hålla på
        och rabbla statistik hur mycket som helst, polisen klarar inte sitt
        jobb

Example 12. Nattöppet, 20/3, 1997, P: Programledare

1 P: men alltså, nu har vi pratat med två kommunpolitiker, men
        du Birger, du tillhör ju, om man får uttrycka sig så, du tillhör-,
        tillhör ju de riktiga pamparna så att säga en ledande figur i ett
        riksdagsparti, men du har också skrivit en tidningsartikel där du
        verkligen har uttryckt nån form av ångest nästan inför det politiska
        uppdraget

Example 13. Nattöppet, 20/3, 1997, P: Programledare, BS: Birger
Schlaug, språkrör (mp)

1 P: ett ögonblick, du ska få komma in, men först ska Birger få
        kommentera det här

2 BS: ofta får man ju höra att politiker har tappat makten att någon har
        tagit makten, men det är ju viktigt precis som Björn säger

3 P: jamen det verkar ju så

4 BS: ja, just det, men det är ju viktigt som Björn säger att politiker, att
        den politiska majoriteten, de flesta politiker har accepterat att steg
        för steg frånsäga sig makten, det är ju väldigt viktigt

5 P: men hur kan ni göra så?

Example 14. Debattakuten, 15/10, 1998, P: Programledare, JN: Joseph
Maria Nilsson, Pater Katolska Kyrkan

1 P: nej, ja, några reaktioner som man kan få, ja, man skulle kunna höra
med en katolsk kyrkoherde här, vad säger du?

2 JN: jag, jag tycker det är uppseendeväckande, att man, när man
då som Elisabeth Olsson ju har gjort med dessa bilder kräver
förståelse och accepterande för en viss grupp och sin egen grupp
då naturligtvis av homosexuella (P: mm) på samma gång kränker
andra människor när hon är medveten om att detta kränker väldigt
många, inte slutar, inte drar sig tillbaka [6 rader saknas]

3 P: är du kränkt?

4 JN: inte jag personligen, men jag-

5 P: ja, ja, nu får du alltså vara lite ärlig här, är du kränkt eller inte (JN:
<u>alltså för mig) man kan inte</u>, du är alltså både präst och person

6 JN: ja, ja, för mig personligen så spelar dessa bilderna ingen roll för
det förändrar inte min Kristusbild, det gör det inte, men jag känner
med dom människorna som känner sig kränkta dom-

7 P: nä men nu får du inte vara sån alltså, vi ska inte vara som jag är
utan som jag lär alltså, så har ju prästerna hållit på hela tiden

8 JN: ja, men du vet, folk som förstår, jag har inte sett, det är första
gången jag ser dessa bilder här, förutom den nattvardsscenen som
har då visats på Aktuellt et cetera (P: mm) äh, men vad, jag tycker
det är inte fråga om bilderna i sig utan om att kränka eller inte, är
en grupp bara (P: mm), har dom rätt att kränka, är det massmedia
eller vem är det som bestämmer (P: mm) vem som får kränka,
nynazister får inte öppna munnen och säga vad dom vill för då är
det hets mot folkgrupp till exempel men en annan som kommer
i sexualitetens namn, dom har rätt och tala precis vad de vill och
kränka, stampar på andra människors gudssyn som är någonting
intimt, som är det innersta i en människa

9 P: (hon /dom?) har kränkt en helighet så att säga, en helighetsgräns
för dig?

10 JN: ja, ja /några applåderar/

Example 15. Svar Direkt, 28/8 1997, P: Programledare, CT: Claes
Tingvall, Trafiksäkerhetsdirektör

1 CT: det går alltid och vända och vrida på såna här siffror, naturligtvis
inte i manipulativt syfte utan för att belysa olika saker (Några
skrattar?), äh, det är ju så, jag menar om man tittar på så att säga

en och samma åldersgrupp så är det naturligtvis så att då sch-,
blir risk-, skillnaderna litegranna mindre, äh, men det, hur man
än vänder och vrider på det så blir det fordon som är långt, långt
farligare att åka på, åtminstone alltså för sig själv va, det är ju helt
rätt att bilen skadar andra och liknande, men för sig själv, men
framför allt det vi pratar om också, att i framtiden går det att göra
så mycket mer för dom som går, cyklar, åker bil, men det är väldigt
svårt att göra nånting på mc-sidan, det, det är bara att tala om som
det är alltså, sen tror jag fortfarande inte nån vill prata om förbud
eller nånting liknande

2 P: mm, men det du säger är ju så nära förbud man kan komma ändå

Responsibility and the conventions of attribution in news agency discourse

Maija Stenvall

1 Introduction

Being 'big' in the world of media can be equated with having power, but power calls for responsibility. According to Tunstall (1999: 191), the American Associated Press (AP) and the British Reuters are the world's 'leading news suppliers'. Together with the French Agence France-Presse (AFP), these global news agencies are commonly called the 'Big Three' (cf. Boyd-Barrett 1998). When defining its company policy, AP stresses 'its commitment to the highest standards of objective, accurate journalism' (About Us – Associated Press; website), and Reuters lists 'accuracy, objectivity, sourcing and freedom from bias' as its 'rigorous standards' in the *Reuters Handbook of Journalism* (2008: 518).

Since the mid-1800s, the big international news agencies have had a key role in shaping the form of news reports and, even more importantly, the very concept of news. As White (1998: 122) notes, news agency reports 'act as a sort of textual common currency for the media around the world and clearly have the potential to establish conventions and 'standards' for journalistic textuality'. In the analysis below, I look into one central convention of news reporting: routines of attribution. I will show how the typical structure of a news story and the news agency journalists' traditional writing style affect the presentation of speakers, often leading to ambiguity and vague language, which can contribute to undermining the alleged factuality or objectivity of news agency discourse.

In this study I discuss the notion of responsibility in various contexts, on various intertwining levels. There is, first, the macro-level, which could be called 'institutional' responsibility: the big question of the responsibility of news agencies as powerful distributors of news, and their responsibility in view of the conventions of news writing, e.g. attribution. Although the policy statements of AP and Reuters cited above show that these news agencies acknowledge their responsibility as important 'agenda-setters' for the world media, the latter aspect – their role in *creating* and *reinforcing* traditions of news reporting – may be overlooked. At the micro-level, in the analysis of attribution, two kinds of responsibility are explored: the responsibility of news actors (i.e. of those who are quoted in news reports) and that of journalists, in particular.

2 Conventions of news reporting

This section examines the role of the big international news agencies in the development of the typical structure of news reports and in that of the conventional objective style. I will also look into some details of news story structure and discuss the notion of journalistic objectivity.

The quest for objectivity is a sign of taking responsibility. Paradoxically, though, the more the journalists strive for objectivity, the more they resort to strategies that tend to obscure the issue of responsibility (e.g. to the use of quotations from unnamed speakers).

2.1 The conventional structure of news reports

Those who want to learn how to write a professional hard news story are commonly advised to apply the 'inverted pyramid' structure. Out of several rather similar instructions found on the Internet, I have chosen the following two for illustration:

> Understand the inverted pyramid structure. Know how to write the traditional AP, or summary lead. (Kearsarge website)

> You are expected to apply AP style, the inverted pyramid, and appropriate lead-writing skills. (Media communications; website)

Scanlan (2000: 153) gives a simple definition of the inverted pyramid structure: 'The inverted pyramid puts the most newsworthy information at the top, and then the remaining information follows in order of importance, with the least important at the bottom'. The 'bottom' corresponds to the narrow tip of the pyramid.

Journalism historians have expressed different views about the origin of the inverted pyramid. According to a popular anecdote (see e.g. Fox 1977: 14–15), this form was invented during the American Civil War (1861–1865). The war correspondents wanted to send the most important part of their report first (a kind of general summary), because they all shared a single telegraph line, which could break down any minute (and was very expensive to use). However, research on the American newspapers of the late 19th century has shown that whether or not the inverted pyramid structure was *invented* during the Civil War, it was not much used before the turn of the century (cf. e.g. Errico et al. 1996). According to Scanlan (2000: 153), 'the invention of the telegraph sparked its development so that it had entered into common use by newspapers and the newly-formed wire service organizations by the beginning of the 20th century'.

Van Dijk's well-known model of the structure of a news report, developed in the 1980s, is also based on the inverted pyramid; he speaks of 'the top down principle of relevance organisation in news' (1988: 43). Since van Dijk's study is discussed in several other studies (see e.g. Bell 1991; Stenvall 1995; White 1998), I will not go into detail here. However, one point is of special relevance for this study: the *instalment* character of topic realisation in news discourse. Van Dijk (1988: 43) states that 'each topic is delivered in parts, not as a whole, as is the case in other discourse types'. High-level, abstract information is given first, followed by lower-level information, specifying details. This kind of discontinuous presentation can mean, for instance, that the same speaker is introduced in two (or even three or more) steps, proceeding from general to specific (see the analysis in Section 3).

White's model (1998: 186) of the typical structure of a news story is somewhat different from the inverted pyramid format. The opening of the news story (that is, the headline and lead) is 'a textual nucleus', which 'enters into an orbital relationship of dependency with a set of satellites'. The second phase – the satellites which follow the nucleus – then specifies the meanings 'through elaboration, contextualization, explanation and appraisal' (p. 194).

2.2 The convention of objectivity

Besides contributing to the birth of the inverted pyramid format, the invention of the telegraph has been credited for another important development in the history of news discourse: a shift in writing style. Scanlan (2000: 195–196) mentions two important factors as leading to this shift: the high cost of sending telegrams and the appearance of 'a new type of news organization, named "wire service" after the technology used to transmit the news'. According to Scanlan, the new writing style was 'concise, stripped of opinion and detail', distinctive from 'the flowery language of the 19th century'. Speaking of the invention of the telegraph and the ensuing birth of the news agencies, Carey (1989: 210) states that the wire services were forced to 'generate 'objective' news', because they supplied news to newspapers of 'any political stripe'.

However, the shift in writing style was by no means drastic; the change was not clearly seen in the language of newspapers until several decades had passed since the invention of the telegraph (cf. White 1998: 156–168, for a survey of US, UK and Australian newspapers in the late 19th and early 20th century). According to White (p. 168), news discourse has undergone a 'fundamental reorganisation' in the 20th century in view of its *interpersonal* aspect (on 'interpersonal metafunction', see Halliday 1994: 36). White (1998: 168) further claims that the 'objective' voice of today's news reports is 'very much a modern invention'.

In news reporting, the convention of objectivity presupposes, above all, that the reporter removes her/his own voice from the story, or at least backgrounds it. Sigal (1986: 15) argues that '[o]bjectivity in journalism denotes a set of rhetorical devices and procedures used in composing a news story'. A central means of backgrounding the role of the journalist is the use of indirect and direct quotes; as Sigal (p. 15) puts it: '[n]ews is not what happens, but what someone says has happened or will happen'. In a similar vein, Fishman (1980: 92) argues that 'the fundamental principle of news fact' is that *something is so because somebody says it*. He adds that, naturally, this 'somebody' cannot be 'just anybody'; s/he must be 'some competent knower or observer' (p. 93).

This is how Tuchman (1978: 83) describes some intertwined notions related to objectivity when exploring what she calls 'the Web of Facticity':

> [N]ewsworkers state that finding facts entails demonstrating impartiality by removing oneself from the story. Impartiality includes demonstrating that one does everything possible to be accurate so as to maintain credibility and avoid both reprimands from superiors and the omnipresent danger of libel suits.

Objectivity, whether we look at it from the point of view of journalists or from that of researchers, is a complex concept. In addition to the notions referred to by Tuchman – impartiality, accuracy and credibility – it can be argued to encompass other ideal notions, too: factuality (or facticity) and neutrality, for example.

3 Conventions of attribution in news agency reports

In this section I examine some of the rhetorical possibilities that journalistic conventions can offer for a reporter when s/he introduces a news actor s/he wants to quote. The discontinuous presentation of a speaker that is discussed in the first part of the section is connected to the typical structure of a news story, to what van Dijk calls its 'instalment character' (cf. above, section 2). It is argued that this kind of presentation often leads to ambiguity by obscuring the responsibility of the speaker in question.

Another important question related to responsibility and attribution concerns the relationship between the news journalist and the news actor who is quoted: i.e. how to share the responsibility between these two parties. In one specific case, the answer is simple: if the news actor has been left anonymous, then, according to Reuters (2008: 562), the responsibility for reporting what s/he says 'resides solely with Reuters and the reporter'. The second part of this section examines the shifting burden of responsibility and some strategies that journalists use to make it lighter for themselves.

3.1 From general to specific: 'Iraq says ...'

As discussed above, the beginning of a news story – the headline and lead – is its most important part. White (1998: 288) argues that the 'angle' included in the 'nucleus' is presented 'as inherently newsworthy, as having compelled itself upon the reporter as obvious subject matter for a report and an unavoidably appropriate starting point'. Each satellite then 'elaborates, contextualises, explains, justifies or appraises some element of that opening burst of informational and interpersonal impact' (p. 288). However, it has to be noted that, strictly speaking, the latter part of this definition does not always apply to news agency reports. News agency reporting differs from newspaper stories in that it is an ongoing process. A big topic, especially a continuing crisis like the one shown in the examples below – i.e. the Iraqi situation, generates a continuous flow of dispatches, none of which can, as such, be regarded as a unity like a single newspaper story.

Dispatches are often summaries which include several news actors' statements, usually interspersed with activity sequences. Paragraphs from earlier reports are repeated and reorganised; the headline and the lead paragraph may change during the day, when a new, more newsworthy statement or event comes up.

At the same time, even the summarising reports tend to conform to the instalment character of a news story, according to which the important information included in the headline/lead is specified later with details given in several instalments. The typical structure of a news report thus makes it possible that a news actor (the source of a newsworthy statement) is presented in general terms in the headline and in the lead, but her/his true identity is not revealed until much later in the report. The later instalment then includes more quotes, giving the full name and title of the speaker and adding other details, such as 'speaking to reporters in Jordan', or 'told reporters Monday'. An important speaker, making a newsworthy statement, is often allotted several instalments within the text body.

The examples below come from AP and Reuters wires, transmitted in September and December 2002.[1] At that time Saddam Hussein still controlled Iraq, but the United States led by President George W. Bush was, together with its allies, already waging the possibility to attack Iraq. The role of the United Nations in the impending war was under vivid discussion. A central question was whether or not Iraq possessed weapons of mass destruction, and the U.N. was urging Iraq to let the U.N. inspectors return into the country. The following two examples illustrate one stage in the reporting of that ongoing crisis (attributions are marked in italics):[2]

(1) **In mixed signals, *Iraq* calls on Arabs to «confront» America, says it wants business, not war, with the U.S.**

—

BAGHDAD, Iraq (AP) – In conflicting signals, *a senior official* on Tuesday called on Arabs to rise and «confront» America, barely a day after *another official* said Iraq wanted to be a trade partner, not a battlefield foe, with the United States.

—

In the most belligerent Iraqi remarks in the current standoff with the United States, *Iraqi Vice President Taha Yassin Ramadan* said: «We categorically believe that the aggression on Iraq is an aggression on all the Arab nation [sic].»
Speaking to reporters in neighboring Jordan, *he* said: «It is the right of all the Arab people, wherever they are, to fight against the aggression through their representatives and on their soil ... by all means.»

—

His remarks came less than 24 hours after *Foreign Minister Naji Sabri*, speaking in Baghdad Monday night, said: «We do not want to fight anybody, we do not hope that a war is waged against our country. We'd

like to live in stability. We'd like to live in peace.»
(AP, 10 September 2002)

(2) ***Iraq* urges Arabs to hit back if U.S. attacks**

—

AMMAN, Sept 10 (Reuters) - *Iraq* called on Arabs on Tuesday to strike U.S. interests in the Middle East if Washington attacked Baghdad, and *the foreign minister* denied his country was trying to produce nuclear weapons.

—

Iraqi Vice-President Taha Yassin Ramadan said U.S. and British claims that Iraq was rebuilding its banned weapons programmes were lies, and restated the Iraqi position that U.N. weapons inspectors could return to Iraq only as part of a comprehensive deal with the United Nations.
'We call for confronting the aggression and aggressors not only by the Iraqi capability but we call on all the Arab masses ... to confront the material and human interests of the aggressors...' *Ramadan* told a news conference in Amman.

—

Foreign Minister Naji Sabri told CNN in an interview late on Monday '... there is no physical existence of anything that is now being promoted by warmongers in Washington and the single warmonger in London who is Mr Tony Blair'.
'It is not only that Iraq has not the material (for a nuclear bomb) but Iraq has no intention in the first place.'
(Reuters, 10 September 2002)

In view of news values[3] – especially the value of negativity – it is hardly surprising that both AP and Reuters have chosen the 'belligerent remarks' of Iraqi Vice-President Ramadan as the new angle to be included in the headline and the lead of their respective dispatches. At the same time, the two news agencies look somewhat differently at the statement by Iraqi Foreign Minister Sabri, which also gets a prominent position in both reports. (AP does not mention CNN as its source like Reuters does, but we can presume that Sabri's quotes have been picked from the same long interview.) In Reuters' example (2), the speaker named 'Iraq' (in the headline and in the lead) refers only to Ramadan; the views of 'the foreign minister' are seen to be consistent with Ramadan's remarks, even if they are less 'belligerent'. In the headline of example (1), AP attributes both Ramadan's and Sabri's sayings collectively to 'Iraq'; in the lead the speakers are presented separately, as two 'officials'. The statements are regarded as 'conflicting', which has compelled the writer to add an implicit, unattributed value of JUDGEMENT[4] in the headline: Iraq speaks 'in mixed signals'. When Sabri's words were cited in the headline of earlier versions, the perspective was more positive: 'Iraq says it wants peace and stability' (AP Sept. 10, 2002).

The writer who introduces an individual speaker as a state, e.g. as 'Iraq', resorts to synecdoche; in other words, the whole is used for a part. Synecdoche is often regarded as a sub-category of metonymy (see e.g. Chandler 1995; Lakoff and Johnson 1980: 36). In the field of international sports, it is quite common to say that 'France' – and not the French team – won a football game, a relay in athletics or skiing, and so on. In international politics, the ambassadors at the United Nations or in the national embassies around the world represent their respective countries so that it is only natural to refer to them by using the name of their home country. However, in those cases the connection between the whole and the part can be easily figured out, because of the unambiguous context. But when a state in a news report headline is given the role of the speaker, the reader has no ready-made context frame to tell her/him who the speaker actually is.

Sometimes the identity is revealed already in the lead paragraph, but often it is hidden among the identities of several other speakers within the text body. One could, of course, claim that the 'Vice President' and the 'Foreign Minister' are entitled to speak for Iraq, but as we see, their words in example (1) are construed as 'conflicting' so that there is not just one 'Iraq' talking.

In my data, there are other examples of this routine of attribution – from general to specific – which, compared to examples (1) and (2), show an even looser connection between 'Iraq' in the headline and the actual speaker mentioned later in the text:

(3) **Iraq says Sept. 11 attacks were 'God's punishment'**

—

BAGHDAD, Iraq (AP) – The Sept. 11 attacks were remembered Wednesday as 'God's punishment' on America among Iraqis fearful and angry at the possibility the United States might attack to topple their president.
(AP, 11 September 2002)

—

(The speaker 'Iraq' is specified later as 'The state-owned weekly Al-Iktisadi'.)

(4) **Defiant Iraq says has no arms of mass destruction**

—

BAGHDAD, Dec 4 (Reuters) – Iraq defied Washington's threats of war, saying it had no weapons of mass destruction to confess to but promising to meet a U.N. weekend deadline to declare all arms programmes.
(Reuters, 4 December 2002)

—

(The speaker 'Iraq' is specified later as 'Hussam Mohammed Amin, head of the Iraqi National Monitoring Directorate'.)

(5) **UN experts at work, Iraq slams US-British 'lies'**

—

BAGHDAD, Dec 20 (Reuters) – U.N. experts resumed their hunt for banned weapons in Iraq on Friday and a Baghdad newspaper said U.S. and British 'lies' were aimed at justifying war.
(Reuters, 20 December 2002)

—

(The speaker 'Iraq' is specified later as 'Iraq's Baath Party newspaper al-Thawra'.)

To use the name of a state to denote an individual speaker in the headline and the lead may look quite natural, since it conforms to the conventional discontinuous structure of news reports. But this, in fact, is a writer's choice, which can be argued to be significant from the point of view of 'rhetorical potential' (cf. White 1998). In the examples above, 'Iraq' – being able to 'speak' – has been personalised; in other words, a state-as-person metaphor is used. Chilton and Lakoff (1995: 39) point out that when states are conceptualised as having personalities, 'they can be trustworthy or deceitful, aggressive or peace-loving, strong- or weak-willed, stable or paranoid, cooperative or intransigent, enterprising or not'. State-persons can also be appraised by JUDGEMENT values, which are used to evaluate human behaviour; for instance, 'Iraq' in example (4) is said to be 'defiant'. As we see in the examples above, the evaluations in the headlines focus on the state-person Iraq, and not on the individual speaker or writer behind the – sometimes aggressive – statements.

In examples (2) and (5) from Reuters, Iraq does not just speak, it 'urges' and 'slams'. This kind of intensification is common especially in the important headline/lead section of a hard news story (cf. White 1998: 287). In (2), the proposal attributed to Iraq – 'urges Arabs to hit back' – is also intensified; it is more concrete than AP's 'calls Arabs to "confront"' in example (1). As a person such a speaker could be described as rather aggressive, but also as purposeful and strong-willed. At the same time, 'Iraq' in example (1) appears to be inconsistent, speaking 'in mixed signals', which can be interpreted as implicit JUDGEMENT on the part of the journalist. In the lead paragraph, the expression 'barely a day after' underlines the inconsistency of Iraq's behaviour.

Distinct from the other examples, the dispatch cited in example (3) looks at the Iraqi crisis from the point of view of ordinary people living in Iraq. On the first anniversary of the Sept. 11 attacks on the United States, AP sent a rather short report including quotes from two ordinary Iraqis: 'Ali Ahmed, a 47-year-old who owns a Baghdad stationary shop' and 'Sameera Kadhim, a 53-year-old housewife'. In addition, there is a quote from the weekly Al-Iktisadi and another quote from the daily Al-Jumhuriya. Of these four sources, Al-Iktisadi is the only one using the expression 'God's punishment', which has been chosen as the headline, and thus gets a prominent position. Notably, the lead of this dispatch differs from the common pattern of attribution in that it does not give a more detailed account of the speaker or her/his words. Instead, the AP journalist has transformed the Verbal Process of the headline (what 'Iraq says') into a Mental Process,[5] depicting how the Iraqis 'remember' the Sept. 11 attacks (as 'God's punishment') and describing how they feel. This kind of process shift involves interpretation on the part of the journalist. Furthermore, the explicit AFFECT values ('Iraqis fearful and angry') could evoke feelings of empathy – or even provoke values of JUDGEMENT – in the reader.

The custom of starting with a general term ('Iraq') is just one of the routines of attribution in news agency reports. Above I have noted that while this mode of attribution opens up a variety of rhetorical choices to the writer, it can be ambiguous from the point of view of the reader. Furthermore, as we have seen above, transforming an individual speaker to a state often involves interpersonal APPRAISAL values, or ideational changes like the one in example (3), which can be argued to affect the objectivity of news agency discourse.

3.2 Manipulating the shifting burden of responsibility

Below I look more closely into the relationship between the news agency journalists and their sources, analysing the sayings of both named and unnamed speakers. According to the *Reuters Handbook of Journalism*

(2008: 3; website), named and unnamed sources are different from the point of view of responsibility: '[N]amed sources ... are responsible for the information they provide', whereas unnamed sources are the weakest. However, in either case, as will be shown, news reporters resort to various strategies which aim at making the quoted source more credible, and which could thus ease the journalists' burden of responsibility.

3.2.1 Named sources

The named sources in news agency reports can be roughly divided into three major categories, on the basis of the different modes used in the presentation of the respective news actors. I have named these groups 'major figures', 'officials' and 'ordinary people'. As for the credibility and the ensuing degree of journalistic responsibility, it can be argued that this issue is related to the status of a speaker; i.e. to how 'elite' or well-known s/he is. The less well-known the speaker, the more responsibility falls on the journalist.

Major figures

Major figures are newsworthy persons whose names are supposed to be recognised by readers all over the world. In news agency reports, these speakers are most often prominent politicians. The presentation of a major figure need not conform to the attribution mode analysed above (from general to specific). In fact, the name of the speaker is usually given at the beginning of the headline, which also stresses the newsworthiness of the – direct or indirect – quote that follows:

(6) **Bush urges Congress to pass spending needed to pay for war**
—
WASHINGTON (AP) – President George W. Bush shrugged off...
(AP, 14 February 2007)

(7) **Castro says Bush presence in Italy hypocritical**
—
HAVANA, April 7 (Reuters) - Cuban President Fidel Castro eulogised Pope John Paul as a fierce critic of savage capitalism during a speech on Thursday night and said it was hypocritical of U.S. President George W. Bush to attend his funeral.
(Reuters, 7 April 2005)

Example (6) refers to a press conference given by President Bush, and example (7) to President Castro's 'televised address'. In both cases, the news agency journalist's burden of responsibility can be argued to be rather light. The speakers are well-known, and the correctness of these indirect quotations can be verified from an audio or a video tape. In addition, verbatim transcripts of the press conferences and television addresses by political leaders can usually be found on several websites.

Officials

This is, by far, the largest of these three categories. I take 'officials' to include all speakers that give information to journalists in their official capacity, as – what Fishman (1980: 93) calls – competent knowers or observers. Besides 'officials', this category includes military officers, policemen, spokespersons, analysts, diplomats, and so on. Should the information given by an official be important enough to make the headline of the report, the presentation usually adopts the 'step-by-step' model discussed above (the steps of attribution are shown in italics):

(8) **U.S. *Army general* sees no new insurgent tactics in helicopter shootdowns in Iraq**

—

BAGRAM AIR BASE, Afghanistan (AP) – There is no basis for believing that insurgents' recent success in shooting down U.S. helicopters in Iraq means they have developed new attack methods or discovered new U.S. vulnerabilities, *the U.S. Army's vice chief of staff* said Saturday.

'I see no change in trends' on the part of the insurgent's targeting efforts, 'and I see no capability gaps' on the part of U.S. forces, *Gen. Richard Cody* said in an interview en route to Bagram Air Base, north of Kabul, Afghanistan's capital.

—

Cody, 56, a career helicopter pilot who flew an Apache attack mission on the opening night of the 1991 Gulf War, said …
(AP, 10 February 2007)

In example (8), typically, the name of the speaker is not mentioned until the third step. This kind of gradual mode of attribution opens up several possibilities to the journalist for boosting the expertise of the speaker, and thus her/his credibility. In this case, the vital detail concerning General Cody's career as an experienced helicopter pilot, comes towards the end of the dispatch, as some kind of final confirmation of the speaker's special competence in the topic area.

Ordinary people

Ordinary people appear very seldom in news reports; usually elite sources are thought to be more newsworthy and more reliable. However, even ordinary people can be quoted, 'if they enter the news arena by some other door' (Fowler 1991: 22); for instance, if they are victims of a bomb attack, eyewitnesses to an accident or witnesses in court. Elite persons as news actors are often personalised, which adds to the newsworthiness of what they say (see e.g. Galtung and Holmboe Ruge 1970).

At the same time, ordinary people as individuals are rather *depersonalised;* as Tuchman (1978: 122) argues, 'people are presented symbolically … made to typify all members of their particular group or class'. As individuals they have no news value, but, paradoxically, they are described in very accurate detail. This kind of detailed presentation can make them more 'factual'; as individuals, with a name and age and maybe profession, they become less anonymous and thus more responsible from the journalist's point of view. Representatives of this category are seldom quoted more than once in a news agency report, so the 'step-by-step' attribution discussed above is not relevant here.

The following example from AP describes the feelings of ordinary Spaniards one week after the train bombings which killed about 200 people near Madrid:

(9) 'I come here many times', said Antonio Ruiz, 68, stopping by the vigil at El Pozo station. 'One's soul falls to the ground.'
Pedro Valdia, 53, said, 'I felt the blow. … Before, this neighborhood had joy. Now people are scared.'

—

Fear has been taken away by pain', said Marco Antonio Heras, a 28-year-old window dresser. Echoing a slogan from last week's peace rallies that drew millions across Spain, he added, 'We were all on that train.'
(AP, 18 March 2004)

Example (10) is taken from a report transmitted one year after the bombing of a revered Shi'ite shrine in the city of Samarra, which triggered 'a wave of bloodletting' in Iraq, as Reuters said in February 2007:

(10) Many worried whether it would be possible to heal the divisions that
      the bombing had sown.
      'It was not just the holy shrine that was targeted, it was the unity of
      Iraq', said Qasim Haddad, 65, a Shi'ite retired teacher sipping tea in
      a Baghdad cafe.
      'Those evil terrorists realised how to break the warm ties between
      Sunnis and Shi'ites. It will take years to repair these sectarian feelings
      and for Iraqis to forget their agonies.'
      Added Ahmed Wael, 35, a Sunni pharmacist:
      'Ties that had linked Iraqis together for ages were destroyed. Families
      who lost loved ones will never forgive.'
      (Reuters, 22 February 2007)

In example (9), the special function of the quotes is to symbolise the
feelings of ordinary Spanish citizens; the only aspect in the attribution that
matters is the fact that the speakers are all Spanish. In example (10), the
attribution itself is more important in that one of the speakers is presented
as 'Shi'ite' and the other one as 'Sunni', so that each of them can be said to
typify all members of his respective Moslem group. At the same time, the
professions given in these examples ('window dresser', 'retired teacher',
'pharmacist') do not make the speakers more credible, as none of them has
been interviewed as a 'competent knower' in his/her own field.

3.2.2 Unnamed sources

Above I quoted *Reuters Handbook of Journalism* (2008), which stresses
the 'weakness' of anonymous sources. In June 2005, AP reminded the staff
about its policy concerning anonymous sources, stating that '[a] story that
identifies its sources is a better piece of journalism, more complete and more
credible, than the very same story pegged to unnamed sources' (Silverman
and Carroll 2005). Further, according to AP guidelines, if a source insists
on remaining anonymous, the journalist has to tell the reader why that
happens. Yet, despite the journalists' good intentions, news agency wires
contain a wealth of unnamed speakers, presented, for instance, as generic
'officials', 'experts', or 'analysts'; or more specifically, as a 'senior Afghan
official', who speaks 'on condition of anonymity' (AP March 7, 2007), or
as 'a senior U.S. military analyst, at an off-the-record briefing' (Reuters
Feb. 14, 2007), and so on.

Referring to this 'curious category ... that of unnamed speakers', Bell (1991: 193) points out that the labellings in the attribution 'claim standing for their anonymous sources' (for unnamed sources as rhetorical constructs, see Stenvall 2008). However, the guidelines AP and Reuters have given to their journalists present the function of the 'labels' from a different aspect. 'AP statement on anonymous sources' says that it is not allowed to simply quote 'a source'; the journalists should be 'as descriptive as possible'. In a similar vein, Reuters (2008: 562) advises its journalists to 'convey to readers as clearly as possible why we believe the source is reliable'.

When the journalist adds an expression stressing the speaker's wish for anonymity and even explains the reason for that, s/he shifts the responsibility of quoting an unnamed source to the speaker, while s/he still retains the responsibility for the quoted words. Sometimes, though, the identity of the speaker is clear enough despite the missing name, and the additional explanations seem superfluous:

(11) Blair's official spokesman, speaking on customary condition of anonymity in line with policy, acknowledged that British officials 'still believed Iranian-supplied ordinance is coming across the border'.
(AP, 21 February 2007)

In this case, it is obvious that the journalist's burden gets lighter, as the readers either know the name of Prime Minister Tony Blair's official spokesman or can get it from the Internet by a simple search. Moreover, the spokesman does not speak for himself, but for the well-known Prime Minister.

In my data, AP tends to explain the reason for a speaker's anonymity more often than Reuters does. A rather common explanation is that the news actor in question actually was not 'allowed' or 'authorised' to speak to the media or that s/he spoke 'too early'. These kinds of explanations raise further questions of journalistic responsibility, at least if the reporter has persuaded the speaker to break the law, as example (12) from AP seems to imply:

(12) Agents from the French anti-terrorism agency were trying to identify the computers from which the e-mails were sent, the official said. The official spoke on condition of anonymity *because under French law information about investigations is secret.*
(AP, 5 April 2007; my italics)

Generic unnamed speakers – officials, analysts, observers, witnesses, diplomats, and so on – are popular sources of information in news agency reports. A whole group of people can thus be hypothesised to stand for the quoted facts or opinions, but who they really are often remains a mystery. However, part of the journalistic responsibility can be shared, if the reporter, after referring to e.g. collective 'analysts', 'observers' or 'officials', names one or two speakers – a model that conforms to the typical convention of 'step-by-step' attribution. The steps of attribution in example (13) from Reuters are marked in italics:

(13) The attack, in which *the military* said insurgents used a suicide car bomber, came as tens of thousands of U.S. and Iraqi forces fanned out across the capital in a new crackdown on rampant sectarian violence that threatens all-out civil war.
A spokesman for the U.S. military in Baghdad said the assault took place in an outpost north of the capital, but declined to provide more specific information on its location.
'It was not just a spontaneous attack. It wasn't just people taking potshots at us', *Major Steven Lamb* told Reuters.
(Reuters, 19 February 2007)

Ordinary people, as discussed above, are presented with their names and other details, wherever possible. When only one name is given, the reason is often said to be the custom of the country in question. This applies especially to Indonesian people; the journalist may refer, for instance, to 'Dr. Alexander who like many Indonesians uses only one name' (AP May 28, 2006). But sometimes the journalist changes the name of the speaker, as example (14) shows – a strategy that could not be found in the category of 'officials'. Here, too, several other details have been added to enhance the factuality and credibility of the story:

(14) One teacher, who asked to be called Aman, said he was paid $100 a month to prepare children for their Rukhnama exams.

'During lessons I explain parts of the book and the children take notes', said Aman. 'The children are not interested in the philosophical parts, but I can't just do the stories in the Rukhnama [book by the late Turkmen President Saparmurat Niyazov] all the time.'
Dressed in a suit, the 41-year-old asked to have his name changed for personal security and spoke to Reuters in a cafe away from school.
(Reuters, 5 March 2007)

4 Concluding remarks

On the basis of the two news agencies' policy statements, cited in section 1, we can assume that for them a vital part of responsibility consists of distributing 'objective' and 'accurate', clearly sourced reports. Today, increased competition poses new challenges. News must be delivered instantaneously, in 'real-time'; 'the world of instant news places huge responsibilities on media organizations and their journalists', Stephen Jukes, the Global Head of News for Reuters, writes. Jukes (2002) stresses that to ensure 'accuracy, objectivity and freedom from bias', one now has to be 'more vigilant than ever'. However, it can be argued that 'vigilance' alone will not help, since some of the very traditions of news writing – starting from the persistent news values – work to undermine its objectivity.

For journalists, the use of quotations is probably the most efficient way to hide their own voice and, in that manner, to transfer responsibility to someone else. White (1998: 278) notes that the media, in this respect, has adopted 'an extreme view', according to which the 'authorial voice' is never 'responsible for any subjectivities it imports into its texts through extra-vocalisation' (e.g. quotations), notwithstanding the fact that it is the writing journalist who has selected the quotation and maybe even given it a prominent position in the report. Thus, despite explicit evaluation, e.g. JUDGEMENT values included in the quotations, the media advocates that 'its texts are neutral, impartial and value-free' (p. 278). The choice of a reporting verb in the attribution can be important, revealing 'the degree of alignment' between the journalist and the quoted source; for instance, 'demonstrate' denotes alignment, while 'claim' puts a distance between the two, as White (p. 275) notes.

My analysis on attribution shows how the traditional structure of a news report – from general to specific – opens up rhetorical possibilities for a journalist, and how the status of a source affects the way s/he is construed in a report. When an individual speaker is transformed into a state, e.g. into 'Iraq', in the headline, this leads to a second transformation; the state in question becomes, metaphorically, a person. After that it is possible to evaluate this state-person – instead of an individual speaker – e.g. with implicit or explicit JUDGEMENT values, as demonstrated in section 3.1. In section 3.2, I have shown that sharing the responsibility between the journalist and the news actor is a complex issue. News agency journalists resort to various strategies to transfer at least some portion of responsibility to the speakers they quote.

News values are often seen to have an inescapable 'institutionalised force' over journalists (cf. Hartley 1982: 81), and some other conventions of news reporting, too, seem to have a similar effect; i.e. the journalists apply them more or less subconsciously. White (1998: 281) states that journalists are perhaps more 'subject to the rhetorical influence of those conventions' than their audience, 'since their continued professional employment relies on them enacting the conventions successfully day after day'. For the news agencies, the increasing competition in the 'world of instant news' means an increase in the volume of news distribution, which again puts even more pressure than before on the agency journalists. In these circumstances – and given the news agencies' committed pursuit of objectivity – one can expect that 'the rhetorical influence' of such conventions, including the routines of attribution, on news agency discourse will rather be strengthened than weakened in the coming years.

Notes

1   These data are part of a larger corpus of news agency (AP and Reuters) reports, which were collected in several batches between 2002 and 2007, as transmitted to one media client of these agencies, the Finnish Broadcasting Company. The total number of words in the corpus is around four million, but as discussed above, news agency reports contain a lot of repetition.

2   Since I only want to show the various steps of attribution, I have not included all the quotes (from Iraqi Vice-president Ramadan and Foreign Minister Sabri) that were included in the two dispatches cited. The byline and the notes to editors between the headline and the lead paragraph have also been omitted.

3   The most influential study of newsworthiness is that of Galtung and Ruge, published in *Journal of International Peace Research* 40 years ago (1965; reprinted 1970). Galtung and Ruge present twelve factors, which are generally known as *news values*: negativity, eliteness, personification, unexpectedness, among others.

4   JUDGEMENT values refer to the APPRAISAL framework, which is an extension of Halliday's Systemic Functional Grammar. APPRAISAL focuses on 'the evaluative use of the language' (see The Appraisal website on a detailed presentation of the APPRAISAL framework). It is divided into three interacting systems: ATTITUDE, ENGAGEMENT and GRADUATION. JUDGEMENT (evaluating human behaviour) is one of the three sub-systems of ATTITUDE; the other two being AFFECT (construing emotional responses) and APPRECIATION (evaluating entities). Values of all three ATTITUDE sub-systems can be either 'inscribed' (explicit), or 'evoked' (implicit). They can also be 'provoked' by values belonging to another sub-type; typically JUDGEMENTS are triggered by AFFECT values.

5 Verbal and Mental Processes refer to the semantic concept of *transitivity*, which belongs to the ideational metafunction in functional grammar (cf. Halliday 1994: 106–146). 'The transitivity system construes the world of experience into a manageable set of PROCESS TYPES' (p. 106). All processes have three elements: the process itself (typically realised by a verbal group), participants of the process, and circumstances associated with the process; for instance, in Verbal Processes the central participant is a Sayer, and in Mental Processes a Senser.

References

[Associated Press] About Us – Associated Press. Retrieved on 10 March 2014 from http://www.ap.org/company/about-us.

[Associated Press] AP statement on anonymous sources. Retrieved on 14 May 2007 from http://www.apme.com/ committees/credibility/052705anonymous.shtml.

Bell, A. (1991) *The Language of News Media*. Oxford: Blackwell.

Boyd-Barrett, O. (1998) 'Global' news agencies. In O. Boyd-Barrett and T. Rantanen (eds) *The Globalization of News* 19–34. London: Sage.

Carey, J. W. (1989) *Communication as Culture: Essays on Media and Society*. Boston, MA: Unwin Hyman.

Chandler, D. (1995) *Semiotics for Beginners*. Retrieved on 13 August 2004 from http://www.aber.ac.uk/media/ Documents/S4B/sem09.html.

Chilton, P. and Lakoff, G. (1995) Foreign policy by metaphor. In C. Schäffner and A. Wenden (eds) *Language and Peace* 37–59. Dartmouth: Aldershot.

Errico, M. (with April, J., Asch, A., Khalfani, L., Smith, M. A. and Ybarra, X. R.) (1996) The evolution of the summary news lead. Retrieved on 13 August 2004 from http://www.scripps.ohiou.edu/mediahistory/mhmjour1-1.htm.

Fishman, M. (1980) *Manufacturing the News*. Austin and London: University of Texas Press.

Fowler, R. (1991) *Language in the News. Discourse and Ideology in the Press*. London: Routledge.

Fox, W. (1977) *Writing the News: Print Journalism in the Electronic Age*. New York: Hastings House.

Galtung, J. and Holmboe Ruge, M. (1970) The structure of foreign news. In J. Tunstall (ed.) *Media Sociology* 259–298. Urbana, IL: University of Illinois Press.

Halliday, M. (1994) *An Introduction to Functional Grammar*, 2nd edn. London: Edward Arnold.

Hartley, J. (1982) *Understanding News*. London: Methuen.

Jukes, S. (2002) Real-time responsibility – journalism's challenges in an instantaneous age. *Harvard International Review* 24: 14–18. Retrieved on 13 August 2004 from http: //hir.harvard.edu/index.html?issue=53.

Kearsarge Regional High School syllabus. Retrieved on 13 August 2004 from http://www.kearsarge.k12.nh.us/ ~klee/166syllabus.htm.

Lakoff, G. and Johnson, M. (1980) *Metaphors We Live By*. Chicago, IL: Chicago University Press.

Media communications course programme. Retrieved on 13 August 2004 from http://www.d.umn.edu/~dpeters1/ comm3505-1/spring04syllabus.htm.

[Reuters] *Reuters Handbook of Journalism* (2008). Retrieved on 10 March 2014 from http://handbook.reuters.com/index.php?title=Main_Page.

Scanlan, C. (2000) *Reporting and Writing: Basics for the 21st Century*. Oxford: Oxford University Press.

Sigal, L. V. (1986) Sources make the news. In R. K. Manoff and M. Schudson (eds) *Reading the News* 9–37. New York: Pantheon Books.

Silverman, M. and Carrol, K. (2005) AP reminds staff about policy. Retrieved on 14 May 2007 from http://www.apme.com/committees/credibility/061705apletter.shtml.

Stenvall, M. (1995) The last round of the Maastricht poker game: a study of news agency language. *Language Forum* 3: 1–57.

Stenvall, M. (2008) Unnamed sources as rhetorical constructs in news agency reports. *Journalism Studies* 9: 229–243.

The Appraisal Website: Homepage. Retrieved on 13 August 2004 from http://www.grammatics.com/appraisal/.

Tuchman, G. (1978) *Making News: A Study in the Construction of Reality*. New York: Free Press.

Tunstall, J. (1999) World news duopoly. In H. Tumber (ed.) *News: A Reader* 191–200. New York: Oxford University Press. Reprinted from Tunstall, J. and Machin, D. (1999) *The Anglo-American Media Connection*. Oxford: Oxford University Press.

Van Dijk, T. A. (1988) *News as Discourse*. Hillsdale, NJ: Erlbaum.

White, P. R. R. (1998) Telling media tales: the news story as rhetoric. Unpublished PhD Dissertation, University of Sydney. Retrieved on 13 August 2004 from http://www.grammatics.com/appraisal/AppraisalKeyReferences.html.

A version of this chapter appeared in *Journal of Applied Linguistics and Professional Practice* 9:3.

Maija Stenvall is a researcher in the Research Unit for Variation, Contacts and Change in English, at the University of Helsinki. She has recently worked mainly on historical news (agency) discourse, but a forthcoming study deals with news agency reports on Europe's migrant crisis.

Who has the power to act in the world? Social actors, agency and voice in a Catholic newspaper

Karin Tusting

1 Introduction

This chapter investigates the construction of social responsibility in British Catholicism, as expressed in the discourse of the weekly newspaper *The Universe*. *The Universe* describes itself as 'the most popular Catholic newspaper in the UK and Ireland', with a circulation at the time this research was carried out of approx. 60,000 (www.totalcatholic.com). It is sold at the back of churches throughout the country. On issues of social responsibility, the newspaper articulates what it sees to be a distinctively Catholic position. In response to a reader's letter, the editor states:

(1)   As a strongly Catholic paper we … feel an obligation to express opinions on all matters affecting society and the common good. Indeed we have a specific duty to do so. In that respect we will applaud anyone who mirrors our Catholic values and concerns, and ask questions of anyone who doesn't.

(2)   Many people do say that the Church shouldn't involve itself in politics, and it may be impossible for we Catholics ever to pin our colours entirely to any party political mast. But politics in its broader sense is about the way society is shaped, and there we do have a duty to put the Catholic perspective.

(3)   A Catholic newspaper has a very special responsibility to lead the way in putting Catholic concerns to the world at large. (1 March 1998)

The repetition of the word Catholic six times (and in addition the reference to 'the Church'), and the strong expression of identification with this identity three times – 'As a strongly Catholic paper *we*', '*our* Catholic values and concerns', '*we* Catholics' – underline the particular responsibility this editor is taking on to express the Catholic moral position, as part of the paper's role in influencing society at large.

This chapter analyses a selection of articles from *The Universe*, collected during fieldwork in Catholic churches in the late 1990s, examining the relationship between representations of society, agency, voice and social responsibility. The focus is to analyse 'the way society is shaped' as it is represented in these articles, and to draw out the implications of this for social relationships and responsibilities.

To address this, I will focus on one specific aspect of discourse: the representation of social actors. Fairclough (2003: 124) describes discourses as 'ways of representing aspects of the world – the processes, relations and structures of the material world, the "mental world" of thoughts, feelings, beliefs and so forth, and the social world'. There are always many possible ways to represent the world, associated with people's positions in the world, identities, social groups and social relationships. One key set of choices made is around the representation of social actors (Fairclough 2003: 145–150; see also Van Leeuwen 1996): that is, who are represented as members of the social world under discussion, what are the relationships between these actors, and what capacities for action are assigned to them. This is a particularly important aspect when addressing questions of social responsibility and agency.

Before asking about the patterns of responsibility in the discourses under study, it is necessary to identify the members of the social world constructed by this discourse who could potentially be assigned such responsibility: that is, the social actors. Social actors can be people, organisations, institutions, or other entities which are represented in the text as acting in the social world. By giving insight into which entities are represented in the discourse as potential actors in the world, and what relationships are constructed between them, analysis of social actors offers a particularly useful tool for generating insight into patterns of responsibility in discourses.

Analysis of the representation of social actors has been used to explore many different questions, including the Uruguayan military's justification of their involvement in the dictatorship period (Achugar 2007); conflicting models of corporate social responsibility in speeches in the Spanish parliament (Canto-Mila and Lozano 2009); gendered discourses in British newspapers (Caldas-Coulthard and Moon 2010); competing socio-political discourses about the Dutch countryside (Frouws 1998); representations of refugees, asylum seekers and immigrants in British newspapers

(KhosraviNik 2009, 2010); and the re-shaping of Mexican national discourses on reproductive rights (Taracena 2002).

This study uses analysis of social actors to identify some significant aspects of the particular discourse of Catholicism, as constructed by *The Universe*, in articles dealing with issues of social concern. I would not wish to suggest that *The Universe* should be seen as representative of Catholicism as a whole, or even of British Catholics. The Catholic Church is made up of a diverse body of people, who draw on a wide range of different discourses to represent the world. Nevertheless, analysis of these articles does give insight into the way social actors and their social responsibilities are constructed by a newspaper claiming to represent 'the Catholic perspective'. This analysis also offers wider insights into how social responsibility can be constructed through the representation of social actors in media texts.

Analysis focuses on how the social world is represented. It will assess who are the principal social actors constructed by the patterns of reference in the text; who amongst these are constructed as playing active roles, and who are not; and which participants are given voice in the articles, and for what purpose. I draw out the relationships and social responsibilities implied by these patterns of reference to assess the distinctive features of Catholic social responsibility as expressed within the pages of this newspaper; that is, who is constructed as having responsibility for dealing with social problems, and in what way they are expected to go about this.

2 Selection of data

The articles analysed here were selected from a corpus of issues of *The Universe* covering the period July 1997–May 1998. These were collected as part of a larger study of the role of textual practices in the constitution of Catholic identity in a single parish (Tusting 2000).[1] The sample articles were taken from the main 'news' section of the paper, as the section which sets out most directly to recount a narrative of events in the world, therefore the section most likely to give insight into constructions of social responsibility and agency. The articles include principally factual reports, rather than purely editorial or opinion pieces, although opinions and arguments are embedded in many.

The initial selection criterion was that the subjects of the articles should fall under the editor's classification of 'matters affecting society and the common good'. This resulted in the selection of 62 articles dealing explicitly with social issues such as poverty, health, crime, and ethical foreign policy. These were then sorted into categories according to their topic. Articles relating to the four topics which gained the greatest amount of coverage during that period were chosen for detailed analysis. These four main topics were poverty, Third World debt, the ethics of foreign policy, and poor working conditions. The 19 articles selected for detailed analysis are listed in Appendix 1.

3 Social actors

Analysis was carried out using Microsoft Word. Each article chosen for analysis was transcribed as a Word file. In the first stage, each reference to a social actor was highlighted in bold, generating sentence-units for analysis like the following example:

> (4)   <SLAVTRAD>8. **The charity** [Christian Aid] is concerned that Third World debt is so severe that **many countries** are struggling to rebuild **their** economies.

The numbers at the start of the sentence units refer to their position in the article by paragraph. Where paragraphs had more than one sentence, letters were used to identify their position within the paragraph, so 7a refers to the first sentence in paragraph 7, 7b to the second sentence in paragraph 7, and so on. The title tags (e.g. <FAITHPOL>) are shortened forms of the article headlines, listed in Appendix 1.

Like the example above, many sentences included reference to two or more social actors. These sentences were therefore copied to produce one unit of analysis for each separate mention of a social actor in the text. The sentence unit above thus became two units, the following example (5) having the charity, Christian Aid, as the social actor in focus for analysis:

> (5)   <SLAVTRAD>8. **The charity** [Christian Aid] is concerned that Third World debt is so severe that many countries are struggling to rebuild their economies.

and example (6) having 'many countries' as the social actor in focus:

> (6)   <SLAVTRAD>8. The charity [Christian Aid] is concerned that Third World debt is so severe that **many countries** are struggling to rebuild **their** economies.

Where social actors were referred to in coordinated groups representing the same type of actor, e.g. in example (9) (c) below, 'The World Bank and the International Monetary Fund', or where mention was made of one specific member as a subset of a larger group, e.g. in (9) (d) 'the supermarkets ... Sainsbury's', these sentence-units were treated as one unit for further analysis, with the participant in focus being understood to be the larger grouping (in these examples: international financial organisations; supermarkets).

These units were then read through many times and sorted and re-sorted, following a 'grounded theory' approach (Glaser and Strauss 1967), to generate and categorise lists of the groups of social actors represented in the articles. These results are summarised in Table 1, overleaf.

The four principal categories emerging from this process are, in descending order of magnitude: social actors representing the Church and related institutions; those represented as needing help; social actors in positions of power; ordinary people without positions of power. In addition to the four principal categories above, there are a small number of references to a range of other types of social actors, including organisations with no link to the Church.

Social actors representing the Church and Church institutions are the largest category, comprising 200 instances. This includes reference to the Church itself and Church institutions; references to agencies and organisations with direct links to the Church (CAFOD (the Catholic Agency for Overseas Development), Christian Aid, Justice and Peace, and others); individuals referred to in their capacity as representatives of Church organisations, fairly evenly divided between clergy and lay people; and a few instances of Church documents being constructed as social actors. According to van Leeuwen (1996), social actors can include both people acting in the world, and other entities which are represented in the way people might be, that is, 'personalised'. This could be, for instance, by performing actions which are normally restricted to human beings, such as speaking. Documents and Church organisations were largely personalised by being given voice, as in 7 (e) below.

The following examples are instances of sentence units where the social actor in focus (in bold) has been categorised as a representative of the Church or of a Church-related organisation. Mgr Diarmuid Martin is a member of the clergy representing a Church institution; Rosemary Read is a lay individual representing a Church institution; a coalition of Catholic aid agencies are church-related organisations; the Vatican is the central Church institution; and a CORI report is an instance of a document being constructed as a social actor in the text by being given voice.

Table 1 Social actors

Social actors representing the Church		Social actors in need of help		Social actors in positions of power, not related to the Church		Ordinary people without positions of power		Other groups of social actors	
The Church itself and Church institutions	32	People in the Third World	18	Governments, politicians and diplomats	37	Church members	7	Organisations with no link to the Church	33
Charities, campaigns and organisations with a direct relationship to the Church	43	The poor	19	Nation states	17	People in general	37	Others	26
Clergy	50	The unemployed	14	International and supra-national organisations	6	Society	10		
Laity speaking from positions within Church or Church-related organisations	58	Young people	15	Companies and business	35	General inclusive 'we' and 'you'	29		
Church documents	17	Workers	24	Generalised references to people in power	3				
		Unspecified people in general, positioned as being in need of help	30	Others in positions of power	9				
		Others	20						
Total: social actors representing the Church	**200**	**Total: social actors in need of help**	**140**	**Total: social actors in non-Church positions of power**	**107**	**Total: social actors positioned as 'ordinary people'**	**83**	**Total: other social actors**	**59**

(7) (a) <PUTLIFE>3. **Mgr Diarmuid Martin, secretary of the Pontifical Council for** Justice and Peace, said the paper was aimed 'at public opinion and at changing the opinion of 7 ordinary citizens' in wealthier countries who may not pay attention to the debt of poor countries.

(b) <PUTLIFE>1b. Spearheading the drive is **Rosemary Read**, the first national Justice and Peace fieldworker for England and Wales.

(c) <PUTLIFE>2. **A coalition of Catholic aid agencies** made the call in Putting Life Before Debt, a document handed to both agencies.

(d) <JPARMS>6. Aware that **the Vatican** has noted with concern that Britain is now one of the world's leading arms exporters, Ambassador Pellew spoke of new guidelines for the export of conventional arms and said that Britain acknowledged that it had 'a particular responsibility to ensure that the arms trade is managed responsibly, so as to avoid the use of arms exports for internal repression or external aggression'.

(e) <RELGPPOOR>3. **A CORI [Conference of Religious of Ireland] report, Surfing the Income Net,** says the current welfare system was introduced when there was almost total employment in Ireland.

The second largest group of social actors, 140 instances, are those represented in the texts as being in need of help. This includes references to the poor, to people in the Third World, to the unemployed, to young people, and to workers, as well as some references to people in general referred to in terms of their need for assistance, as in the following examples:

(8) (a) <FAITHPOL>7a. **Many people living in poverty** are in the grip of debt to loan sharks: the Church can help by supporting credit unions.

(b) <RELGPPOOR>4. Now, with almost **100,000 long-term unemployed,** welfare is a permanent source of income for many, something it was never intended to be.

(c) <ASIANWORK>13b. '**The workers** need to be given a copy of the codes so **they** know how **they** can act to defend **their** rights against violation', he said.

The third significant grouping of social actors, 107 instances, is that in which reference is made to people or institutions in positions of power in the broader social structure: governments and politicians, nation states, international and supra-national organisations (the International Monetary Fund, the European Union), companies and business organisations.

(9)   (a)   <FIGHTPOV>3. And a new group, Jubilee 2000 Coalition, will try to persuade **governments around the world** to cancel Third World debt to celebrate the new millennium.

(b)   <NEWPLEA>8b. 'BAe and **the British Government** have broken international law by applying Hawk aircraft to be used on population of East Timor. I myself have seen the planes in action', he said.

(c)   <PUTLIFE>6a. Putting Life Before Debt praises recent efforts by **the World Bank and the International Monetary Fund** to ease the burden on some of the world's most indebted countries.

(d)   <FAITHPOL>11e. She is also delighted with the work Christian Aid and others have done with **the supermarkets**, and was very impressed to see three fairly traded products in **Sainsbury's** top 100, voted for by customers.

Reference is also made, 83 times, to what I have called 'ordinary people', that is, people who are referred to without positioning them with reference to a particular institution: as ordinary Church members not representing Church institutions, as people in general using a generalised *we* and *you*, or simply in a reference to 'society':

(10)   <LOSTFOLK>3. 'Over the last 20 years **we** have seen a destructive form of individualism which has broken up the whole fabric of **our communal society**', said Fr. McCartney.

These four categories – Church organisations, people in need of help, people and groups in positions of social power, and ordinary people – constitute the main significant groupings of social actors across these texts. There is also a smaller grouping (33 instances) of representations of organisations with no direct link to the Church and no particular position of social power, such as in the following example:

(11)   <ASIANWORK> 2. **Apo Leong, the executive director of the Asia Monitor Resource Centre (MRC)** based in Hong Kong, visited the UK recently as a guest of the World Development Movement.

Finally, there are 26 references to social actors specified in a range of different ways which did not fall into any of these categories:

(12)   (a) <SLAVTRAD>7. The advert features **two bailiffs** entering a run-down hospital in search of goods which can be seized and sold.

(b) <GOSPARMS>12. Some of **the cons** found his presence in prison strange but many applauded his stance.

Although the identification of these categories of social actors is only the first stage of the analysis, it is already suggestive about the construction of the social world here. There are many more references to institutions and authorities of various sorts than to the 'ordinary person'. A clear distinction is being made between 'those in need of help' and 'those in a position to help'. This suggests that in these texts, social responsibility may be placed largely in the realm of the authorities and institutions, rather than in that of the 'ordinary person'. Further analysis is, however, necessary to explore this hypothesis in more depth.

4 Who is the active agent?

The next stage explores the suggestion that responsibility may be placed largely with the authorities, examining in more detail how the different social actors are positioned in the articles. Starting from the premise that assigning responsibility to a social actor must also entail the assignation of agency, this stage examines how agency is attributed. The set of sentence-units analysed above was categorised according to whether the social actor in focus in the unit was an active grammatical agent or not. For instance, in the sentence unit:

(13)   <CUTSDIGN>1. **The Scottish bishops** have slammed the Government's removal of lone parent benefit as 'divisive' and at odds with the Church's social teaching.

the social actor in focus, 'the Scottish bishops', is grammatically an active agent, whereas in the sentence unit:

(14)   <SYNDEBT>2. They also called for an international talks on related economic policies, saying **their communities** were being squeezed by globalisation.

the social actor in focus, 'their communities', is a passive participant being acted on by 'globalisation'. Finally, in a small number of sentence-units, the same social actor is referred to more than once, both as an active agent and otherwise, as in (15) below, where 'every Church member' is an active agent while 'we', referring to the same grouping of 'the Church', is in the passive position of having been anointed by someone else:

(15)   <FAITHPOL>11b. Pointing out that at baptism **we** are all anointed as priests and prophets, she stresses that **every Church member** has a part to play.

The results of this analysis are given in Table 2.

This analysis shows clear divisions in the patterns of grammatical agency in the articles. The majority (103 of 140, 73.5%) of social actors referred to as needing help are not active agents in the clause. Social actors representing the Church were slightly more likely to be active agents: 116 (58%) of the 200 sentence-units having an agentive social actor in focus; 75 (37.5%) a non-agentive social actor in focus; and 9 (4.5%) having both. These proportions are reversed for the third main category, people in non-Church positions of power. These actors are in the majority referred to in non-agentive ways, 65 references of 107 (60.7%) being non-agentive as against 39 (36.4%) agentive. 'Ordinary people' are positioned as non-agentive in the majority (50 of 83, 60.2%), although nearly a third of references (24 of 83, 28.9%) are agentive, and in a tenth of references (9 of 83, 10.8%) as both. These patterns can be seen more clearly represented in a chart, as in Figure 1.

These clear differences in the patterns of agency ascribed to different social actors begin to show some nuances of the discourse in the articles. The marked tendency is for the people positioned as being in need of help to be non-agentive. There is a lesser tendency for people in power and ordinary people to be non-agentive. The only groups in these articles referred to more often as agentive are those relating to Church organisations, their

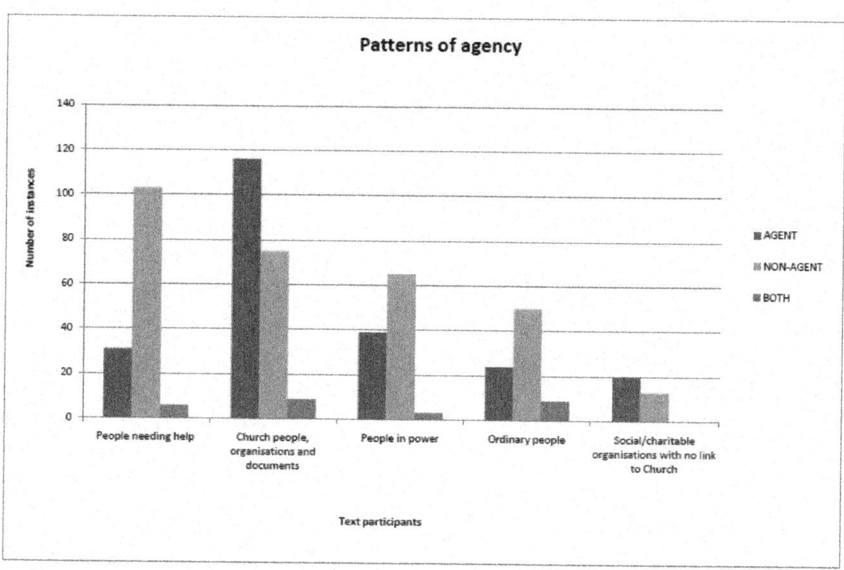

Figure 1 Patterns of agency.

spokespeople and documents emanating from them, and non-Church social or charitable organisations.

However, identifying patterns of agency is of limited value unless it is also possible to identify what is being done with this agency. Halliday (1994) identifies six types of processes in the English language. The three principal types are material processes (processes of doing), mental processes (processes of feeling, thinking and perceiving), and relational processes (processes of being). Halliday (1994: 138) claims that these tend to account for the majority of clauses in a text. There are also three subsidiary process types. Behavioural processes refer to processes of physiological and psychological behaviour. Existential processes represent that something exists or happens. Verbal processes are processes of saying, or of any kind of symbolic exchange.

Taking the category of Church organisations and their representatives and analysing the types of processes they were engaged in when they were agentive shows what they are referred to as doing in these articles. Of these 125 processes (116 where they were solely agentive plus 9 where they were referred to in both agentive and non-agentive positions), a two-thirds majority (84) refer to verbal processes, either directly or metaphorically, as in the following examples (participant in focus in bold, verbal processes underlined):

Table 2 Patterns of agency

Social actors representing the Church	Number of instances	Agent	Non-agent	Both	Social actors in need of help	Number of instances	Agent	Non-agent	Both
The Church itself and Church institutions	32	19	12	1	People in the Third World	18	5	13	0
Charities, campaigns and organisations with a direct relationship to the Church	43	20	23	0	The poor	19	0	19	0
Clergy	50	36	8	6	The unemployed	14	3	11	0
Laity speaking from positions within Church or Church-related organisations	58	34	23	1	Young people	15	3	10	2
Church documents	17	7	9	1	Workers	24	8	14	2
					Unspecified people in general, positioned as being in need of help	30	8	21	1
					Others	20	4	15	1
Total: social actors representing the Church	**200**	**116**	**75**	**9**	Total: social actors in need of help	140	31	103	6

Social actors in positions of power, not related to the Church	Number of instances	Agent	Non-agent	Both	Ordinary people without positions of power	Number of instances	Agent	Non-agent	Both
Governments, politicians and diplomats	37	13	23	1	Church members	7	0	6	1
Nation states	17	3	13	1	People in general	37	9	25	3
International and supra-national organisations	6	2	3	1	Society	10	1	9	0
Companies and business	35	12	23	0	General inclusive 'we' and 'you'	29	14	10	5
Generalised references to people in power	3	1	2	0					
Others	9	8	1	0					
Total: social actors in non-Church positions of power	**107**	**39**	**65**	**3**	**Total ordinary people**	**83**	**24**	**50**	**9**

Other groups of social actors	Number of instances	Agent	Non-agent	Both
Organisations with no link to the Church	33	20	13	0
Others	26	11	10	5
Total: other social actors	**59**	**31**	**23**	**5**

(16)   (a)   <LOSTFOLK>8. 'We need compassion, and we need to be able to look into young people's hearts', <u>said</u> **Bishop Brain**.

(b)   <SYNDEBT>1. **Latin-American participants at the Synod of Bishops for America** <u>have pleaded</u> for a reduction of the continent's huge foreign debt.

The majority of the other processes where Church organisations and agencies are active agents are material, that is, processes of doing, as in the following examples (participant in focus in bold, processes underlined):

(17)   (a)   <JOINDEBT>11. Before going to Birmingham, **Mulima** <u>will travel</u> the country to urge Catholics to join her in the Human Chain.

(b)   <NEWPLEA>2. **Church campaigners** <u>joined</u> other protesters effectively laying siege to the annual meeting of British Aerospace (BAe) on Wednesday.

There are also a few relational processes, as in the following:

(18)   (a)   <HELLFACT>8a. As a priest working in one of the poorest areas of Sao Paulo, **Fr. Fernando** <u>is</u> no stranger to poverty.

(b)   <SYNDEBT>7b. They have the most success among society's marginalised – immigrants, the imprisoned and the sick; sectors where **the Catholic Church** <u>should be</u> more active.

and one mental process:

(19)   <LOSTFOLK>20. '**THOMAS** <u>wants</u> to work with businesses, police, probation, social services and statutory agencies looking at how we can reconcile people with each other.

So those participants who are most often the active agents in the texts tend to be saying, rather than doing, and doing, rather than being or sensing. This focus on saying is foreshadowed by the phrasing of the editor's letter quoted above, in which he states that the newspaper's responsibility is: 'to *express opinions* on all matters affecting society and the common good (…) we will *applaud* anyone who mirrors our Catholic values (…) we have a duty *to put the Catholic perspective*' (my emphasis). We can see from this that the social responsibilities most commonly engaged in by this group of social actors are those of speaking out, rather than of acting.

5 Who speaks?

One of the key ways in which social responsibility can be carried out is through speaking out to others in the social world. Things can rarely be achieved or changed without at some point justifying the need or rationale for such actions to others, and politics is always carried out at least in part through discursive engagement in the public sphere. As we have seen, the explicit position of *The Universe*, as expressed in the editor's letter, is that a central part of their social responsibility is to speak out and express opinions. We have also seen that for the group 'Church organisations and their representatives', engaging in verbal processes forms the greater part of what they are represented as doing in these articles. Further analysis showed that this is not the case for some of the other groups of social actors represented in these articles.

The sentence units in focus were then classified according to whether the social actor in focus was given 'voice', either through the use of direct speech, indirect speech, or the narrative report of a speech act by the participant in focus (following Leech and Short 1981). The following have the verbal process and representation of speech in focus underlined, in an example of direct speech:

(20)   <ONMARCH>3a. **Kailash Satyarthi, the march's international co-ordinator**, said: 'The time has come to initiate a real endeavour to make the whole world one family for the future citizens of this planet.[']

indirect speech:

(21)   <RELGPPOOR>10. **CORI** say that at the moment unemployed people are receiving social welfare payments on condition they stay idle while being available for a job.

and a narrative report of a speech act:

(22)   <HELLFACT>3a. Fr. Fernando had never actually been inside shoe factories until invited by **CAFOD** to help investigate conditions for its campaign.

The results of this analysis can be found in Table 3.

Table 3 Analysis of voice

Social actors representing the Church	Direct speech	Indirect speech	Narrative report of speech act	Total	Social actors in need of help	Direct speech	Indirect speech	Narrative report of speech act	Total
The Church itself and Church institutions	0	4	7	11	People in the Third World	0	0	0	0
Charities, campaigns and organisations with a direct relationship to the Church	2	2	9	13	The poor	0	0	0	0
Clergy	24	13	8	45	The unemployed	0	0	1	1
Laity speaking from positions within Church or Church-related organisations	25	7	7	39	Young people	0	0	0	0
Church documents	2	2	6	10	Workers	0	0	2	2
					Unspecified people in general, positioned as being in need of help	0	0	0	0
					Others	0	0	1	1
Total: social actors representing the Church	**53**	**28**	**37**	**118**	Total: social actors in need of help	0	0	4	4

Social actors in positions of power, not related to the Church	Direct speech	Indirect speech	Narrative report of speech act	Total	Ordinary people without positions of power	Direct speech	Indirect speech	Narrative report of speech act	Total
Governments, politicians and diplomats	3	1	5	9	Church members	0	0	0	0
Nation states	2	0	3	5	People in general	1	0	4	5
International and supra-national organisations	0	0	3	3	Society	0	0	0	0
Companies and business	1	2	6	9	General inclusive 'we' and 'you'	0	1	4	5
Generalised references to people in power	0	0	0	0					
Others	4	1	4	9					
Total: social actors in non-Church positions of power	**10**	**4**	**21**	**35**	**Total: ordinary people**	**1**	**1**	**8**	**10**

Other groups of social actors	Direct speech	Indirect speech	Narrative report of speech act	Total
Organisations with no link to Church	6	3	5	14
Others	2	1	7	10
Total: other social actors	**8**	**4**	**12**	**24**

This demonstrates that in these articles, only certain types of social actor were given voice. The most notable result is that social actors making up the group 'People in need of help' are almost never given voice. Of 140 references to people in need of help, their own words are never used, either in direct or in indirect speech. On only 4 occasions is there a narrative report of a speech act they are (potentially) engaging in. And in fact, on examination, on each of these occasions, the social actors are referred to in such a way that the speaker is disempowered further, either by being prevented from speaking, requiring permission to speak from others, or 'begging' and therefore being positioned as being at the mercy of others:

(23)　(a)　<HELLFACT>9b. **Hundreds of unemployed people** hang around the factory doors every day <u>begging for work</u>.

　　　(b)　<HELLFACT>9a. None of **the workers** dare <u>protest about working conditions</u> for fear of losing their jobs.

　　　(c)　<ASIANWORK>10. When **the workers** attempt to organise and set up unions <u>to collectively bargain</u> they are victimised.

　　　(d)　<ONMARCH>9. Each continent will select **a number of children** to participate in the march, providing them with the opportunity <u>to speak about their experiences of childhood disappearing into misery at the hands of callous employers</u>.

This can be contrasted with the figures for social actors representing the Church, in which of 200 references in total, there are 37 references to speech acts they are involved in, 28 indirect speech citations and 53 direct speech citations. These social actors are given voice in the texts in a way that the people in need of help are not.

A slightly more surprising result comes from an examination of the voice given to the group 'people in power', which includes States, governments and politicians, multinational companies and the like. Since these social actors are capable of action on a global scale, we might expect them to be given voice in the articles to a greater degree than other actors. However, this is not the case. Of 107 references to these social actors in total, there are only 10 direct speech citations, 4 indirect speech citations and 21 narrative reports of speech acts. In general, people in power are spoken to in the texts, rather than speaking themselves.

Similarly, members of the social world in the group 'ordinary people', which includes references to ordinary Church members and participants referred to as 'ordinary citizens' or 'the people around us', are rarely given voice here. Out of 83 references in this category there are only 8 references to speech acts and one instance each of direct and indirect speech, both from the same article, and both representing hypothetical, rather than real speech. (Note that the underlining highlights the particular speech representation in focus at this point, since both of these are examples where the speech representation in focus is embedded within another representation of speech.)

(24) (a) <GOSPARMS> 4. 'It's not going to be brought about by one person smashing the nose cone of a jet but by **ordinary people** <u>saying "no this is wrong"</u>.'

(b) <GOSPARMS> 21. But he added: 'I think **we** <u>have to say</u> <u>**we** need to stop this</u> and **we** need to put **our** bodies on the line.'

These articles construct a particular representation of the world in which only certain groups of social actors are given voice. The Church, Church organisations, charitable organisations and their representatives all speak in these articles. Ordinary people outside these organisations rarely speak. People in power are spoken to, rather than having their own voice. And those who the organisations are trying to help have little or no voice at all.

6 What is spoken about?

The final part of the analysis asks not only who speaks, but also what is spoken about, in order to assess the nature of the social responsibilities which are being requested or taken on by the social actors given voice in these articles. Speaking publicly is one way of taking on social responsibility, but this can be done in a variety of ways. Stating an opinion or reporting facts in a neutral manner is different from asking for or demanding action. Pledging to act is an active engagement in social responsibility, different from demanding action from others. This part of the analysis will focus on the groups of social actors who are given voice most often, that is, social actors representing the Church, and will explore what these representatives actually do with this voice. This group of social actors is given a voice on 118 occasions. These sentence-units were sorted to allow categories relating to what is being said to emerge from the data, through a process of repeated classifying, coding and re-coding.

Four main categories of reported speech content emerged from this process. The majority of verbal processes reported (55 instances) were ones in which the speaker stated an opinion, either speaking in support of something, criticising something, or stating a neutral opinion, that is, neither explicitly critical nor explicitly supportive of a particular organisation or event (verbal processes and verbiage underlined). The following examples show speaking in support:

(25)   <EUINNER> 1. **Parish priests in Leeds** have welcomed a huge cash investment from the European Union into two poverty stricken areas of the city.

Criticising:

(26)   <CUTSDIGN> 7. **Ms Ure** stresses that the policy 'betrays a lack of imagination' and is at odds with the Labour Party's principles.

And stating a neutral, non-evaluative opinion:

(27)   <PUTLIFE>9. 'Politics is about how we organise society, and religion is about how we relate to the people around us', **she** says.

But there was another category which emerged from the sorting and re-sorting process, in which rather than simply stating an opinion, the speaker explicitly called for action in regard to this situation, either on the part of themselves or the group they represent:

(28)   <GOSPARMS> 3. 'We have to create a culture where the arms trade isn't acceptable any more', **he** said.

Or from someone else:

(29)   <CUTSDIGN> 13. **Niall Cooper, national co-ordinator of CAP,** urged Tony Blair to 'match rhetoric with resources' and to challenge the 'vested interests of the more wealthy'.

There were 48 instances where the speaker was calling for action in this way. There was also a small number of incidences of reported speech which were neither stating an opinion nor calling for action on social problems, as in the following examples:

(30) (a) <PUTLIFE>13b. But, **she** <u>pleads: 'Please don't come back in the year 2000 and ask me if I've done it!'</u>

(b) <GOSPARMS>10. A former CAFOD worker **he** has found himself increasingly drawn <u>to proclaim the Gospel</u> by peace-campaigning.

The results of this analysis are given in Table 4 below:

The patterns which emerge from this give further insight into the underlying ideology of social responsibility constructed by these articles. Firstly, Church organisations were more likely to be critical than supportive, with nearly twice as many critical statements as supportive ones. Secondly,

Table 4 What do social actors representing the Church say?

Stating an opinion		Calling for action		Other	
Speaking in support	12	Pledging action	5	Other	15
Criticising (Criticising Government 8; criticising other specific things 6; criticising society or the world in general 7)	21	Announcing campaigns	5		
Stating a neutral opinion, neither critical nor supportive	22	Stating that some action is necessary	17		
		Calling for someone else to act (Governments and politicians 4; international organisations 6; the Church 3; people in general 5; other specified people 3)	21		
Total stating an opinion	**55**	**Total calling for action**	**48**	**Total other**	**15**

with regard to calls for action, on only 10 occasions does the organisation pledge to act themselves, either through running a specific campaign, or in the form of a vaguer general pledge to act or to make a difference (verbiage in focus underlined):

(31) (a) <FIGHTPOV>2. **CAFOD** has announced <u>Challenge 2000, a radical new fund-raising scheme which will focus on one area for aid each year.</u>

(b) <LOSTFOLK>16. Drawing the conference to a close, **Universe editor Joe Kelly** said that <u>the day's events had confirmed 'not only that we can make a difference in society, but that we have an obligation to['].</u>

There are a far greater number of occasions when the representative is saying that action should be taken, either with (21 instances) or without (17 instances) a specific actor being mentioned. Action is often demanded from others, whether from Governments or international organisations, from the Church or from society or people in general:

(32) (a) <CUTSDIGN>3. In a separate move, **Church Action on Poverty (CAP)** has challenged Tony Blair <u>to make sure that the new unit does more than simply 'hear the views of the socially excluded' and matches resources with rhetoric.</u>

(b) <SYNDEBT>4b. **He** said <u>the Church should propose a remittance of the debt, and encourage an examination of the unfavourable conditions placed on debtor nations by lenders.</u>

(c) <LOSTFOLK>7. In his opening address, **Bishop Terence Brain of Salford** spoke <u>of society's responsibility to 'understand and give hope' to young people who had lost their way.</u>

In these articles, Church organisations are far more likely to criticise other bodies or to call other people to act than to pledge action on their own behalf, or indeed to support the actions of other bodies.

7 Interpretation: Who has the power to act in the world?

To summarise, the discourse of these articles constructs a social world in which members fall into three main groups. There are those who are in need of help; those who are in a position to provide help; and those – mainly representatives of Church organisations – who speak on behalf of the former to the latter.

Everyday readers of this newspaper, if they are not members of any particular organisation or institution, are not positioned as having particular responsibility for the general social problems the articles discuss, or for helping to deal directly with their consequences. Ordinary individuals are largely only responsible for acting to help those in need insofar as they are acting as members of particular groups or organisations – a collective, rather than an individualised sense of responsibility. And any actions they take as part of these organisations tend to involve speaking to those in power, rather than taking action themselves.

Representatives of Church organisations are not described in these articles as having the power to act directly, either. Their principal social responsibility is neither to help people in need directly, nor to help them to help themselves. Rather, it is to speak about them to other social actors: to powerful individuals, companies and Governments. And the people who are actually in situations of social difficulty are deprived of voice and agency, while Church organisations and institutions speak on their behalf, representing their case to the powerful.

It is the groups of people who are spoken to – the Governments, multinational corporations and politicians – who are the ones positioned as having the responsibility to act. However, in these articles at least, the actions that they are to take often remain unspecified. We have seen, in Table 2 above, that these groups of social actors are rarely in agentive positions. So the explicit nature of their power and the sorts of actions that they are or could be taking are not often made explicit in these articles. Rather, these groups function principally in these articles as audiences for the calls for action from representatives of Church organisations.

This is by no means an inevitable way of constructing the social world. An alternative approach would be to report on the poor and the dispossessed speaking for themselves, calling for the actions that they feel need to be taken, or taking direct action. But this would run counter to the principal discourse on which these articles draw, a representation of society in which the power to act for change is not given to individuals, but is held in the hands of small elite groups. The response of ordinary people, and even of activist institutions, in the face of social injustice becomes mainly to appeal to those with the 'real' power to change things – who, at least in these articles, rarely respond. The Church organisations' main role in these articles is to criticise those in power, and to call for action to be taken that might help those groups of people in need of help – who are rarely, if ever, positioned in such a way that they can speak for or help themselves.

So we see that the discourse of *The Universe* in these articles is representing a social world in which ultimately social responsibility is not assigned to ordinary people, but is assumed to be in the hands of institutions and powerful individuals. This resonates with a broader argument that power is increasingly removed from people at a local level and operates on a global scale, as in Bauman's (1998) dichotomy between powerful 'globals', free to act and move across boundaries, and disempowered 'locals', trapped in localities and situations from which they do not have the agency to free themselves, or Giddens' (1991) identification of the tendency for decision-making powers to be taken away from ordinary people and passed over to 'expert systems'. In such expert systems, knowledge and responsibility associated with the individual person are transformed and become transferable within the system – just as responsibility is, in these articles, associated with institutions rather than people. This is a vision of social responsibility in which the role of the activist organisation is to call for action, and the role of the ordinary person is to spectate – a fairly disempowering model for most readers.

Notes

1   I am grateful to the Economic and Social Research Council for supporting the doctoral study which enabled this research.

References

Achugar, M. (2007) Between remembering and forgetting: Uruguayan military discourse about human rights (1976-2004). *Discourse & Society* 18: 521–547.

Bauman, Z. (1998) *Globalization: The Human Consequences.* Cambridge: Polity Press.

Caldas-Coulthard, C. R. and Moon, R. (2010) 'Curvy, hunky, kinky': using corpora as tools for critical analysis. *Discourse & Society* 21: 99–133.

Canto-Mila, N. and Lozano, J. M. (2009) The Spanish discourse on corporate social responsibility. *Journal of Business Ethics* 87: 157–171.

Fairclough, N. (2003) *Analyzing Discourse: Textual Analysis for Social Research*. London and New York: Routledge.

Frouws, J. (1998) The contested redefinition of the countryside: an analysis of rural discourses in the Netherlands. *Sociologia Ruralis* 38: 54–68.

Giddens, A. (1991) *Modernity and Self-Identity: Self and Society in the Late Modern Age*. Cambridge: Polity Press.

Glaser, B. and Strauss, A. (1967) *The Discovery of Grounded Theory*. Chicago, IL: Aldine.

Halliday, M. A. K. (1994) *An Introduction to Functional Grammar*, 2nd edn. London: Edward Arnold.

KhosraviNik, M. (2009) The representation of refugees, asylum seekers and immigrants in British newspapers during the Balkan conflict (1999) and the British general election (2005). *Discourse & Society* 20: 477–498.

KhosraviNik, M. (2010) The representation of refugees, asylum seekers and immigrants in British newspapers: a critical discourse analysis. *Journal of Language and Politics* 9: 1–28.

Leech, G. and Short, M. (1981) *Style in Fiction: A Linguistic Introduction to English Fictional Prose*. London: Longman.

Taracena, R. (2002) Social actors and discourse on abortion in the Mexican press: the Paulina case. *Reproductive Health Matters* 10: 103–110.

Tusting, K. (2000) Written intertextuality and the construction of Catholic identity in a parish community: an ethnographic study. Unpublished doctoral thesis. Lancaster University, Lancaster.

Van Leeuwen, T. (1996) The representation of social actors. In C. Caldas-Coulthard and M. Coulthard (eds) *Texts and Practices: Readings in Critical Discourse Analysis* 32–70. London: Routledge.

A version of this chapter appeared in *Journal of Applied Linguistics and Professional Practice* 9:3.

Karin Tusting received her PhD in Linguistics from Lancaster University and is currently Senior Lecturer in Linguistics and Literacy Studies at Lancaster University. Her research interests include workplace literacies, accountability and audit culture; learning and identity in communities of practice; and linguistic ethnography. Her current research focuses on academics' everyday writing practices in university workplaces.

Appendix 1: Texts analysed and tags

October 19 1997 p. 5 Fighting poverty from two fronts. <FIGHTPOV>

January 4 1998 p. 17 A slave trade for today? <SLAVTRAD>

April 26 1998 p. 15 Put life before debt, says coalition. <PUTLIFE>

December 7 1997 p. 17 On a thin line between faith and politics. <FAITHPOL>

November 30 1997 p. 11 Synod calls again for end to debt. <SYNDEBT>

May 10 1998 p. 1 Join us to help end debt misery. <JOINDEBT>

October 26 1997 p. 12 Priests welcome EU inner-city cash boost. <EUINNER>

March 15 1998, p. 2 Poor need help in Budget, Brown told. <POORHELP>

October 12 1997 p. 4 Religious group's plan to help poor. <RELGPPOOR>

February 22 1998 p. 9. Church called to support latest jobless initiatives. <JOBLESS>

December 7 1997 p. 6 We don't give the lost folk a hope! <LOSTFOLK>

December 14 1997 p. 1 Benefit cuts 'an attack on human dignity'. <CUTSDIGN>

October 12 1997 p. 1 Bold plan to beat poverty. <BOLDPLAN>

May 3 1998 p. 1 New Plea to halt UK arms exports. <NEWPLEA>

January 11 1998 p. 8 Proclaiming Gospel against arms trade. <GOSPARMS>

February 8 1998 p. 2 John Paul's warning to Britain over arms trade. <JPARMS>

November 9 1997. p. 19 Hell in the factory: Ordeal of workers too busy to smile. <HELLFACT>

January 19 1998 p. 16. Asian workers still suffer in 'appalling conditions'. <ASIANWORK>

January 25 1998 p. 6 On the march for justice. <ONMARCH>

Construing professional norms in journalism: Responsibility and risk reporting

Anna Solin

1 Introduction

Open any newspaper and you are likely to come across stories about risks. International news talk about global warming and the Ebola virus, home pages about food poisoning and air pollution. Risk stories are frequent not only in the quality press, but also in the popular press, local papers and online news sites. Besides being frequent, risk news are influential: for most people, they are a key source of understandings about risks (Hansen 2010). They influence everyday choices such as where people live, how they travel from place to place and what they buy in the supermarket. While most news reports do not contain explicit advice, information provided for instance about the relation between pollution and asthma or sunbathing and cancer is likely to be interpreted as advice by many readers.

Questions of responsibility are therefore highly relevant in the context of discussions of risk reporting. With the increase in risk headlines, the media have come under attack for not providing adequate reporting; they have been blamed for sensationalism, playing on people's fears and even causing 'hysteria' among the public. Indeed, they have been criticised for failing to live up to their self-assumed responsibility to keep the public informed of issues of social, political and personal relevance.

This chapter is concerned not with the overall public responsibilities of the press in democratic societies, but with the way in which individual journalists construe their sense of professional responsibility in the context of risk reporting. The assumption is that responsibility relations are defined and negotiated in different ways in different institutional and cultural contexts of media production, and that it is therefore not possible to establish a stable and universally acceptable definition or norm of what counts as responsible reporting.

I start from the premise that there are particular shared ideals which are a key element in the self-understanding of the journalistic profession – an example is the strive for accuracy. Reference to such ideals is a typical way of beginning discussions around journalistic responsibility. However, my analytic focus is how such ideals are drawn on or evoked in specific organisational settings where journalists negotiate their day-to-day practices. More particularly, I analyse the way journalists talk about professional ideals and norms in the context of risk reporting. Following Deuze (2005: 444), the professional norms of journalism are seen as an 'ideal-typical value system' through which journalists give meaning to their work and which is continually being construed in discourse about journalistic writing.

The main data are a set of interviews with British press journalists who specialise in environment and science reporting. In line with a discourse studies perspective, the interview data are interpreted as situated accounts delivered from particular positions. The descriptions that journalists provide about their writing practices are not treated as 'eyewitness accounts', but as contextualised narratives, which construe particular kinds of professional and institutional identities (cf. Briggs 1986: Potter 1996; Smith 2002). Thus, responsibility relations and normative principles are seen as emergent, dynamic constructs, not simply established qualities or states which interviewees reproduce in their talk.

The study focuses on the tension between institutional representations of professional responsibility (as encoded for example in journalism text-books, stylebooks and codes of practice) and representations of journalistic practice in the interview talk.[1] The data illustrate the complexity of responsibility relations in newsrooms: local normative systems constraining journalistic writing are affected not only by accountability to the public or to sources but also responsibilities to colleagues, editors, managers and owners.

The data studied are four interviews, which I conducted with British environment and science journalists in London, UK, in 1998. The interviewees are Paul Brown (*Guardian* environment reporter – PB), Nigel Hawkes (*Times* science reporter – NH), Roger Highfield (*Daily Telegraph* science reporter – RH) and Nicholas Schoon (*Independent* environment reporter – NS).[2] All four interviewees have extensive experience of journalism, though not exclusively in the areas of environment or science. The interviews were semi-structured and lasted between one and one and a half hours each. Three of the interviews were conducted in the journalists' workplaces (i.e. in newsrooms), one (with Nicholas Schoon) in a cafeteria in central London. The interviews focused on two issues: the particularities of environment and risk reporting and the production practices of news texts (e.g. practices of source use and practices of editing source texts).

2 Evaluating risk news

The evaluation of media performance is necessarily related to the kinds of normative frameworks that are evoked, that is, the kind of criteria that 'responsible reporting' needs to fulfill. McQuail suggests the following 'public sphere expectations' as a general starting point:

> ... publishing full, fair and reliable information; assisting in the expression of diverse and relevant opinions, including criticism of government; giving access to significant voices in society; facilitating the participation of citizens in social life; abstaining from harmful propaganda. (McQuail 1997: 514)

However, more specific criteria that are acceptable across cultural and political boundaries are notably difficult to establish (see e.g. McQuail 1996; Rao and Lee 2005), so principles of adequate reporting are often debated in local contexts. A typical result of such debates is the publication of a 'code of practice', a formal codification of norms regarding professional conduct analogous to codes of conduct in medicine, law and academia (see e.g. Hafez 2002; Laitila 1995; Wilkins and Brennen 2004). In journalism, such codes typically provide guidelines on issues such as accuracy, respect for privacy and journalistic autonomy. In the UK, the relevant codes for press journalists are the Press Complaints Commission code (now the Independent Press Standards Organisation code)[3] and the National Union of Journalists (NUJ) code. An important international code is that published by the International Federation of Journalists (IFJ).[4]

As noted above, the aim here is not to discuss specific criteria for the evaluation of risk reporting though such attempts do exist (see for instance Lofstedt 2010; Sandman et al. 1987), but rather to analyse how journalists talk about broader professional ideals and norms. It is, however, worthwhile to review the most frequent types of criticism that have been directed at risk news, since the way the interviewees talk about risk reporting can be expected to respond and refer to such critique, even if mostly in an implicit manner.

In public debates, risk reporting is perhaps most often criticised for sensationalism and exaggeration. Indeed, research has found that reports often focus on dramatic and extraordinary risks and on the human interest element in risk scenarios. For instance, stories focus on particular, striking events and on victims rather than on long-term processes or complex political questions. (See Allan et al. 2000; Anderson 2006; and Kitzinger 1999, for reviews.)

An example of the focus on dramatic events is provided by Kitzinger and Reilly's (1997) study into the reporting of the risks of BSE-infected beef. The first peak in UK media reporting on BSE occurred already in 1990, but reporting all but ceased between 1991 and 1995 even though the problem had not gone away. In late 1995, the number of reports surged again with news of new cases of CJD in young people. As one of the journalists interviewed for the study put it: 'We needed dead people, well, we've got them now' (Kitzinger and Reilly 1997: 344; see also Shih et al. 2008).

Another aspect of sensationalism is overstatement and exaggeration. For instance, Bell's (1994) study on the reporting of climate change in the New Zealand press shows that news stories reported scientific claims as more certain than the original reports had done. Estimates were presented as certainties, and claims presented as 'what-if assumptions' within science were turned into firm predictions in news reports. The stories also overstated the sea level rises expected to result from climate change. For instance, in a number of reports no time scope was provided, thus suggesting that huge rises were imminent.

Fowler (1991: 147–207) provides even more striking examples of exaggeration in his study of the reporting of salmonella in eggs in the UK press in the late 1980s. For instance, the press labelled the episode *the food fight, the salmonella epidemic* and the *eggs panic*. Headlines included *Fears over toxic cocktail* and *20 ways to beat the killers in your kitchen*. Towards the end of the episode the risks were even further generalised in the headline *The poisoning of our world*.

A comprehensive study of US news reports on environmental risks indicates that risk reporting 'tends toward the extremes' – that is, a situation or event is reported as being either risky or not risky, rather than representing uncertainty or intermediate positions (Sandman et al. 1987: 100). Particularly headlines were found to contain overstatements. The data collected for the study include examples where the news text itself provides no grounds for alarm, but the headline creates a 'feeling of impending doom' (1987: 43). That is, headlines were found to set a tone which was not in line with the report itself.

Solin (2004) came to similar conclusions when analysing news reporting on air pollution in the UK press. The analysis focuses on the relations between news reports and their source texts and shows that the headlines and lead paragraphs of news reports tend to present the strongest possible risk claim warranted by the source. For example, headlines and lead paragraphs express strong causal relations between pollution and health risks (e.g. *Pollution is killing people*) instead of using the weaker expressions typical of scientific reports (such as *correlations* and *associations*). Markers of uncertainty (e.g. *may, possibly*) are also seldom used.

Finally, a type of criticism of risk reporting put forward particularly by US researchers is that stories lack information about risks (see e.g. Cox 2010: 209–211; Major and Atwood 2004; Sandman et al. 1987: 40–43). For instance, studies have suggested that much risk reporting fails to explain how great the risks are in comparison to other risks or to situate the risks in a broader context. Wilkins and Patterson (1987) argue that the 'body counts' typical of risk reports are problematic in the sense that no context is given for interpreting the numbers, such as an indication of how many lives are lost per thousand.

Media research has pointed to many aspects of newswork which underlie such tendencies. Perhaps the principal factor influencing risk reporting is the importance of news values in the selection of stories for publication. News values are a set of qualities which journalists and editors have been found to rely on to determine whether a story is worthy of being published (see e.g. Bell 1991: 155–160; Galtung and Ruge 1973). Some of the key news values in risk reporting are negativity, novelty, unexpectedness and unambiguity. It is evident that overstatement is related to the value of negativity; the more dramatic the consequences, the more newsworthy a risk is. The values of novelty and unexpectedness are fulfilled, for example, in stories about an everyday product or practice which was assumed to be safe but turns out to be potentially risky (e.g. eating beef). Another central value is unambiguity: news about risks need to put forward concise 'facts', not uncertain estimates. As Anderson (1997: 118) argues, 'the less ambiguous an event the more it is likely to be covered'. This value is evident in the presentation of risk claims as certain rather than tentative and by the use of numbers (such as 'body counts') to communicate the extent of risks.

3 Construing journalistic responsibility

In the talk of the journalists interviewed, a clear duality emerges between journalistic ideals and various types of local demands in the newsrooms the interviewees worked in.[5] While the interviewees do refer to professional ideals and norms, most of the discussion revolves around constraints such as competition, lack of time and editorial intervention. Newswork, and even the relatively independent practice of a specialist journalist, emerges as wrought with tensions and competing demands.

In the following, the data are discussed from the point of view of two salient professional ideals: accuracy and autonomy. Both ideals are well-established and extensively recycled in the discourse of journalists, as illustrated, for example, in journalism textbooks and professional codes of practice.

3.1 The ideal of accuracy

The ideal of accuracy is perhaps the most salient element in the public self-understanding of the journalistic profession. It is prominently established in the codes of practice of various professional bodies. For instance, the code published by the UK Press Complaints Commission (2011) states that 'the press must take care not to publish inaccurate, misleading or distorted information', while the code published by the National Union of Journalists (2014) states that '[a] journalist … strives to ensure that information disseminated is honestly conveyed, accurate and fair'. Journalism textbooks also emphasise this ideal. The manual *Writing for Journalists* states that '[f]actual accuracy is vital to credible news journalism' (Hicks et al. 2008: 13), while Frost (2010: 15) emphasises that 'the reporter should [go] to considerable pains to ensure the material is truthful' (see also Cotter 2010: 36–43).

In the interviews, the ideal is referred to a number of times: the interviewees refer, for example, to the need to *report facts* and *stick to the scientific data*:

(1)   my job is to try and report the facts as I see it, and obviously I don't always report them right, but I try to get it right (PB)[6]

(2)   I try very hard to stick to the scientific data so far as so far as it's known, you know that's my loyalties, is to the truth as revealed by science, I mean it isn't, you know, not every truth is revealed by science and sometimes scientific truths turn out to be untrue, but that's that's the that's the process (NH)

It is striking here how cautious the interviewees are in the way they talk about accuracy. Besides references to the possibility of presumed truths being untrue and reporting not always being right, the extracts contain modals suggesting uncertainty (e.g. the verb *try* and the modification of the nouns *facts* and *data* in the phrases *facts as I see it* and *data so far as it's known*). Thus, achieving accuracy is not construed as straightforward, but as a challenge.

Indeed, the interviews contain a wealth of accounts of how the journalists are prevented from achieving the ideal of accuracy. A key tension which emerges in the data is the clash between the ideal of accuracy and the news value of unambiguity in day-to-day writing. As noted above, the value of unambiguity is at work when editors show a preference for stories where risks can be presented as having definite effects. For Roger Highfield, a science reporter, this translates into the need to produce *strong stories*:

(3)   half of what I write never gets into the paper, so there is pressure
       on us within the paper to you know come up with strong stories

Highfield describes the way he writes a science story on the basis of a scientific paper as follows:

(4)   [you] go in, pluck out what look like the most sensational things
       you can find, ring up the scientist, and just harry them until
       they you know until you come up with a kind of compromise
       statement that you feel is something significant to say in news
       terms and they're happy to stand by that

That is, in order to turn a story into something *significant in news terms* the journalist needs to negotiate and identify the strongest and least ambiguous claims in what the source has said; simply restating the original scientific claims is not likely to be acceptable as a news story.

Nigel Hawkes, a science reporter, similarly refers to a distinction between *story* and *non-story*, between *obscure* stories and stories that *leap out at you*:

(5)   if [the source] is a slightly obscure paper in a journal you're not
       going to ring up [the author] on the offchance that talking to him
       will turn a non-story into a story, because there are lots of stories

out there and you pick the ones that leap out at you and you don't
dig around for the ones that are a bit obscure

It is illustrative of the relations between journalists and editors that
the interviewees construe themselves as being under an obligation to
write strong stories. This is evident, for example, in the use of modals of
obligation, such as *have to* and *can't* in descriptions of news writing. In the
following extracts, the frequency of such modals is particularly striking
(the modals are in italics):

(6)   you *have to* write a news story with a hard lead, the lead *has to*
       say something definite, you *can't* start a news story by saying a
       small, badly designed study has produced unconvincing evidence
       […] you *can't* do that, that may be your personal opinion, but you
       can't do that (NH)

(7)   we *have to* convince our news editors that it's a story at all, so we
       can't write a story that says on the one hand air pollution might
       be a problem, on the other hand it might not, because it won't get
       in the paper (PB)

Notably, such 'obligation talk' does not occur when the interviewees
talk about accuracy, suggesting that newsworthiness is a more pressing
professional requirement than accuracy. The key challenge for a journalist
writing a risk story is to convince the editor that the story is *significant* or
interesting, not that it is completely faithful to sources.

Nicholas Schoon, who was on leave from the *Independent* at the time
of the interview, talks in a way which suggests a great deal of tension
between editors and reporters. In the following passage Schoon talks about
the editors (*they*) not being interested in *maybe* and follows this with a
hypothetical representation of how editors would be likely to react to a story
representing scientific uncertainties: *why bother with these uncertainties ...
we'll use something else.*

(8)   [editors] are not interested in maybe […] if you're kind of not
       sure about this, then why are we bothering to put it in the paper,
       you know, there's lots of other stories, every day there's five
       times as much around that we could use as we do use, so why
       bother with these uncertainties and subtleties, just forget the story
       then, we'll use something else

Such talk construes the journalist as someone who is sensitive to nuances, while editors are represented as dismissing *subtleties* in a rather offhand manner. Paul Brown, environment editor, describes a similar scenario as being typical; editors look for drama while journalists aim for accurate and *reasonable* reporting:

(9)   there's always a tension in newspapers between news editors and editors who want to make a story more dramatic than it is and a specialist reporter who wants to report it like it is […] there's a constant tension between what is reasonable to say and what is more dramatic to say

Here, *reporting it like it is* is construed as an ideal that specialist reporters aim for but whose achievement is a struggle.

From the point of view of the construction of responsibility relations, it is evident that journalists are in a dilemmatic position. In the interview talk they align themselves with accuracy as a professional norm in a relatively straightforward manner – the status of the norm is not questioned, nor do the interviewees question the possibility of achieving accuracy. Such talk emphasises their responsibility towards readers, and more generally to the 'public sphere expectations' referred to above. However, at the same time the interviewees provide plenty of descriptions of their immediate daily accountability to the editor, where different local demands emerge, often clashing with the ideal of accuracy. Nigel Hawkes describes his position bluntly:

(10)   nobody ever got sacked for exaggerating, people get sacked for missing stories (.) it's a greater journalistic sin to miss a story than to exaggerate a story

This example is illustrative of the friction between local norms (journalists have a responsibility not to downplay or miss stories) and broader professional norms as outlined in ethics codes (journalists have a responsibility not to exaggerate). The local demands are described as severe; what is at risk is not simply occasional failure to get stories published but job security. Reference to the risk of job loss is a dramatic way of describing the journalists' position. Raising the possibility of such harsh sanctions also functions to limit the journalist's personal accountability.

This discussion illustrates the tension between an abstract but well-established professional norm and the immediate local demands which journalists need to orient to in the context of a competitive newsroom. The data suggest that while the ideal of accuracy is not seen as irrelevant, it is variably adopted as a norm of news writing. Overall, the influence of news values (and particularly the demand for 'strong stories') is described as being a stronger influence on risk reporting than the ideal of accuracy. Responsibilities towards editors and the requirement to produce a competitive news product are construed as more acute than the responsibility to live up to an ethics code. Thus, there appears to be a deeply-rooted conflict between a professional norm and the day-to-day local circumstances of news writing.[7]

3.2 The ideal of autonomy

The notion of journalistic autonomy and the free press is another revered ideal among newsworkers. As Deuze (2005) notes, the journalistic profession prides itself on autonomy; the ideal journalist is understood to be resistant to outside pressure, whether it comes from owners, the marketing department or public opinion. This is also reflected in professional codes of practice. The UK National Union of Journalists code contains references to the importance of 'media freedom' and the need for the journalist to resist 'inducements to influence, distort or suppress information', while the International Federation of Journalists states that 'the journalist shall at all times defend the principles of freedom in the honest collection and publication of news'.

The ideal is also referred to in the interview data, though mostly implicitly. The interviewees talk about *making up their own minds* (Paul Brown) or *doing the thinking themselves* (Nicholas Schoon). However, as with accuracy, the way the journalists talk about their work construes their journalistic autonomy as constrained by day-to-day concerns such as lack of time and relations with colleagues.

The data construe lack of time as a daily constraint on news writing – a finding supported by other research on environmental news production (see e.g. Sandman et al. 2006). On the day of our interview, Roger Highfield had entered seven stories into the *Telegraph*'s news queue, while Nigel Hawkes described days when he was writing four or five stories. The interviewees also described themselves as regularly using source materials already written as news (mainly press releases and news agency dispatches) in order to save time.

When discussing practices of source use, Nigel Hawkes said he would normally like to talk to the scientists whose work he was writing about, something he referred to as *following up*, instead of relying only on written sources. However, he described a number of scenarios where such *follow up* was not necessary, as in the following:

(11)   if you've got a paper from a journal and you're only writing 250 words, you don't really need to follow up (.) and of course you've got the news agencies too, sometimes I'll take something, sometimes they'll do an interview with a scientist and there'll be a quote in there, I'll just take that out and use that, so it saves me actually having to make the phone call

It is striking that, in Hawkes' account, the tempo of newswork is such that the journalist has to be 'saved' from talking to sources.

Reliance on source material already written as news can be assumed to curtail the journalist's autonomy in the sense that it influences both the selection and framing of stories: out of all the stories offered to newspapers for publication, those stories are selected which are easy to turn into news. Nigel Hawkes is candid about such influence:

(12)   what tends to happen is you look at the Nature press release and find out what they think is interesting and those are the ones you tend to look at, you tend to ignore the others

Hawkes also makes a distinction between *simple rewrite jobs* (for example taking off the material for a story from a press release) and writing a story on the basis of a journal article; the latter is *not quite so press friendly because you've got to understand the science.*[8]

Source texts which imitate the news report genre are useful not just because they save time (they need little rewriting) but because they already conform to the criteria of newsworthiness assumed to guide the journalist's selection of sources. Source texts written as news *make it a story*:

(13)   we're a bit vulnerable to the press release because they draw out the implications of the work and make it a story, where you might not otherwise realise it was a story (NH)

However, the reference to vulnerability here suggests that Hawkes is ambivalent about such source use. Nicholas Schoon explicitly refers to press releases as something to avoid:

(14)   as a journalist you're kind of wary of the press release [...] I
         never like to read the press release cause actually cause everyone
         gets the press release, and it's very lazy sort of journalism, and
         it'll lead everyone to interpret things in the same way

This kind of talk positions the journalists as concerned about the risks
that the tempo of newswork poses to journalistic autonomy. However, the
practice of drawing on press releases is not described as something that
the individual journalist can control. Predictably, none of the interviewees
describe themselves as using press releases out of laziness or indifference.
As with accuracy, responsibility for such practices is placed in the realm of
editors and managers; if journalists were not pressured to produce several
stories a day, they would be less dependent on carefully designed, ready-
to-print source material.

As discussed in the previous section, the interviews also contain a
wealth of descriptions of the sometimes tense relations between journalists
and editors. Many comments by the interviewees construe editorial pressure as a daily presence which shapes writing, and the editorial process
(sub-editing and headline writing, for example) as something they cannot
influence. This orientation towards editors is clear for example in what
Nicholas Schoon says at the very beginning of the interview, when asked
about the particularities of being an environment reporter:

(15)   the sort of journalism you do is no different from any other kind
         of journalism fundamentally, it's got to have to produce stories
         that interest news editors and get used in the paper, otherwise
         you're not doing your job

What is notable here is that in describing his work Schoon only refers
to his responsibilities to editors – his main duty is to produce *stories that
interest news editors*.

In the journalists' talk, journalists and editors are typically placed
in opposing positions, with editors construed as controlling the news
product and journalists as having to orient to the editors' expectations.
When discussing the competitive news market in the UK, Roger Highfield
describes his situation as follows:

(16)   you're very aware of what you're you're judged every day on
         what your colleagues [in other newspapers] do, and if they have
         a stronger line on a story then you will, you know you'll have to
         explain yourself to your news editor (RH)

Here, the journalist is positioned as having to 'explain himself' to the editor, if he fails to produce competitive stories.

Notably, the power over (and responsibility for) the final product on the newspaper's page is placed solely with editors. Nigel Hawkes suggests that he gives up the rights over his own writing once he submits his story:

(17)   you know it's not my job to determine what goes in the paper, or in what form, that's their [the editors'] job [.] so I don't hassle them and I don't make difficulties

The responsibility for inaccuracies is thus also placed with editors. Even though a news story usually contains an individual journalist's byline, that journalist is not construed as being accountable for possible problems in the story, given that s/he does not have final control over it. The interviewees describe themselves as *complaining* and *moaning* if there are mistakes, but it is not possible for them to intervene in the production process:

(18)   often what happens is that there are stupid mistakes made that's when something is shortened or in the headline (.) then I'd, you know, then you'd, all you can do is complain about it (NS)

(19)   a lot of stories I write won't get into print or are in a truncated form, occasionally there'll be bad headlines [...] you can moan after it's happened, but yeah, you're not sort of considered or informed (RH)

These accounts construe the journalists' authorial role as narrower than suggested by the convention of attributing stories to individual writers. While the interviewees describe themselves as being responsible for the overall framing of stories and the way sources are represented and claims worded, the final form of stories (e.g. which paragraphs of the journalist's text are included in the final layout) is placed as out of their control.

4 Discussion

This chapter has analysed how journalists talk about professional responsibility, and more specifically professional ideals and norms in the context of risk reporting. The setting analysed is the highly competitive UK press, which is marked by 'compulsive consumption of competitors' output' (Aldridge and Evetts 2003: 560). The analysis illustrates, in particular, the tension between well-established and broadly accepted but relatively abstract ideals such as accuracy and autonomy and local constraints on day-to-day writing in newsrooms. The analysis points for example to clashes between the news value of unambiguity and the ideal of accuracy, as well as the way in which the tempo of newswork affects journalistic autonomy. Such tensions raise questions about responsibility relations: the 'public sphere expectations' associated with journalism appear to be in conflict with journalists' accountability towards editors and managers.

It is evident that journalists have to negotiate different and sometimes competing responsibilities in their everyday writing: while ethical ideals are not questioned or construed as irrelevant, they are often in conflict with acute local demands on writing. Moral responsibilities (such as avoiding exaggeration) are rarely referred to in the interview talk and seem to be relatively distant from day-to-day writing in newsrooms. The immediate local concern is the journalist's accountability to the editor: at the end of the day, the journalist has to have produced stories acceptable 'in news terms'. We may interpret this as two normative orders clashing, with the one influencing daily writing in the form of editorial gatekeeping and control and the other having a more diffuse presence, involving less direct sanctions.

Belsey (1998) argues that there is necessarily a clash in newswork related to a 'two-sided reality', where the two sides are contradictory. He analyses journalism as a profit-making industry, where the journalist's position is that of a worker making a living, and as a profession, where ethical principles both define and regulate the profession. One of the particularities of the journalistic profession is that there are few sanctions resulting from non-adherence to codified norms. Belsey (1998: 5) notes that a journalist who fails to respect professional codes 'may get a scoop and a promotion' – a scenario which is unlikely in medicine, law or academia. The uncertain status of professional codes of practice is also evident in the interview data analysed here: interviewees do not refer to sanctions related to inaccurate reporting or being led by influential sources, while the failure to produce 'strong stories' is cited by all interviewees as a risk to job security. The responsibilities outlined in ethics codes may thus remain abstract and distant from the perspective of newsrooms.

Overall, the interview talk is rather pessimistic in tone: while the interviewees suggest that journalistic ideals such as accuracy and autonomy have a reality for them, they also confess to being unhappy with some of their writing in this respect. Moreover, they construe themselves as lacking agency in relation to organisational constraints. Some talk about the problems of risk reporting using emotional and even confessional language:

> I've never kind of been ashamed, I hope I would never be ashamed of an intro [xxx] taking it in isolation I hope I could still justify it [...] I personally think I kind of try and be responsible about it and I would never you know I'd hope I could defend every story. (NS)

> I wrestle with this and I don't I don't really know what the answer is (.) I try and avoid creating unnecessary scares, but if I look back at my cuttings, I find I've I find I have written a lot of scare stories over the years, less than some but plenty. (NH)

Such talk points to a sense of powerlessness and uncertainty: the interviewees are *hoping* and *trying*, and even *wrestling* with the question of how to report risks.

It needs to be noted, however, that the journalists' representation of themselves as torn between ideals and constraints is also likely to be strategic. Most of the journalists gave the interview at their workplace in the middle of the working day. They talked as members of their profession and did not ask for anonymity. What they say is therefore also to be seen as a form of construing professional identities and as profiling their newspaper and its orientation to journalistic ideals.[9]

The analysis of the journalists' descriptions of their practices shows that the different types of norms affecting journalistic writing are not necessarily coherent with one another, but often in conflict. One conclusion that we can draw is that responsibility relations in journalism – who is responsible to whom for what – need to be analysed as they are tied to specific local contexts of discourse production and consumption, since local norms of news production vary across different settings. As such norms vary and change, responsibility relations are also negotiated and defined in new ways.

One type of change which is affecting responsibility relations in journalism is the increasingly dominant role of online journalism. The producers of online news on risks (e.g. bloggers) do not necessarily subscribe to the same normative codes as newspaper journalists nor are they necessarily accountable to editors or managers. Moreover, the criteria for news selection and the practices of source use can be expected to differ significantly across different online media. As Singer (2007: 82) notes, in online journalism 'an infinite number of participants simultaneously serve as sources, audiences and information providers'. Moreover, online news allow for instant dialogue with readers, as well as a forum for interaction between readers (see Horlick-Jones and Farré 2010 on formal vs. informal risk communication).

This is likely to influence writing on risks in an important way: readers may, for example, instantly question or criticise risk claims or refer other readers to additional or competing representations of the risks being reported on. In such a scenario, writing is affected not just by editorial pressure and in-house competition, but by pressure and input from readers. Editors no longer function as gatekeepers and agenda setters, and professional codes of practice lose some of their relevance. This results in shifts in the sources of and authority over professional norms in news production (Singer 2007). From the point of view of risk reporting, this could mean developments in two directions: on the one hand, there is an increase in the demands on journalists in the form of instant audience feedback, but on the other hand, perhaps a loosening of the role of news values and the tyranny of the 'strong story'.

Notes

1   See also Hafez (2002: 226), who distinguishes between 'formal journalism ethics' as expressed in codes of practice and 'informal discourse(s) on journalism ethics', going on in newsrooms and in public debate.
2   All four interviewees agreed to be identified by name.
3   The UK Press Complaints Commission ceased its activities in September 2014 and has been replaced by the Independent Press Standards Organisation (see www.ipso.co.uk/IPSO).
4   See www.pcc.org.uk/cop/practice.html for the Press Complaints Commission *Editors' Code of Practice*, www.nuj.org.uk/about/nuj-code for the UK National Union of Journalists' *Code of Conduct* and www.ifj.org/about-ifj/ifj-code-of-principles/ for the International Federation of Journalists' code *Declaration of Principles on the Conduct of Journalists* (all accessed September 2014). For a selection of European codes of practice, see ethicnet.uta.fi.
5   This duality relates interestingly to empiricist and contingent repertoires in the discourse of biochemists, as analysed by Gilbert and Mulkay (1984).
6   In the interview transcripts, three dots within square brackets indicate that an excerpt of talk has been omitted. The symbol (.) marks a short pause. [xxx] indicates that the interviewee's speech was incomprehensible when transcribing from the tape.

7   For an example of similar tensions in a healthcare setting, see Arribas-Ayllon et al. (2009).

8   It is notable that in this interview, language and texts were explicitly referred to as 'raw material', suggesting that news writing is a craft of turning specialist writing into something more accessible: '[text is] just raw material, you know, I'm just shovelling that raw material (.) I mean words are just they're like you know they're like oil or coal or something, they're just the raw material we deal with, in they come and I process them and pass them on'. Interestingly, this processing metaphor downplays the practice of selection and transformation involved in news writing as well as the role of news values in the production of news stories.

9   Curran (1996: 99) talks about the 'cult of professionalism' as a way of reconciling the need for credibility with increasingly aggressive market demands, while Starck (2001: 144) notes that ethics may become 'a marketing rationale for news media'. See also Tuchman (1972) on objectivity as a 'strategic ritual'.

References

Aldridge, M. and Evetts, J. (2003) Rethinking the concept of professionalism: the case of journalism. *British Journal of Sociology* 54: 547–564.

Allan, S., Adam, B. and Carter, C. (2000) Introduction: the media politics of environmental risk. In S. Allan, B. Adam and C. Carter (eds) *Environmental Risks and the Media* 1–26. London: Routledge.

Anderson, A. (1997) *Media, Culture and the Environment*. London: UCL Press.

Anderson, A. (2006) Media and risk. In G. Mythen and S. Walklate (eds) *Beyond the Risk Society: Critical Reflections on Risk and Human Security* 114–131. Buckingham: Open University Press.

Arribas-Ayllon, M., Sarangi, S. and Clarke, A. (2009) Professional ambivalence: accounts of ethical practice in childhood genetic testing. *Journal of Genetic Counselling* 18: 173–184.

Bell, A. (1991) *The Language of News Media*. Oxford: Blackwell.

Bell, A. (1994) Climate of opinion: public and media discourse on the global environment. *Discourse & Society* 5: 33–64.

Belsey, A. (1998) Journalism and ethics: can they co-exist? In M. Kieran (ed.) *Media Ethics* 18–31. London: Routledge.

Briggs, C. (1986) *Learning How to Ask. A Sociolinguistic Appraisal of the Role of the Interview in Social Science Research*. Cambridge: Cambridge University Press.

Cotter, C. (2010) *News Talk. Investigating the Language of Journalism*. Cambridge: Cambridge University Press.

Cox, R. (2010) *Environmental Communication in the Public Sphere*, 2nd edn. London: Sage.

Curran, J. (1996) Mass media and democracy revisited. In J. Curran and M. Gurevitch (eds) *Mass Media and Society* 81–119. London: Edward Arnold.

Deuze, M. (2005) What is journalism? Professional identity and ideology of journalists reconsidered. *Journalism* 6: 442–464.

Fowler, R. (1991) *Language in the News. Discourse and Ideology in the Press.* London: Routledge.

Frost, C. (2010) *Reporting for Journalists.* London: Routledge.

Galtung, J. and Ruge, M. (1973) Structuring and selecting news. In S. Cohen and J. Young (eds) *The Manufacture of News. Social Problems, Deviance and the Mass Media* 62–72. London: Constable.

Gilbert, G. N. and Mulkay, M. (1984) *Opening Pandora's Box. A Sociological Analysis of Scientists' Discourse.* Cambridge: Cambridge University Press.

Hansen, A. (2010) *Environment, Media and Communication.* London: Routledge.

Hafez, K. (2002) Journalism ethics revisited: a comparison of ethics codes in Europe, North Africa, the Middle East and Muslim Asia. *Political Communication* 19: 225–250.

Hicks, W., Adams, S., Gilbert, H. and Holmes, T. (2008) *Writing for Journalists.* London: Routledge.

Horlick-Jones, T. and Farré, J. (2010) On the communicative constitution of risk objects in mediated times. *Catalan Journal of Communication and Cultural Studies* 2: 131–143.

Kitzinger, J. (1999) Researching risk and the media. *Health, Risk and Society* 1: 55–59.

Kitzinger, J. and Reilly, J. (1997) The rise and fall of risk reporting: media coverage of human genetics research, 'false memory syndrome' and 'mad cow disease'. *European Journal of Communication* 12: 319–350.

Laitila, T. (1995) Journalistic codes of ethics in Europe. *European Journal of Communication* 10: 527–544.

Lofstedt, R. (2010) Risk communication guidelines for Europe: a modest proposition. *Journal of Risk Research* 13: 87–109.

Major, A. M. and Atwood, L. E. (2004) Environmental risks in the news: issues, sources, problems, and values. *Public Understanding of Science* 13: 295–308.

McQuail, D. (1996) Mass media in the public interest: towards a framework of norms for media performance. In J. Curran and M. Gurevitch (eds) *Mass Media and Society* 66–80. London: Edward Arnold.

McQuail, D. (1997) Accountability of media to society: principles and means. *European Journal of Communication* 12: 511–529.

Potter, J. (1996) *Representing Reality. Discourse, Rhetoric and Social Construction.* London: Sage.

Rao, S. and Lee, S. T. (2005) Globalising media ethics? An assessment of universal ethics among international political journalists. *Journal of Mass Media Ethics* 20: 99–120.

Sandman, P. M., Sachsman, D. B., Greenberg, M. R. and Gochfeld, M. (1987) *Environmental Risk and the Press: An Exploratory Assessment.* Oxford: Transaction Books.

Sandman, D. B., Simon, J. and Valenti, J. A. (2006) Regional issues, national norms: a four-region analysis of US environment reporters. *Science Communication* 28: 93–121.

Shih, T.-J., Wijaya, R. and Brossard, D. (2008) Media coverage of public health epidemics: linking framing and issue attention cycle toward an integrated theory of print news coverage in epidemics. *Mass Communication & Society* 11: 141–160.

Singer, J. B. (2007) Contested autonomy: professional and popular claims on journalistic norms. *Journalism Studies* 8: 79–95.

Smith, D. E. (2002) Institutional ethnography. In T. May (ed.) *Qualitative Research in Action: An International Guide to Issues in Practice* 17–52. London: Sage.

Solin, A. (2004) Intertextuality as mediation: on the analysis of intertextual relations in public discourse. *Text* 24: 267–296.

Starck, K. (2001) What's right/wrong with journalism ethics research? *Journalism Studies* 2: 133–152.

Tuchman, G. (1972) Objectivity as a strategic ritual: an examination of newsmens' notions of objectivity. *American Journal of Sociology* 77: 660–679.

Wilkins, L. and Brennen, B. (2004) Conflicted interests, contested terrain: journalism ethics codes then and now. *Journalism Studies* 5: 297–309.

Wilkins, L. and Patterson, P. (1987) Risk analysis and the construction of news. *Journal of Communication* 37: 80–92.

A version of this chapter appeared in *Journal of Applied Linguistics and Professional Practice* 9:3.

Anna Solin is a senior lecturer at the Department of Modern Languages, University of Helsinki, Finland. She gained her PhD in Linguistics at Lancaster University, UK, in 2001. She currently directs a research project on language regulation in academia, with a particular focus on the shifting norms of English use.

Index

CPSIA information can be obtained at www.ICGtesting.com
Printed in the USA
BVOW06s0958250416

445293BV00004B/1/P